Ian Robertson and Mark Oxbrow are respected writers and speakers on Arthurian and Grail legends, British folklore, Freemasonry and the history and legends of Rosslyn. They are both Fellows of the Society of Antiquaries of Scotland.

Ian Robertson is the co-author of *The Quest for the Celtic Key*, acclaimed as a 'must-read book for all who sense the mystery and magic of our distant past'. Robertson is the custodian of a private craft guild museum in Edinburgh and keeper of a renowned relic said to be linked to the Crusades.

Mark Oxbrow is the author of *Halloween*, widely considered the definitive history of Hallowe'en. Mark also contributed to the bestselling *Cracking the Da Vinci Code*, UK and US TV and DVD documentaries and has lectured widely, including guest lectures for the Folklore Society and Université de Bretagne.

Caroline Davies is a fine-art and editorial photographer, represented by John Stevenson's gallery in New York. Her photographs have appeared on the covers of *US News*, *World Report* and *Phenomena* magazine, and inside *Condé Nast Traveller*, *Newsweek*, *Time Life* and many other international publications. Caroline's work can be found in private collections and gallery exhibitions around the world. She was also the expedition photographer and contributing producer of the Emmy-nominated, award-winning television documentary *Mystery of the Sphinx*. **www.carolinedavies.com**

ROSSLYN
AND THE
Grail

MARK OXBROW
AND IAN ROBERTSON
with additional photography
by Caroline Davies

MAINSTREAM
PUBLISHING

EDINBURGH AND LONDON

Reprinted, 2007

First published in Great Britain in 2005 by
MAINSTREAM PUBLISHING COMPANY (EDINBURGH) LTD
7 Albany Street
Edinburgh EH1 3UG

ISBN 9781845961152

A catalogue record for this book
is available from the British Library

Typeset in Apollo

Printed and bound in Great Britain by
Cox & Wyman Ltd

ACKNOWLEDGEMENTS

This book is dedicated to the many people who have helped along the way, and to William, Elisabeth and Gilbert.

Especial thanks are due to our proofreader Ed Davies of Ancient World Research, copy editor Susan Davies, editor Simon Cox, creative director, layout, design and cover artist Mark Foster, photographer Caroline Davies, and Danny, Robert Kirby of PFD agency, and Bill Campbell and Ailsa Bathgate at Mainstream.

With thanks to Pat and Charlie Napier, Robert and Lindsey Brydon, Gordon Strachan, Anna Munro, Julia Fowler for Latin translations, Henry Lincoln and in memory of Jay Lincoln, John and Joy Millar of the Saunière Society, and Rat, Rua and family, John Ritchie for our many discussions of Sir Gilbert Hay and the Earthly Paradise, the staff of Midlothian Library, the National Library of Scotland, the Scottish Text Society, Edinburgh Central Library, RCAHMS, Penicuik Historical Society, Loanhead and Rosslyn Rotary Club, Mr Harris of Ye Olde Original Rosslyn Hotel, Lodge St Kentigern, Penicuik and West Linton No. 429 (formerly St Kentigern, Penicuik and Rosslyn No. 429 until 1877), Lodge Rosslyn St Clair, Rosslyn No. 606, Grand Lodge of Ancient Free and Accepted Masons of Scotland, Society of Rosicrucians in Scotia, Society of Antiquaries of Scotland, Trades Maiden Hospital, Torphichen St John Association of West Lothian, Priory of Scotland of the Most Venerable Order of the Hospital of St John of Jerusalem, the Mitchell and Hillhead Libraries in Glasgow, the reading room of the British Library, the Museum of Scotland, the National Gallery of Scotland, Judy Fiskin, Claudine and Herve Glot, Maggie of Hocus Pocus, Porteous Peacock, Stuart Beattie of the Rosslyn Chapel Trust and all the staff at Rosslyn Chapel, Helen and Peter Rosslyn, Joe Lang, Stuart McHardy, Judy Shoaf and all the members of Arthurnet.

Love and enormous thanks to my fiancée Vivienne for her great patience (sometimes!), which I've often tested. To Sam for being such a wonderful daughter. To Dad and the Penicuik Crew, and to Is and the Libyan connection. To Josef, Michael, Ian, Brian, Christine, Heather, Martinez de Pascally and other like-minded people! To all my friends who put up with my Rosslyn conversations always. To my friend, colleague, and co-writer for our years of discussions, research and debate. And finally, to the place that has enchanted me for a lifetime – Rosslyn.
Ian Robertson

For Jill. With love and thanks to all my family; to my brothers Craig and Lewis, to Dad, Mum and Gran for years of support. Especial love to Fleur. Love to Pam and John, Geoff and Stephanie. Huge thanks and love to Ian and Viv. There are so many people who have believed we could do this and pushed us to get our act together. We would need another book to include everyone, so thank you all.
Mark Oxbrow

www.rosslyngrail.com

Rosslyn Chapel official website: www.rosslynchapel.org.uk

Rosslyn Castle is owned by the Earl of Rosslyn and managed by the Landmark Trust: www.landmarktrust.co.uk

CONTENTS

FOREWORD
by Simon Cox

Rosslyn Chapel is a true enigma. On the one hand, this chapel amidst the woods is a living, breathing, working chapel of worship, with a congregation and a place in the community. On the other, it's a place of mystery, enlightenment and wonder. Written about in a plethora of books both old and modern, this wonderful edifice stands to remind us that faith endures throughout the ages, whatever is put in its way and however many stories and legends grow up around it.

I first encountered Rosslyn Chapel many years ago when I attended the wedding of Dr Karen Ralls, the Celtic historian and author. Unbeknown to me at the time, Ian Robertson was in attendance that day, along with the gathered great and good of Rosslyn studies. I have travelled to Rosslyn many times since this event, a place you could never get bored of nor tire of its surroundings in the sleepy village of Roslin, with its more modern spelling.

The chapel has featured in many of the biggest-selling alternative history books of the past 25 years, becoming a pilgrimage for many, with tales of buried treasure, buried bodies, knights' gold, holy relics, scrolls from Jerusalem and much else besides. However, it wasn't until the publication of the novel *The Da Vinci Code* by Dan Brown in the last few years that sleepy little Roslin and its even sleepier chapel have really caught the public imagination. Visitor numbers have soared to unprecedented levels, with tourists from all over the world desperate to see the site of the dénouement of the novel. Of course, as Mark and Ian will explain in these very pages, much that Dan Brown wrote about the chapel was simply fiction, as befits a novel. The Rosslyn Chapel Trust, headed by the redoubtable Stuart Beattie, are, I'm sure, still thankful for the added revenue and numbers as they battle to make sure the chapel is fit for the twenty-first century and beyond, a job they do with great patience and a steady hand in trying circumstances.

It was during the writing of my book, *Cracking The Da Vinci Code*, that I turned to Mark Oxbrow for input on the Rosslyn Chapel section, going on to meet Ian Robertson as part of the process. It became immediately clear to me that these two historical researchers had real passion for this magical place. A passion born of 20 years of visits, research and enduring much of the written inaccuracies that have been published about Rosslyn over that period. It was time to put the record straight, and there were only two people who could do it with real conviction and weight. Mark and Ian have earned the right to put this book before you now. They have amassed a huge amount of research and data on Rosslyn Chapel, its legends, myths and stories, on the people and events that have carved out its very existence and the most important factor in any investigative undertaking: the truth.

In short, I have no hesitation in recommending this book to everyone interested in finding out more about Rosslyn Chapel, the real Rosslyn Chapel, the true Rosslyn Chapel.

Simon Cox
Bedford
Summer 2005

INTRODUCTION
The Round Table

THE KNIGHTS RODE OUT onto the tournament field, clad in plate armour and chain mail, their warhorses churning up the damp earth. Their squires rode alongside, bearing lances, swords, axes and daggers. The pale afternoon sun glinted on polished steel. Bright pendants and banners waved from tents and pavilions as the king, his earls, lords and ladies watched from the wooden stands.

It was a pageant worthy of the court of King Arthur and the Knights of the Round Table, but this tournament actually happened in fifteenth-century Scotland.

The year was AD 1448. The three Scots knights rode out 'very splendidly', accompanied by the lords of Scotland and, according to contemporary chronicles, four to six thousand men. They took the field at Estrellin, now Stirling, after a night of feasting and dancing in the king's castle. The king bestowed the honour of knighthood on worthy squires. He was King James II, King of Scots, then just a boy in his early teens.

11

The Scots' opponents were three knights of the household of the Duke of Burgundy, in France. Just 14 years earlier, the Scots and Burgundians had been mortal enemies. During the Hundred Years War, the Burgundians had fought alongside the English, facing the French and their Scots allies in a succession of terrible battles. In 1448, the war still raged, but the Duke of Burgundy had switched sides to support the King of France.

That day, the Burgundians were first upon the field. Sir Jacques de Lalain, Simon de Lalain and Hervé de Mériadec wore the finest steel plate armour and robes of black velvet edged in sable martin fur. Their squires wore black satin.

The Scots knights were nobles of 'high lineage': Sir James Douglas of Heriotmuir, John Ross of Halket and James Douglas, a brother of Douglas of Lochleven. The knights dismounted at their pavilions. Their squires checked the straps on their armour and armed them with the agreed weapons. As the crowds looked on, the knights faced off across the tournament field.

At a trumpet blast, the warhorses leapt forward and the mounted knights charged 'with great force on their adversaries'. The tournament was a mock battle with firmly established rules governing the conduct of knights during jousts and in the mêlée. The swords and axes were blunted, but the tournament could still prove fatal.

At the last moment, the Burgundians threw away their lances, attacking with axes. James Douglas broke rank and wounded Hervé de Mériadec in the arm, splitting his body-armour. Hervé countered with a ferocious axe blow to Douglas's helm. The Scots knight reeled. A second blow knocked him from his horse. Hervé rounded on the Scot, bringing his axe down again and again on his steel helm. Hervé turned from the fallen knight, thinking that he 'was rid of him' for the day.

Across the field, the Burgundian knight Simon de Lalain 'fought most bitterly' with the Scot, John Ross of Halket. Sir Jacques de Lalain was fighting hand to hand with Sir James Douglas of Heriotmuir.

Hervé de Mériadec rode to the aid of Simon de Lalain but was astonished to find that his own opponent, James Douglas, had stubbornly dragged himself to his feet and regained his horse. Hervé turned and charged down the Scot, dealing him a 'heavy blow' with his axe then repeatedly striking the Scot with his chain-mailed fist. As the Scots knight fell, Hervé turned to join his fellows. At that moment, the king threw down his baton and the tournament guards separated the combatants.

The tournament was chronicled by Matthieu d'Escouchy, Castellan of Péronne, for the Duke of Burgundy. One surviving manuscript bears the signature of 'James Douglas, knight, of the Kingdom of Scotland', who honours his 'valiant and gallant' opponents.

The Scots knight Sir James Douglas of Heriotmuir was the second son of Archibald, fourth Earl of Douglas and Duke of Touraine. Matthieu's chronicle does not record the names of the lord and ladies who attended the tournament at Stirling, but it is likely that Sir James's sister Elizabeth Douglas and her husband would have watched as her brother took the field.

Elizabeth was married to Sir William St Clair, third Earl of Orkney and Lord of Rosslyn. Sir William was a powerful Scots noble. He had land and titles, and was grateful to God for all the blessings He had bestowed upon him. Two years before the tournament, in AD 1446, Sir William had founded a collegiate church by his castle at Rosslyn.

Over 500 years later, Sir William's church is known as Rosslyn Chapel. It has become one of the most famous, and most mysterious, buildings in the world.

In the last few years, the phenomenal success of Dan Brown's novel *The Da Vinci Code* has brought Rosslyn Chapel to the attention of millions of readers. Before this bestseller, the chapel appeared in a series of 'alternative history' books. Their authors claimed that the chapel hides a fabulous secret treasure: the Holy Grail, the Ark of the Covenant, the embalmed Head of Christ, the True Cross, the golden plate of the Chartres Cathedral labyrinth, the Lost Gospels of Jesus or the treasure of the Temple of Jerusalem. With each new book, the theories grew more bizarre.

Many people believe that the truth about the chapel is lost for ever, that it is a secret we can only guess at. But Rosslyn's story is not lost. By going back to original sources and conducting in-depth research, we have finally separated the facts from the fiction and unlocked the chapel's secrets.

After ten years of research and writing, *Rosslyn and the Grail* is complete. We have made some startling discoveries and met many wonderful people. Throughout, we have been determined to uncover the truth about Rosslyn.

Truth is a tricky thing. You should always be wary of anyone peddling 'the truth'. Histories and chronicles are often biased. Evidence can be circumstantial and it is easy to speculate when there is a gap in your knowledge. We have tried to tell the real story of Rosslyn as accurately as we can, and we hope we have remained faithful to the memories of the men and women whose lives we have documented.

It is easy to leap to conclusions about Rosslyn Chapel. There has never been a truly accurate guide to all of the thousands of carvings within the chapel. At first glance, you can interpret a carving based on your prior knowledge and imagination. If you stop there, then you simply make an intuitive guess at what the carving depicts. This interpretation may have special meaning for you, but was this the reading that was intended when it was carved in the fifteenth century?

There is a group of carvings of strange furred and feathered angels on the east wall of the chapel. They are pointed out as 'Masonic angels'. As the chapel pre-dates the establishment of the Freemasonic Grand Lodges by hundreds of years, these angels are said to be proof that the early roots of Freemasonry can be traced to Rosslyn. There is just one small problem with this theory. These particular carvings were not part of the medieval chapel; they were carved in the nineteenth century.

If you don't thoroughly investigate the history of Rosslyn,

you miss the fact that controversial restoration work was carried out at Rosslyn Chapel in the 1860s under the direction of the freemason and architect David Bryce. New angels were carved and added to the east wall: 'Masonic' angels. Without careful research, it is easy to make serious mistakes.

We have investigated the chapel and castle in the context of the history and culture of medieval Scotland. We have read the books that were written at Rosslyn as the chapel was being built and have traced the lives of the people who shaped Rosslyn's past. If we can find out what the chapel's carvings would have meant in fifteenth-century Scotland, we can come close to truly understanding the real story of Rosslyn.

In this book, we have followed the example of Robert Graves' *Greek Myths* and Geoffrey Ashe's *Mythology of the British Isles*. In each chapter, we tell one of the legends of Rosslyn then carefully examine that legend and the history of the chapel, the castle and the St Clair family.

The Oxford English Dictionary defines a legend as 'a traditional story popularly regarded as historical but which is not authenticated'. The word 'legend' is derived from the Latin *legendae* meaning 'things to be read'. We read legends as fanciful tales but expect history books to be historically accurate. Yet our history books are often full of legends and tales that have simply become accepted as historical fact.

In the early fourteenth century, King Robert the Bruce sat alone in a dark cave. He had lost every battle he had fought against the English. His men were cold and tired, and he was close to abandoning the war. As his eyes grew accustomed to the inky blackness, he saw a tiny spider trying to build a web. It dangled from a thin wisp of cobweb. The Bruce watched as the spider climbed up its thread and tried to weave a web. Suddenly, it fell. Again it climbed up and again it fell. As the king watched, the spider fell again and again until eventually it managed to spin a web. At that moment, the Bruce realised that he too would eventually win. 'If at first you don't succeed, try, try again.' A year later, in AD 1314, King Robert the Bruce led the Scots army to victory at the Battle of Bannockburn.

The story of Bruce and the spider is still widely accepted as history, but in reality it is a legend. It didn't actually happen, but it has become one of the most famous events in the life of the Bruce. 'Bruce's cave' is a popular tourist attraction set into a sheer rock face above the River Kirtle near Gretna in Dumfries and Galloway.

The Battle of Bannockburn began with a cavalry charge. The English knight Sir Henry de Bohun rode out recklessly and was met by King Robert the Bruce. With a single blow from the Bruce's battleaxe the English knight's head was cleft in two. The only problem is that historians now strongly dispute that 'Sir Henry de Bohun' ever actually existed.

We accept that Hollywood movies usually have little regard for historical accuracy. The Oscar-winning movie *Braveheart*, directed by and starring Mel Gibson, may have been a good movie, but it was hardly an accurate portrayal of Sir William Wallace or the history of medieval Scotland!

Among the many inventions and inaccuracies are the blue woad-painted faces that actually date to about a thousand years before Wallace's time, the kilts that weren't actually worn in Scotland till hundreds of years after Wallace's time and the fact that the French Princess Isabella (portrayed by Sophie Marceau) was only 13 years old when Wallace was executed and never actually met him. It is said that at the movie's world premiere in Stirling, a local man asked Mel Gibson why the Battle of Stirling Bridge had been filmed in a field without the bridge that was crucial to the Scots victory. 'Oh, the bridge would have got in the way of the action,' Gibson is said to have replied. The local noted, 'Aye, the English found that too!'

'It's just a movie' and we expect a movie to simply tell a good story, regardless of how true it is to the historical facts. But we expect books that sell themselves as historical non-fiction to actually be historically accurate.

Stories about the Knights Templar secretly fleeing to Rosslyn and hiding their treasure under the chapel are now so widely repeated that they will probably never be forgotten. The fact is that these 'Templar myths' are utterly false. They are inventions without a shred of credible evidence to back them up. But if the stories are repeated often enough, and no one challenges their accuracy, then eventually they may be written into Scots history.

If I told you stories of trolls secretly escaping from France and living at Rosslyn, no one would believe me. If I told you that Smaug the Dragon, from J.R.R. Tolkien's book *The Hobbit*, lived in a cave beneath the chapel guarding his hoard of gold and treasure, you'd look at me strangely. I only have to take these stories and push them a little bit too far and suddenly you lose your suspension of disbelief. You realise that the story you are being sold is nonsense.

The odd thing is that the real history of Rosslyn is far more incredible and spellbinding than any of the theories and fantasies.

As stonemasons cut blocks of sandstone to build Rosslyn Chapel, books on chivalry and knighthood were written at Rosslyn Castle. Sir William was patron to Sir Gilbert Hay, one of Europe's foremost scholars who translated the Book of Battles, the Book of the Order of Knighthood and a Life of Alexander the Great. Sir Gilbert had studied at the University of St Andrews, had been chamberlain to the Dauphin of France, and had lived in the French court for over 20 years. Sir Gilbert Hay was also a knight who may have fought alongside Joan of Arc.

Joan led the French and Scots against the English and their allies. Her legend begins with her life as a simple peasant girl from the tiny village of Domrémy. The young Joan heard the 'voices' of Michael the Archangel, St Margaret and St Catherine of Alexandria. Her voices guided her to seek out the Dauphin and to ask him for an army to drive the English from her beloved France.

Joan met the Dauphin at the castle of Chinon, where, 100

years before, Jacques de Molay and other Templar knights were held captive. The Dauphin gave Joan a horse, a suit of armour and an army. Legend says that her sword was a magical weapon, uncovered from beneath the altar of the chapel of St Catherine in Fierbois. She was known as 'Jeanne la Pucelle' – 'Joan the Maiden'. She carried a banner, made by a Scots soldier named Hamish, into battle. Joan described her banner at her trial and said she liked it '40 times better' than her sword:

> I had a banner of which the field was strewn with lilies. The world was painted there, with two angels at the sides; it was white of the cloth called boucassin; there was written on it, I believe, 'Jhesus Maria'; it was fringed with silk.

In AD 1429, Joan led her army in a series of bloody battles and saw the Dauphin Charles crowned King of France. Among the Scots who attended the coronation was Sir Gilbert Hay.

If Sir Gilbert watched the tournament at Stirling he may have remembered that it was the Burgundians who finally captured Joan of Arc. They sold her to their English allies for 10,000 gold crowns. She was tried as a heretic and was burnt at the stake. As the flames leapt about her, Joan cried out to Jesus and 'the saints of Paradise' for aid. She was only 19 years old.

When Sir Gilbert Hay returned to Scotland in AD 1445, he lived at Rosslyn Castle in the household of Sir William St Clair as his trusted friend and adviser. There, he tutored William's children and translated French books into Scots, with a scribe carefully copying down his words. Among thousands of lines on chivalry and knighthood, Sir Gilbert describes the game of 'golf', where two opposing teams struck a ball back and forth with 'golf-staffs', and notes that claret wine 'makes a man wise'. When William decided to found a collegiate church at Rosslyn, it seems likely that he turned to Sir Gilbert Hay for counsel.

In truth, it is impossible to say that Sir Gilbert Hay definitely knew Joan of Arc or if he was without doubt involved in the design of Rosslyn Chapel. He was chamberlain to Joan's patron, the Dauphin of France. Both Joan and Sir Gilbert are recorded as being in attendance at the coronation at Rheims, but there is no surviving proof that we know of that they actually met. Sir Gilbert did return from France to live at Rosslyn as the chapel was founded, but that could simply be a coincidence. There is no 'old book' that tells us that Sir Gilbert Hay worked with Sir William to create Rosslyn Chapel.

The history of Rosslyn is fragmented and full of legends. What is more, the legends of Rosslyn Chapel and Castle are closely connected to the legends of King Arthur, the Knights of the Round Table and the quest for the Holy Grail.

The Arthurian legends were immensely popular in medieval Scotland. Nobles named their children Arthur, Merlin, Tristran, and Yseult. Knights and ladies emulated King Arthur's court at tournaments, pageants and spectacles. Storytellers recounted the valiant deeds of Arthur's knights and writers composed verse romances and tales of battle and courtly love.

At Stirling, where the tournament of 1448 took place, there was a 'Round Table'. As early as the fourteenth century, John Barbour mentions this Round Table in *The Brus*. In 1478, the chronicler William of Worcester wrote that King Arthur 'kept' the Round Table at Stirling Castle.

The Round Table can still be found near Stirling Castle. It is a huge mound, about 40 to 50 feet (12 to 15 metres) in diameter. It lies at the heart of 'the King's Knot', a royal garden created in AD 1627. The garden is lost now, but its earth embankments and paths still encircle the Round Table. It is thought that the mound was the centrepiece for medieval pageants and tournaments. It may have become known as King Arthur's Round Table, as the lords and ladies of Scotland played the knights and maidens of Camelot at Stirling. To Sir William St Clair of Rosslyn, King Arthur was a real figure who lived in story and song.

The Arthurian legends say that the wizard Merlin built the

Round Table so that all Arthur's knights could meet as equals. In the early-thirteenth-century prose romance *Le Queste del Saint Graal*, Sir Perceval is told that the world has seen three great tables: the Table of Jesus Christ, the Table of the Holy Grail and King Arthur's Round Table that suggested the roundness of the earth and the spheres of the planets. Today, Leonardo da Vinci's depiction of the Last Supper at a long straight table has captured our imaginations, but in medieval images of the Last Supper, Christ and his disciples are often pictured at a round table.

There is a local tradition that there was once a Round Table kept in Rosslyn Chapel, where knights from the noble families of Scotland would meet.

Rosslyn and the Grail is a book of legends and stories. It is also a study of the surviving historical evidence and a quest to discover the real story of Rosslyn. Our aim is not to debunk the myths or to explain away the magic and mystery of the chapel and castle. We simply think that the story of Rosslyn should be told.

We leave you to decide what you believe is true.

PREFACE
Dark And Secret Things

THREE MILES FROM ROSSLYN, in the depths of a shadowy cave, a mysterious Latin inscription is carved into a solid stone wall.

> *Tenebrosa Occultaque Cave*
> which translates as;
> Beware of dark and secret things

The cave, known as Hurley's Cove, was created by Sir John Clerk of Penicuik about the year 1742. It is said to be a copy of the grotto near the tomb of the pagan poet Virgil. Clerk's cave was at once a celebration of the classical world and a sacred space designed for secret gatherings. It lies in the private grounds of Penicuik House in Midlothian, Scotland. Clerk's grand designs for his family estate included 'green grasses, avenues of trees, shady walks, banks and water works, groves and secret places for Gods and Goddesses'.

Clerk is acknowledged as a 'master of all the liberal arts'. He was a politician, lawyer and architect, an antiquarian and noted collector of antiquities, a writer and baroque composer. Clerk's collection of Roman antiquities was to become a centrepiece of the National Museum of Antiquities in Edinburgh and is now gathered together in the 'Early Peoples' area of the Museum of Scotland.

Sir John Clerk was also a Freemason, a member of an eighteenth-century druidic order and a 'Roman Knight'. The Society of Roman Knights, also known as 'the Order of the Book', was founded by the noted antiquarian William Stukely to save the ancient monuments of Britain from destruction.

In the early eighteenth century, Rosslyn Chapel lay neglected and forgotten. It had been attacked by a Protestant mob, condemned as a Catholic 'monument of idolatrie' and abandoned to ruin.

It was Sir John Clerk who saved Rosslyn Chapel. He intervened with Sir James St Clair, the Lord of Rosslyn, and in 1739 drew up conservation plans and personally supervised the restoration of the fragile medieval building.

Things become secret. In the fifteenth century, when Rosslyn Chapel was first founded and built, its carvings could be 'read'. The Catholic congregation that met to worship within the Collegiate Church of St Matthew the Apostle would have known exactly who each figure represented, what each stone flower symbolised. There was nothing secret or mysterious in the characters, stories and scenes that William St Clair's masons and stone carvers had depicted.

When Sir John Clerk began restoration work at Rosslyn Chapel, 250 years after it was first built, the meanings of most of the carvings were already lost; they had become 'secret'.

CHAPTER ONE
Amidst The Woods

A THOUSAND YEARS AGO, Rosslyn was simply a bend in a river in the depths of the native wildwood. The ancient Britons told tales of the Wood of Celidon. They said it was the haunt of Merlin the Wyld, a magical prophet who lived with the wolves and wild boar. The forest was an enchanted place where druids gathered in sacred hazel groves and King Arthur rode into battle.

Legend tells that the first dwelling built at Rosslyn was founded by 'Asterius'. His daughter was a Pictish lady named 'Panthioria'. The pagan maiden Panthioria married King Donaldus, the first Christian king of the Scots.

Rosslyn and the Wood of Celidon lay between two vast Roman walls that stretched from sea to sea. The Antonine Wall was a deep ditch and embankment and Hadrian's Wall was an immense stone battlement fortified with towers and forts garrisoned by Roman Legions. The lands between were a battlefield from the time of the Romans, the Picts and the Caledonians.

We imagine maidens, ladies and princesses as fair young women with long, plaited golden hair and fairy-tale dresses. A Pictish maiden like Panthioria would have been expected to fight and kill on the battlefield alongside the men. She would have been a skilled warrior who fought with sword, axe and bow. Her body would have been tattooed with an iron needle, marked with images of serpents, crescents, wild animals and birds.

According to the early chroniclers of Scottish history, King Donaldus 'coined gold and silver, and embraced the Christian faith', although he was unable to banish the 'old heathenish rites and ceremonies' practised in his kingdom. On desolate mountaintops and in forest glades, the tribes worshipped their ancient gods and goddesses.

In truth, it is highly unlikely that either Donaldus or Panthioria ever really existed. The legend of their marriage may be some small fragment of an ancient tale of the pagan Picts and the Celtic Christian Scots finally forging a lasting peace. Equally, it may be a romantic invention of the seventeenth century.

When the Romans arrived in northern Britain around AD 100, they encountered the native Pictish tribes. As the Roman Legions marched north into the highlands they encountered fierce resistance from the Caledonians and the Picts. The natives launched a vicious guerrilla war against the invaders and *circa* AD 122 the Emperor Hadrian decreed that a frontier wall must be built to divide the Romans from 'the Barbarians'. The defensive wall stood about 20 feet tall and was over 70 miles long. Thousands of men were stationed in milecastles, watchtowers and forts.

Antiquarians like Sir John Clerk of Penicuik, archaeologists and academic historians have thoroughly studied and documented the Roman history of the British Isles. In comparison, the study of the Picts is in its infancy. The Picts have long been seen as a mysterious people; they left virtually no written records to tell their story. Early descriptions of them are often fantastical and bizarre, little better than 'here be dragons'.

The name Pict is usually assumed to derive from the Latin 'Picti', so the Picts are described as the 'painted' or 'tattooed' people. They were said to be an ancient native people: 'noble savages' painted with blue woad or tattooed with iron needles. The Picts, both male and female, went into battle naked, with their bodies covered in strange magical symbols.

A *History of the Picts*, written in 1706 by Mr Henry Maule of Melgum and dedicated to Sir James Balfour, Lyon King at Arms in the time of Charles I, makes some curious claims about the Picts in the lands around Rosslyn. 'Pictlandia' was the 'easter, middle and wester Lothians'. The Pentland Hills were the 'Pictlandi Montes', the 'Pictland Hills'. Edinburgh was founded by 'Cruthenus Camelonius', the 'first Pictish king'. Edinburgh was known as the Castle of Maidens, as Pictish 'virgins of the blood' were 'closely kept' there. Early histories of the Picts often recounted local legends and tales of the Picts, or 'Pechts', as small people, the origins of tales of faeries.

What we do know with some certainty about the Picts is that they were a group of tribes that flourished for over 800 years from the first century to the mid-ninth century on Orkney and across most of what is now Scotland. Initially, the tribes had warred against one another, but when faced by the threat of the invading Romans, the Picts finally gathered together to fight their common enemy. The Romans called them 'Picti', the Irish Celts called them the 'Cruithne', the Welsh Britons 'Pethwyr', the Norse 'Petta' and in Old Scots they were called the 'Pechts'.

The Picts were highly skilled craftspeople. They created exquisite silver jewellery and carved incredibly beautiful symbol stones. These fabulous works of stone carving feature a unique set of symbols including deer, eagles, serpents, boar, bulls, salmon, magical sea creatures, armed warriors on horseback, battle scenes, hand mirrors, combs, crescent and V-rods, and double disc and Z-rods. With the advent of Christianity among the Picts, they incorporated carved wheel crosses covered in intricate knotwork and decorative spirals.

Among the Pictish symbol stones collected in the small village of Meigle, near Glamis Castle, is a cross-slab stone known locally as 'Vanora's Stone'. 'Vanora', 'Ganora' or sometimes 'Wander' was said to be the real Queen Guinevere of Arthurian legend. According to local legend, Vanora, the wife of King Arthur, was left behind as Arthur set out for Rome. In Arthur's absence, the Pictish King Mordred plotted to steal his throne and take his wife. It is not clear if Vanora was forcibly abducted or willingly consorted with Mordred, but she ended up ruling alongside the usurper Mordred and cuckolding her husband Arthur. The pair ruled from 'Mordred's Castle', the Iron Age fort on Barry Hill a few miles from Meigle.

When Arthur finally discovered what was happening in his absence, he headed back north, raising an army as he went. Mordred and Vanora rode out from their stronghold near Meigle with a force of Pictish warriors to meet Arthur and his army. Arthur and Mordred fought a dreadful battle that cost both of them their lives. Vanora was taken from the field to await the judgement of Arthur's wise men. She was condemned to death for the crime of adultery, for betraying the true king.

At Meigle, in the small museum full of Pictish symbol stones, 'Vanora's Stone' stands over eight feet tall. On one side is a magnificent Christian cross, on the other a carving said to be the execution of Vanora, wife of King Arthur. There, carved in stone, is a lone figure in a long robe being attacked by wild beasts. Some say this is actually a depiction of the biblical story of Daniel in the Lions' Den, but local tradition insists that this is the punishment of Vanora. She was torn to pieces by wild dogs or pulled apart by horses.

Vanora's body was said to be buried beneath a mound known as 'Vanora's Grave'. It lies in the churchyard in Meigle and it has long been believed that any maiden who is foolish enough to wander into the kirkyard and stand on 'Vanora's Grave' will become barren. In the 1860s, John S. Stuart Glennie climbed Barry Hill to see Mordred's Castle while researching Arthurian

Scotland. He met a local man who told him that in fact Vanora had four graves, as her dismembered body was buried in four separate places.

In the twelfth century, the monks of Glastonbury would claim that the graves of Guinevere and Arthur were within their Abbey grounds in Somerset. Over the centuries, Glastonbury became the heart of Arthurian England. Glastonbury was said to be the mythical Avalon, the Isle of Apples where nine sorceress-queens tended Arthur's wounds after his tragic last battle at Camlann. It was said that Joseph of Arimathea brought the Holy Grail to Glastonbury.

When Christ died upon the cross, Joseph of Arimathea convinced Pontius Pilate to let him take Christ's body and lay it to rest in his own rock-cut tomb. Medieval legend says that Joseph left the Holy Land with the Grail and sailed to Europe. On Wearyall Hill in Somerset, England, a strange thorn tree grows: this is the Glastonbury Thorn. When Joseph arrived at Glastonbury, he planted his staff in the hilltop. Miraculously, his staff took root and flourished into the Holy Thorn tree that flowered twice a year: in the spring and at Christmastide, to mark the birth of Christ. The Thorn at Glastonbury today was grown from a cutting from the legendary Holy Thorn. Each midwinter, a single bough is still cut from the Glastonbury Thorn and placed upon the ruling British monarch's table on Christmas morning.

Arthur has become a king and hero of England. Legends say he was conceived and born at Tintagel in Cornwall and that Merlin the Wizard raised the immense monoliths of Stonehenge. At Westminster in London, the boy Arthur pulled the Sword from the Stone and became King of all the Britons. Arthur fought his battles against the invading Saxon hordes in the fields and rolling hills of England. It is King Arthur's Round Table that hangs in a medieval hall in Winchester. Camelot, the legendary stronghold of King Arthur, is said to be Cadbury Castle, in Somerset. He fell at the battle of Camlann, fighting his son and bitter enemy, Mordred. His sword Excalibur was taken from the battlefield and cast into the waters of the Dosmary Pool in Cornwall, returned to the Lady of the Lake. 'Arthur's Grave' at Glastonbury Abbey became a site of pilgrimage, but the Welsh believed that Arthur had no grave. He was not dead but dreaming, awaiting the day when he would rise again to lead the Britons in their hour of greatest need. The real Arthur was not the king of legend.

According to the early chronicles, the Arthur of history would have lived 500 years before the medieval kings. He was not married to a romantic Queen Guinevere dressed in fine silks. He did not have a Round Table of chivalrous knights and a grand castle at Camelot. The historical Arthur was a war leader, a fighter who led a cavalry force in battle against the enemies of the Britons. He is thought of now as England's greatest hero, but in reality he fought against the ancestors of the English in pitched battles across Britain. The real Arthur fought invaders on all sides, including the warrior Picts whom he met in battle in the Wood of Celidon: the great wood that covered much of what is now southern Scotland.

The first settlement at Rosslyn was cut from the Wood of Celidon. Legend tells us it was founded by Asterius the Pict. The archaeological evidence shows that Roslin Glen was inhabited long before the time of Picts and the warrior Arthur: over 2,000 years before the birth of Christ.

Overlooking the River Esk, between the castles of Rosslyn and Hawthornden, is a small rockface. Carved into its surface are ancient rock art designs that date to the Bronze Age. Each design was carefully 'pecked' into the surface using stone tools. Circles and triangles have been interpreted as a human figure; other symbols are more mysterious. There are concentric circles, spirals, circles and double 's'-shaped spirals. Upstream, cut into a dramatic rock outcrop that overlooks the river, a rock art fish survives amid centuries of carved graffiti.

The rock art is thought to date to around the late Neolithic era or the early Bronze Age, *circa* 2500 BC, although rock art is notoriously difficult to date. Without other datable finds and artefacts, archaeologists have to compare the style of rock art designs to make an estimate of age. In 1939, the rock art in Rosslyn Glen was described as 'Rock scribings at Hawthornden' pecked into an overhanging shelter in 'a precipitous cliff'. Initially, they were compared to Bronze Age cup-and-ring markings, but the lack of 'cups' – small pecked hollows or shallow holes – suggested an earlier date.

The spirals were thought to be similar to examples at Newgrange and Lough Crew in Ireland. The closest parallel in Scotland was a huge flat stone that once covered an ancient grave, a stone cist-cover discovered on a burial mound in Drumelzier, Peeblesshire. The Drumelzier cist-cover was removed in the early twentieth century and is now stored in Edinburgh in the National Museum archives in Leith. When we tracked it down, it was secured in a wheeled wooden storage crate amid huge shelves stocked with antiquities and ancient stones. The cist-cover stands about six feet tall. Its surface is cracked and weathered, marked by double concentric circles created 4,000 years ago. The stone was found less than a mile from a site traditionally thought to mark Merlin's Grave.

An ancient thorn tree grew to mark the wizard's final resting place. The Border prophet Thomas the Rhymer foretold that when the Powsail Burn met the river Tweed at Merlin's Grave, the warring nations of Scotland and England would finally be united. It is said that when the two countries were finally joined in 1603, at the Union of the Crowns, the rivers flooded and flowed together. The rock art downstream from Rosslyn Chapel and Castle has the same circles as the cist-cover from near Merlin's Grave.

North of Rosslyn, near the village of Lasswade, a burial ground with over 100 long cists was excavated in the 1950s. These stone slab graves were between five feet and six feet three inches long, aligned west to east, and were thought to date to somewhere between the third and ninth centuries AD. The long cist cemetery belonged to the age of the Romans and the Britons, the Picts and the early Christian Church.

In August 1754, a farmer was ploughing a furrow in his field at Roslin village when he stuck something solid. A 'stone coffin' was uncovered, nine feet long, containing human bones. 'The bones were much decayed, except the skull and teeth.' It was thought that this was the grave of 'some British warrior'.

This patchwork of evidence shows that the land about Rosslyn has been inhabited for thousands of years. From at least 2000 BC, people have fished the River Esk and hunted in the native forest. Over the centuries, villages were built, fields were sown and harvested, cattle were raised and slaughtered. Long before the time of the legendary Pictish lady Panthioria, people lived in settlements at Rosslyn.

The St Clair family was first granted the lands and barony of Rosslyn in AD 1280. Over the following 400 years, the St Clairs of Rosslyn would become one of the most powerful families in medieval Scotland. In the fifteenth century, they built Rosslyn Chapel. Within 200 years, the chapel lay abandoned and the St Clair family fortunes had turned.

In 1700, Father Richard Augustine Hay, Canon of St Genevieve in Paris and Prior of St Piermont, compiled a genealogy of the Rosslyn St Clairs. According to Hay, the St Clair family was founded in Scotland by Sir William Sinclare, who was known as 'William the Seemly' as he was fair of face and yellow haired. Hay tells us that William was the second son of Woldonius or Wildernus in France. He settled in Scotland in the time of King Malcolm Canmore and became the 'cupbearer' of Queen Margaret. He is said to have married 'Dorothe or . . . Agnas Dunbar', daughter of the Earl of March, and obtained the Barony of Rosslyn.

In recent years, pseudo-history writers have turned 'William the Seemly' into a wondrous figure descended from Vikings, French Dukes and Counts, and an Archbishop of Rouen. Some writers even allege that the St Clairs are descended from a

Holy Bloodline that goes back to a union between Jesus Christ and Mary Magdalene. They claim that William and the knight Bartholomew Ladislaus Leslyn escorted the Saxon princess Margaret to Scotland. She brought with her the Black Rood: a piece of the True Cross enshrined in a silver and gold reliquary. Margaret was the granddaughter of Edmund Ironside, who was buried at Glastonbury, the legendary Isle of Avalon where Joseph of Arimathea brought the Holy Grail. Like Joseph of Arimathea, the Saxon princess Margaret brought with her a fabulous sacred relic.

The reality is a little less romantic. 'William the Seemly' is just as legendary as the Pictish lady Panthioria.

Queen Margaret was eventually to become Saint Margaret. She is credited with bringing Roman Catholic Christianity to Scotland, as symbolised by the 'Black' or 'Holy Rood' she bore. 'William the Seemly' was simply invented to connect the St Clair family with the Christian Saint Margaret. In reality, he doesn't appear in any other historical documentation and Hay's genealogy is widely seen as deeply unreliable.

King Malcolm Canmore and Margaret were married 'with great magnificence' in AD 1070. They reigned from 'Dumfermling in the Wooden' in Fife, but their cupbearer was not 'William the Seemly'. Queen Margaret was a devout Christian who paid for ships to ferry pilgrims across the waters of the Firth of Forth as they journeyed to St Andrews on holy pilgrimage. North and South Queensferry are named for Margaret's pilgrim ferry. King Malcolm Canmore died in battle near Alnwick in 1093. Queen Margaret was in Edinburgh when she heard that her beloved husband had fallen and was said to have died of grief. She was laid to rest in the oldest building in Edinburgh, now known as Saint Margaret's Chapel, a tiny simple building on Castle Hill. It has survived all the wars that have seen Edinburgh Castle burned, besieged, destroyed and rebuilt around it.

The first William St Clair 'of Rosslyn' did not exist until AD 1280, over 100 years after the wedding of King Malcolm and

Queen Margaret. The real Sir William appears in early historical records as the Sheriff of Edinburgh in 1266 and from 1288 to 1290, the Sheriff of Haddington and of Linlithgow from 1264 to 1290, the Sheriff of Dumfries in 1288, and the 'Justiciar of Galwythie' from 1288 to 1289. It was this William who married Agnes, daughter of Patrick, Earl of Dunbar.

Surviving early Scottish charters show that 'Rogero de Rofelyn' and 'Henricus de Rofkelyn' owned the lands of Rosslyn before the St Clairs. Henry of Rosslyn resigned his lands to King Alexander III and on 14 September 1280 Sir William de Sancto Claro was granted a Charter by the King of the lands and barony of Rosslyn. Rosslyn passed from father to son as the St Clair knights, lords and earls fought alongside William Wallace and King Robert the Bruce, built Rosslyn Chapel and Castle, and remained the faithful servants of Mary Queen of Scots and the Catholic faith. The history of Rosslyn and the St Clairs can be untangled from centuries of legends and folktales. Things that have become secret can finally be revealed.

CHAPTER TWO
The Haunted Castle

THE RUINS OF ROSSLYN Castle are hidden deep amid the wooded hills and rolling fields of Midlothian, perched on a rocky outcrop high above the twists and turns of the River Esk. The river has cut a deep ravine through the fiery orange and red sandstone, sometimes flowing gently, sometimes raging white water that tears down trees and drags boulders.

The crumbling battlements of Rosslyn Castle appear to grow from the living rock. Deep down, carved from the solid stone of the hill, is an underground world of chambers and corridors.

Today, this labyrinth of chambers, stairways and narrow passageways lie dark and empty, but once this was the bustling heart of the medieval castle: kitchens and storerooms, bedchambers and dungeons.

Some say there is nothing to fear in the shadows. Others say that these abandoned medieval halls are home to the wandering spirits of the dead. Down in the depths, beneath the ruined tower, the castle dungeons echo with the savage growl of the Black Dog of Rosslyn.

The year was AD 1303 and Scotland was a nation without a king. The sudden death of King Alexander III, with no clear heir to succeed him, had left the throne empty. Thirteen men came forward, each claiming the crown for themselves. These Scottish nobles, their families and allies, fell to bickering and feuding amongst themselves and Scotland was left divided, leaderless and vulnerable. Unable to decide who should succeed, the Scottish nobles invited King Edward the First of England to intercede and choose a king. True to form, Edward chose a weak puppet ruler that he could manipulate. The divisions within the Scots nobility deepened. John Balliol, the puppet king, was deposed, Edward laid claim to the Scots crown, and England and Scotland were at war.

William Wallace, Guardian of Scotland, had led the Scots to victory at Stirling Bridge and to grim defeat at Falkirk. Wallace spent years in self-imposed exile negotiating trade deals, petitioning the Pope, rallying support wherever he could. In February 1303, Wallace was back in Scotland and King Edward sent a force of 30,000 troops north to destroy the Scots. The stage was set for the Battle of Roslin.

Legend says that among the 30,000 was an English soldier who led a huge black war hound. As battle was met, amid the bloody chaos of knights, archers, foot soldiers, axes, arrows and broadswords, the black dog stood by its master defending him from the Scots soldiers. In the mêlée, the English soldier was slain, at which the hound viciously set upon the Scot who had killed its master. So ferocious was the hound's attack that the Scots soldier had to kill it as he fought for his own life.

As the sun set, the battlefield was covered with the dead and dying. The slaughter was horrendous, with tens of thousands of men slain and thousands more grievously wounded. But, as darkness fell, the Scots had won the day.

That night, at Rosslyn Castle, some Scots soldiers sat and

celebrated in the guardhouse. Battle-weary and the worse for drink, they sang songs and recounted tales, then without warning a horrific apparition appeared amid them: an enormous black dog. The ghost dog growled and bore its sharp fangs. Its pitch-black hair stood on end, hackles raised and eyes wild. The soldiers fled, running in terror from the guardhouse, screaming as they fought to get away.

In the small hours of the morning, the bravest soldier returned. He could find no sign that the ghost dog had ever been there. However, the following night, as the Scots soldiers rested from a long day among the dead, the phantom hound appeared again, all teeth and claws, as hellish as before. Each night the black dog came to haunt and torment the Scots, and in time the frightened soldiers nicknamed it the 'Mauthe Doog'.

One night, the soldier who had killed the hound's master took his turn to stand guard. Nervously he paced the silent passageways, rattling the castle keys for company. From nowhere came the black dog, snarling and staring him down with its cold, dead eyes. The Scots soldier ran in blind panic. His screams woke the castle as he clawed at doors and scrambled up spiral stairs on his hands and knees with the dog's howls ringing in his ears. He never told what he saw, he never spoke a word to anyone again and after three days he died.

It is said that the black dog was rarely seen from then on, but on dark lonely nights its baying can be heard and its footfalls still echo in the deserted chambers of Rosslyn Castle.

'Never let the truth get in the way of a good story' the saying goes. The truth is that, in reality, Rosslyn Castle was not even built when the Battle of Roslin took place. So, is the ghost dog haunting the wrong castle?

The name 'Rosslyn' has at its root two Scots words: 'Ross' – hill, and 'Lynn' – waterfall. In 1303, the hill in the water was just that: a bare hill at a bend in the River Esk. At that time, the castle at Rosslyn was further down river, and was an earlier, far less sophisticated fortress built of stone and wood on a low mound.

The St Clairs of Rosslyn were Scots knights whose family had been granted the lands and barony of Rosslyn by King Alexander III on 14 September 1280. Sir William and his son Sir Henry had been at Dunbar in 1297. They were captured by King Edward the First's forces as the English army overwhelmed the Scots. Knights and the nobility were valuable prizes in medieval warfare. The St Clairs, along with other Scots nobles, were held prisoner in English castles to be traded for English prisoners or ransomed back to their families and allies. Sir William languished in Gloucester Castle while Sir Henry was held at St Briavels Castle on the Welsh border near Monmouth. In all, 171 Scots knights and esquires were taken prisoner at Dunbar.

We imagine that chivalry, the laws of knighthood, ensured that medieval warfare was bound by rules of conduct and that knights would protect the poor and the innocent. The reality of the medieval Wars of Independence was brutal and appalling. Entire towns of men, women and children were butchered as both the English and Scots troops committed what we would term 'war atrocities'. The value of a knight in ransom was the only thing that made his life worth anything to the opposing force.

There was nothing heroic or romantic about battle. Men were hacked to death with axe, sword and pike. Towns and villages became slaughterhouses as troops looted, raped, burned and murdered. The Scots nobles switched sides and allegiances as they squabbled for power. They traded their loyalty as the Scots commoners fought and died under William Wallace.

By 1303, the St Clairs had been exchanged for English knights and were back in Rosslyn. It was early February. The days were short and the sun offered little warmth; the icy cold froze the morning dew in the fields. Through the chill winter, the English army of 30,000 men trudged north towards a Scots force of only 8,000. The Scots marched to Roslin under the leadership of Sir Simon Fraser and John 'the Red' Comyn. It is thought that

William Wallace fought at the Battle of Roslin, suggesting battle tactics but declining to lead the Scots after his defeat at the Battle of Falkirk.

The English army split into three separate forces, planning initially to attack three different Scottish strongholds. Just before dawn, the Scots fell on the first English encampment as they rested near Roslin. The surviving English troops, under the command of Sir John Seagrave, surrendered as the sun rose. At first light, the Scots were exhausted from battle and from an overnight forced march with little or no sleep. Then the cry went up: a second English force was sighted on its way. The English knights were kept for ransom, but the infantry were massacred so they could not rise up to join the new force.

The river already ran red with blood. Thousands lay dead and dying as the second battle was met.

The River Esk cuts a deep gorge in the sandstone at Roslin. The deeply wooded glen gives way to sudden, deadly cliffs. The English cavalry galloped recklessly through the trees, chasing down the Scots soldiers, trying to trample them underfoot. Without warning, the English knights saw the ground vanish from beneath them as they fell headlong into the gorge.

The day wore on and in time the third English force came into view. Fraser and Comyn tried to rally the Scots, but their men were broken and bloody. In the fields to the north of Roslin, the Scots began the last battle. The lands around Roslin village still bear names that commemorate that day: 'Shinbanes Field', where the ploughs would turn up acres of bones in the soil; and 'Kill Burn', the river that was filled with the dead and dying.

At twilight, the Scots Prior Abernethy of Mount Lothian had a huge wooden cross raised in the far Pentland Hills. As the dying sun set behind the cross, the Scots troops took heart at this sign from heaven. Night fell and the tide of battle turned as the ragged Scots army defeated the last of their enemy. In one bloody day, 8,000 Scots had beaten a force over three times their number.

The Battle of Roslin is now largely forgotten. It is often overlooked entirely or relegated among skirmishes and minor engagements. 'History is written by the victors' and the Wars of Independence were narrated by Blind Harry in *The Wallace* and John Barbour in *The Brus*. Sir Simon Fraser fell at the terrible Battle of Halidon Hill. The Red Comyn was murdered before the high altar of Greyfriars Monastery in Dumfries by Robert the Bruce. The knights that led the Scots to victory at Roslin were dead within a few years and effectively written out of history.

The English lieutenant Sir John Seagrave, who led the English forces, was ransomed back to Edward the First. Though we will never know for sure, it is interesting to think that Wallace may have met Seagrave at Roslin. It would probably have been their first meeting but not their last. Two years later, when the tables were turned and Wallace was the prisoner, it would be Seagrave who was charged with delivering Wallace from Edinburgh to London. Sir John Seagrave would sit at the trial of Wallace and bear witness as Wallace was hung by the neck, disembowelled, hacked into quarters and beheaded.

As Wallace was being butchered in London, a new castle was being built at Rosslyn. Father Richard Augustine Hay, in his *Genealogie of the Sainteclaires of Rosslyn, circa* 1700, tells us that an English soldier captured at the Battle of Roslin advised the St Clair family on where and how to build their new castle.

If Hay is to be believed, the unnamed English soldier was 'a man of no small estimation in England'. He advised the St Clairs that the original site of the castle was not 'strong enough' and chose another location, at a bend in the River Esk, where the new castle was build on a foundation of solid rock.

This new Rosslyn Castle was a traditional fourteenth-century tower, an imposing and easily defendable fortress built for a century of war. In the decades that followed, the Lords of Rosslyn added high walls, towers and underground chambers to their stronghold. Sir William St Clair, the third St Clair Earl of Orkney and founder of Rosslyn Chapel, remodelled the castle in the flamboyant continental style of fifteenth-century France.

Hay compiled the genealogy for his stepfather-in-law, James Sinclair, around the year 1700, 400 years after the battle. In 1688, when a Protestant mob attacked the castle and chapel, Hay was staying at Rosslyn Castle:

> Those monuments, with some other part of the Chapell . . . were a little defaced by the rabble; the eleventh of December 1688, about 10 of the clock att night, after the castle had been spoiled, where I lost severall books of note . . .

Hay is not exactly noted as a terribly reliable genealogist or historian. Despite the fact that pseudo-historians seem to happily accept every word he writes, it has long been noted that Hay tends to exaggerate and occasionally make things up to fill in the gaps in his sources. As Dr Rev. Professor H.J. Lawlor, D.D., FSA Scot once observed, it is 'probably universally admitted that Father Hay is not a writer whose unsupported testimony can be implicitly accepted'. Hay's genealogy may not be a great work of history but it is certainly a wonderful collection of local legends.

Rosslyn Castle has attracted many legends over the years: the supernatural White Lady of Rosslyn protects a hidden treasure, a dark knight on horseback gallops across the castle drawbridge, phantom flames engulf the castle and chapel when a St Clair dies, and the ghost dog still prowls the castle's underground passageways.

Phantom black dogs have appeared across Great Britain for hundreds of years. The Church Grim or Kirk Grim haunted graveyards. Its appearance was a portent of death, though it was also said to protect the dead from the devil and his demons. The Barguest was a fearsome creature with razor-sharp claws and fangs, a black shaggy coat and fiery eyes. Guytrash, Shriker and Padfoot were Yorkshire and Lancashire names for the phantom black dogs that haunted deserted trackways. The Gurt Dog was the benevolent ghost dog of Somerset while Old Shock appeared in Suffolk, Black Shuck haunted East Anglia and Black Angus appeared in Scotland.

On Sunday, 4 August 1577, a Black Dog appeared in two Suffolk Churches. In Bungay, during a violent thunderstorm, the beast burst into the church and killed two of the terrified worshippers. In the church at Blythborough, more villagers died and the creature left claw marks in the church door.

Supernatural black dogs also ran with the Wild Hunt across the skies of Britain. The Wild Hunt was a terrifying apparition: monstrous hounds led by a fearsome dark rider chased human prey down lonely roads and across empty fields. Near Cadbury, in the West Country, is King Arthur's Lane. It is said that on winter nights King Arthur himself leads a pack of ghostly black hounds along the ancient track. In France, the Wild Hunt is known as *'la chasse Artu'*. In Wales, the Wild Hunt was led by Arthur or by Gwyn ap Nudd, the lord of Annwfyn, ruler of the faerie underworld. On Dartmoor, the Wild Hunt legend tells of the Wish Hounds led by the mysterious Wistman, thought by some to be the devil but probably a name derived from the local dialect word 'whisht', meaning uncanny or eerie. The Wish Hounds haunted Wistman's Wood, an ancient copse of gnarled and twisted oak trees covered in moss and lichens. In Cornwall, it was Dando and his Devil's Dandy Dogs; in Peterborough, the Wild Hunt was led by King Herla. In the north, the Gabble Retchets or Gabriel Hounds of the hunt were not named for the Archangel but for an old name for 'corpse'. Across Britain, the Black Dog was a portent of death, an ill omen. William Wordsworth wrote of the Wild Hunt:

> He oftentimes will start,
> For overhead are sweeping Gabriel's Hounds,
> Doomed, with their impious lord, the flying hart
> To chase for ever through aerial grounds.

A legend from the Isle of Man closely resembles the tale of the Ghost Dog of Rosslyn Castle. Tradition says that Peel Castle is haunted by a spectral hound known as the 'Mauthe Doog' or 'Moddey-dhoo'. As night fell and candles were lit, the dog would appear in the guard chamber and lie down by the fire. At first, the soldiers of the castle were terrified of the beast, but in time they learned to avoid it, fearing its malicious nature. Then, one foul night, a drunken soldier made to attack the Mauthe Doog 'whether it were dog or devil!' He never spoke another word and died three days later 'in agonies more than is common in a natural death'. The legend of the Mauthe Doog of Peel Tower was noted by Sir Walter Scott in *Peveril of the Peak* and in *The Lay of the Last Minstrel*:

> 'Twas fear'd his mind would ne'er return;
> For he was speechless, ghastly, wan,
> Like him of whom the story ran,
> Who spoke the spectre Hound in Man.

Sir Walter Scott, *Peveril of the Peak*, 1882

Scott was an avid collector of ballads, traditional tales and fairy lore. He was bewitched by Rosslyn's chapel and castle and is probably responsible for creating some of the legends of Rosslyn. It is certainly an amazing coincidence that legends of the Mauthe Doog of Man and the Mauthe Doog of Rosslyn are so similar. It appears that the phantom hound of Rosslyn Castle may be nothing more than a ghost story relocated to Scotland by Sir Walter Scott. But there is one final twist to the tale.

Some decades ago, on a Saturday afternoon near the end of February, two boys about twelve years old were playing in the underground chambers and stone-cut passageways of Rosslyn Castle. Neil's aunt, Miss Leitch, was the caretaker. She lived in the castle after the Second World War and often found Neil and his friend John Ritchie running around the ruined castle exploring all its dark nooks and crannies. This particular day the pair were investigating down on the second level when they suddenly became aware of a light coming from the far end of the corridor.

The light began to grow brighter. The two boys stared at each other, turned and ran for it. John recalls that as they ran up the castle's stone stair the light 'moving towards us down the corridor was what appeared to be a large wolfhound-type dog, which ran underneath us and appeared to go straight through the wall'. The large grey dog vanished into the wall at the site of a blocked-up doorway.

The boys kept running until they were suddenly met by Miss Leitch. As the two boys blurted out their story, Miss Leitch smiled back then said softly, 'Aye, boys, it's an auld castle, with lots of strange things like that, but dinnae worry about them. They will no' harm ye. Now, come and have a bottle of lemonade!'

CHAPTER THREE

Robert The Bruce And The White Deer

A KNIGHT ON HORSEBACK gallops through a dark forest 700 years ago. Thundering hooves fall heavily on the ground as the rider and his party approach Rosslyn Castle.

Nearing home, the knight and his companions approach the stone fortress deep within the glen. The forest was a wild place then, with tangled trees and patches of moorland stretching for miles in every direction. The riders dismount and the stable boys tend to the horses. The knight, Sir William St Clair, enters the tiny private chapel in the castle and drops to his knees to give thanks. Through the family's patron saint, St Catherine, William prays to Christ and the Blessed Virgin. He is especially grateful this day for their divine intervention and for his two fine hunting hounds, 'Help' and 'Hold'.

Legend has it that in 1296 William Wallace, Guardian of Scotland, knighted Henry St Clair, the father of this Sir William. The ceremony was said to have taken place at a religious house based at Mount Lothian. Both Henry and William fought under

Wallace and King Robert the Bruce. In the years after the Battle of Bannockburn, the king and his knights were able to engage in the lordly pursuit of the deer hunt.

During the age of chivalry, the nobility had three passions: warfare, courtly love and hunting with hawk or hound. The art of the hunt, although described as a leisurely pursuit, was in fact a very serious affair. Hunting not only provided meat for the banqueting table but also gave an opportunity to practise skills required for battle. Both required cunning, perseverance, fortitude, zeal and courage. Medieval hunters had a great deal of respect for their prey. The 'sacrifice' of the hunt described by medieval writers suggests that the death of the deer was often viewed as a metaphor for the sacrifice of Christ.

In his castle, the Bruce received word that a mysterious 'white faunch deer' had been spotted at Pentland, in the king's forest. White deer are rare and magical. In legends and tales, they are otherworldly creatures associated with the realm of faerie. Some accounts say the white deer was a stag whilst others suggest it was a hind.

A hunt was arranged, messengers were dispatched and the king and his nobles headed out to a stone landmark far beyond the outskirts of Edinburgh. The 'Buckstane' was an ancient standing stone that sat upon the brow of a hill. Here, the buckhounds and huntsmen gathered to prepare for the hunts in the royal forests. The Buckstane has now been relocated and lies within the modern city limits near to Mortonhall Golf Clubhouse at the Braids.

Randolph de Clerc of Penicuik, then a village a few miles from Rosslyn, was responsible this day for blowing the hunting horn to signal the start of the royal hunt. The horn had a vital role within the pageant. Various blasts that day signalled when groups of hounds were to be released, the distance between the deer and the hounds, when the deer took to water to escape and, finally, the end of the chase.

Local villagers were strategically placed around the hunting ground to contain the deer within the hunt area. The hunting party itself consisted of only a privileged few. Accounts name Sir William St Clair, the Good Sir James Douglas, Randolph de Clerc, the Earl of Forfar and, as Master of the Hunt, King Robert the Bruce.

To the south of the Buckstane, the hunt arrived at the tiny village of Pentland, an ancient burial place of the St Clair family. Today this area is among open fields but 700 years ago it was on the edge of dense woodlands beneath the moors of Pentland. From Pentland, the king as the Master of the Hunt led the knights deep into the forest. First they headed down alongside the River Esk and then, once they reached the river, they next headed off towards the holy site at Mount Lothian. Very shortly, along this trail, a commotion broke out. In the distance, a hunting horn could be heard. The blast notified the king that the white deer had been spotted and at the king's order the hounds were released.

The hunters pursued the white deer towards the rising ground near House of Muir not far from Glencorse burn. The terrified deer desperately tried to lose the hunt by changing direction at Turnhouse. The hounds sped on as the deer raced frantically over the slopes of Logan Glen towards a narrow outlet. With the hounds snapping and snarling a few strides behind, the exhausted deer bounded a stream in the hills called the March Burn in a final attempt to escape. Across the water, it darted off into overgrown brushwood and into the depths of the forest, disappearing from sight.

Randolph signalled his huntsmen, but there was no sign of the deer. King Robert knew that all was lost for the day and ordered that the hunt be abandoned. The hounds were recalled and the hunting horn was blasted once more. Disappointment was apparent on the faces of the hunters, but the king vowed that this beast would not escape him again.

Various accounts of the legend differ about what happened next. Some are far more elaborate than others, no doubt having been embellished over the years. One version says that the royal party retired to nearby Logan House in the valley between Black Hill and Carnethy Hill or to the nearby Threipmuir Farm ('threip' is old Scots meaning to argue or quarrel). Sir William, drunk on ale, boasted that his two red fellow hounds, Help and Hold, could have easily caught the white deer if they had led the hunt. In a drunken boast, he wagered his head that they would kill the deer before it crossed the March Burn.

Another version records Sir William as the lead huntsman. Being a favourite of the king, William thought nothing of innocently suggesting that his hounds would succeed should the king wish to use them. Again, he wagered his head against the deer being caught before it crossed the March Burn. Unheard by the king, who was deep in thought, Sir William's remarks deeply offended some of the nobles, who took his suggestion as an arrogant boast. The Earl of Forfar approached Sir William, furiously shouting down the young knight. Hands flew to swords and at this point the king intervened. The king chastised Sir William for staking his life in such a rash boast. He proclaimed that the young knight would be held to the wager and matched it: staking all the lands of the Pentland Hills and Moors, and the forest, should Sir William's hounds succeed.

Word of Sir William's foolish wager spread quickly and people from across over the land came to witness the spectacle of the hunt. At daybreak, people were allocated their places around the hunt area in accordance to their rank and social standing. Sir William knelt in silent prayer at the Buckstane. He prayed to 'Chrift, the bleffed Virgin Marie, and Sainte Katherine' to save him from danger.

Some miles away, the king waited at a place now called King's Hill. From there he could watch the final stages of the hunt, down in the valley, by the March Burn. Assembled with the king were members of Sir William's family: his father, his uncle the Bishop of Dunkeld, and his betrothed the Lady Elizabeth de Spar. Other ladies from the castles of Rosslyn, Dalhousie and Dirleton joined them. Suitable judges were appointed and placed near to the March Burn. Assisting the contest were men deployed to direct the deer towards the spot where it had previously escaped.

The horn sounded and the hunt began. A little way into the hunt, Sir William and Randolph de Clerc heard a second horn blast: a huntsman named Cleland of Rosslyn had spotted the deer. His slow hounds gave chase. As the white deer passed, Help and Hold were released. The life-and-death challenge had begun. A mile west of Auchendinny, the hounds almost caught the deer, but it escaped and headed towards Beeslack on the outskirts of Penicuik. Racing ahead, the white deer once more ran towards House of Muir and the March Burn.

At the foot of the Pentland Hills, the huntsmen cheered on the hounds. Moments later, the king and the gathered nobles watched as the knights, the hounds and the white deer tore towards the March Burn. Help and Hold had gained some ground but Sir William, fearing that all was lost, dismounted. Randolph de Clerc charged past with the hounds still in hot pursuit as the white deer splashed into the waters of the burn. Sir James Douglas is said to have cried, 'Help, Hold, gin ye may or Rosslyn tynes his head this day' – 'Help, Hold, if you may or Rosslyn loses his head this day'.

As the deer made to cross the March Burn, the Lady Elizabeth looked on in horror. Suddenly the white deer stopped in the middle of the burn. At that moment, Sir William's hound Help leapt upon the deer and bit its hind leg. Then Hold launched its attack, tearing at the white deer's throat. As Father Hay describes, William had thought his life was forfeit:

> . . . he saw the hind pass to the middle of the burn, whereat he fell on his face, beseeching Christ to have mercy on him, but the hound called Hold came to the deer, and made her stay in the burn, and then Help made her go to the same side where Sir William was, and there slew her.

The magical white deer was slain. A circle of knights led by the king formed in the clearing where Sir William stood, thereafter known locally as the Knight's Field. Sir William and Randolph stood at its centre. Robert the Bruce warmly congratulated Sir William on his fine hounds and happily granted the young knight the lands and forests of Pentland. Randolph, for his part, was knighted Sir Randolph de Clerc of Penicuik. Thereafter, his family were given the privilege of always sounding the horn when the king came to hunt. The town of Penicuik still bears the hunting horn on its crests in acknowledgement of its ancient laird.

Near the spot where the white deer fell, Sir William built a church dedicated to St Catherine, known as St Katherine of the Hopes. The ruins of an early church are now beneath the waters of Glencorse reservoir.

One account of the Royal Hunt adds a family tragedy to the legend. That night, back within the castle, Sir William felt uneasy and retired to his bedchamber with a terrible sense of foreboding. He fell into a restless sleep haunted by dreadful nightmares in which his dead mother appeared to him. Woefully she warned him that to cruelly dispose of a white deer would bring misery and ill luck to the house of Rosslyn.

Her prophecy was soon realised as Sir William received news that his betrothed, here named the fair Rosabelle, had been drowned in a dreadful storm. She had set sail from Ravenscraig Castle in Fife to be with him, but her ship went down in the Firth of Forth:

> O listen, listen, ladies gay!
> No haughty feat of arms I tell,
> Soft is the note, and sad the lay,
> That mourns the lovely Rosabelle;
>
> . . . Last night the gifted Seer did view
> A wet shroud swathed round ladye gay;

Then say thee, Fair, in Ravensheuch:
"Why cross the gloomy firth today?"

. . . There are twenty of Roslin's barons bold
Lie buried within that proud chapelle;
Each one the holy vault doth hold —
But the sea holds lovely Rosabelle!

Sir Walter Scott, *The Lay of the Last Minstrel*, 1805

In truth, the lady Rosabelle belongs to a different century and Ravenscraig Castle was not owned by the St Clairs till the fifteenth century. The church of St Katherine of the Hopes was already built before the St Clairs were granted the lands of Pentland.

Sir William St Clair certainly fought alongside Robert the Bruce at the Battle of Bannockburn in 1314. William's father, Henry, was one of the signatories of the letter to Pope John XXII, dated 6 April 1320, better known today as the Declaration of Arbroath. Ten years later, Sir William stood on a battlefield in Spain with his brother John, Sir James Douglas, Sir Robert and Walter Logan of Restalrig and Sir William Keith of Galston. The heart of Robert the Bruce was carried by Douglas in a silver casket. The Scots had set sail after the death of Bruce on a last quest to place his heart in the Church of the Holy Sepulchre in Jerusalem. In Spain, the Scots joined the Christian army of King Alfonso XI to attack the Moors. At Teba on 25 August 1330, the Scots charged headlong into the enemy. Sir William was separated from his fellows and surrounded by Moors. He was cut down as Douglas fought to reach him.

After the battle, William Keith boiled the flesh from the dead knights' bodies and returned their bones and hearts to Scotland. William's bones went to Rosslyn, the bones and heart of Douglas to the church of St Bride and the heart of Bruce to Melrose Abbey.

At Melrose, under the Eildon Tree, Thomas the Rhymer is

said to have met the Queen of Elfland riding a milk-white horse. White was one of the colours of the faeries: white ladies, white horses, white hounds and white deer. These were supernatural creatures and their appearance marked the crossing of the boundary from the mortal world to the realm of faerie.

The white deer appears in legends, folktales and saints' lives throughout the Middle Ages. In the collection of Welsh legends known as *The Mabinogion*, Pwyll the Prince of Dyfed hunts a white stag with his pack of hounds. At a clearing in the woods, Pwyll sees another pack of hounds, shining, glittering white hounds with red ears led by Arawn, lord of Annwn. Gawain hunts the white hart with his two hounds in Malory's *Morte d'Arthur*. In another tale from *The Mabinogion*, King Arthur hunts the white stag:

> 'In the Forest I saw a stag, the like of which beheld I never yet.'
> 'What is there about him,' asked Arthur, 'that thou never didst see his like?"
> 'He is of pure white, Lord, and he does not herd with any other animal through stateliness and pride, so royal is his bearing.'

> *Geraint Son of Erbin*, Lady Charlotte Guest, trans.

In *Erec and Enide*, the twelfth-century French Arthurian romance, King Arthur wishes to revive the traditional hunt of the white stag. In this romance, Chrétien de Troyes tells us that Gawain sponsored a tournament on the 'plain below Tenebroc', identified by Arthurian scholars as Edinburgh.

At Edinburgh, in the century that Chrétien was writing his Arthurian Romances, legend has it that David, the King of Scotland, encountered a white stag. David was out hunting on Sunday, 14 September 1128, having ignored his priest's advice not to hunt on the Sabbath. In the wilds around what is now

Arthur's Seat, he was startled by a huge white stag that appeared from nowhere. The king was thrown from his horse and lay on the ground in fear of his life. Miraculously a vision of a brilliant shining crucifix appeared between the stag's antlers. King David built an Abbey for Canons devoted to the cross. This led to the founding of Holyrood Abbey, which in turn has given its name to Holyrood Palace and to the Scottish Parliament.

Over 500 years after Sir William St Clair and his hounds, Help and Hold, are said to have hunted the white deer, James Alexander St Clair Erskine became the 3rd Earl of Rosslyn. From 1841 to 1846 and from 1852 to 1853, James was Master of the Buckhounds, in a strange echo of the medieval legend.

The magical creatures of legend and folklore still appear today. There really are white deer among herds in Scotland. Ghostly black dogs and mysterious black cats are still spotted across the British Isles. The faeries of the medieval age are still seen on wild nights and at the first light of dawn. The white deer may not be as fearsome as a dragon nor as wondrous as a unicorn but it still appears in our most popular fantasies. In *The Chronicles of Narnia* by C.S. Lewis, in *The Hobbit* by J.R.R. Tolkien and in *Harry Potter and the Prisoner of Azkahban* by J.K. Rowling, the white deer, a creature of the medieval imagination, appears and has lost none of its magic and wonder.

CHAPTER FOUR
The Murdered Apprentice

THE APPRENTICE PILLAR LIES in the south-east corner of Rosslyn Chapel. Its exquisite beauty hides a dark legend of envy and murder.

In the year AD 1446, Sir William St Clair, the third Earl of Orkney and Lord of Rosslyn, was grateful for the many blessings that he had experienced in his life. He decided to build a sumptuous church in thanks to God for all that had been bestowed upon him. When the foundations had been laid and the walls gradually began to rise, Sir William discussed the creation of an intricate pillar with the Master Mason. On viewing the design, the master craftsman shook his head and admitted that carving a pillar of such beauty would be the greatest challenge of his life.

The Master Mason gained his patron's permission to travel to Rome to study the city's architecture and to learn from the finest Italian craftsmen. Some versions of the legend suggest that he travelled to Rome to view the original pillar on which the Apprentice Pillar is based.

Months slipped by and there was no news of the Master Mason. Rumours began to circulate. Many were convinced that he had died on the journey. Others thought that the Master Mason had taken a job in Rome. Sir William grew concerned about the fate of the Master Mason and that work on the chapel was falling behind.

One day, in his master's absence, a young apprentice stonemason approached Sir William and sought his permission to carve the pillar. Some say that the boy had a vision of the finished pillar in a dream, whilst others claim that a heavenly angel guided his actions. Sir William allowed the apprentice to begin work.

Gradually, to the amazement of Sir William and the chapel craftsmen, the most incredible pillar began to appear from the rough stone. The boy's skills were equal to, if not superior to, those of his master. After weeks of devoted work, the pillar was eventually finished.

Then, to everyone's surprise, the Master Mason returned. He was eager to begin work immediately and strode into the half-completed choir. The Master Mason stared at the pillar in horror. His disbelief turned to anger. This was far superior to anything he himself could have created, and his anger and envy gave way to violent rage. He demanded to know who had carved this work in his absence. When he learned that his very own apprentice had surpassed him, his pride would not allow him to suffer this humiliation. Driven mad with envy, he grasped his mason's maul (wooden mallet) and viciously struck the boy in the head. The blow proved fatal and the young apprentice fell dead to the ground.

Some say that the Master Mason was apprehended and put to death for his heinous crime; others say that he took his own life. Either way, the Master Mason died with a noose about his neck. For years, the guides within the chapel have pointed out a head, said to be the murdered apprentice, carved high up in the south-west corner of the building. This head has a gash cut into its right brow. To his left is the head of a weeping woman, supposedly his mother, lamenting the untimely death of her son. She is always referred to as the widow but does not feature in any of the earliest written accounts of the tale. High up in the north-west corner, opposite the apprentice, is the worn head of a man said to be the Master Mason. It is said that for his terrible crime he was placed in this position so that he will look down upon the pillar carved by his apprentice for all eternity.

Finally, high in the north-east corner is a hideous swollen face said to be the bloated face of a hanged man, perhaps another depiction of the Master Mason. Carved on the outside of the building, beside the south door, are two worn figures, one with a noose around his neck. In recent years, some writers have suggested that this carving could be some kind of initiation ceremony. If the legend of the Apprentice Pillar is true, it could equally be the murderous Master Mason.

The legend of the murdered apprentice of Rosslyn Chapel has been recounted for hundreds of years, yet no contemporary fifteenth-century evidence exists. So, is there any truth to the tale?

Father Hay tells us that Sir William founded Rosslyn Chapel when he felt

> . . . his age creeping on him, made him consider how he had spent his time past, and how to spend that which was to come. Therefore, to the end he might not seem altogether unthankful to God for the benefices he received from him, it came in his mind to build a house for God's service, of most curious work . . .

But Father Hay was writing in 1700, over 250 years after the founding of the chapel. In reality, Sir William decided to build a collegiate church at the height of his power and influence. He would live for almost another 40 years, watching as his church slowly took shape.

Work halted with the death of Sir William in 1484. At this point, only the quire of the church was nearing completion. Sir Oliver St Clair, the eldest son from Sir William's second marriage, inherited the lands and properties of Rosslyn. He and his sons roofed the building but stopped work on the original grand plan for a huge cruciform church. In time, the quire became known as Rosslyn Chapel.

There has been much speculation that the chapel was deliberately left incomplete so that it would remain as an unfinished temple for 'esoteric' reasons. There is no evidence to support this. Stone foundations for the larger church have been excavated and Rosslyn's unfinished state is by no way unique. Many collegiate churches in the area, including Seton Collegiate Church in East Lothian, were also left unfinished.

The full name of Rosslyn Chapel, as recorded in a 1523 charter, is the Collegiate Church of St Matthew the Apostle and Evangelist of Rosslyn, in the diocese of Saint Andrew. Rosslyn was one of around 40 collegiate churches built in Scotland during the reigns of King James I to King James IV (1406–1513). The wealth and power of Sir William must have been vast if we are to believe his many titles according to Father Hay:

> Sir William Saintclair, called Prodigus, Knight of the Cockle and Golden Fleece, Prince of Orkney and Shetland, Duke of Holdembourg, Earl of Caithness, Lord Saintclair and Nithsdale, Sherieff of Dumfries, Admirall and Chancellor of Scotland, Wardine and Justiciar of the three Marches betwixt Scotland and England, Baron of Eckfoord, Caverton, Cousland, Roslin, Pentland, Herbertshire, Dysart, Newburgh in Buchan, Cardine, Polmese, Greneslaw, Kirkzetoune, Roxburgh, Kenrusi, &c. – titles to wearie a Spaniard.

Hay tells us that Sir William 'caused artificers to be brought from other regions and foreign kingdoms . . . masons, carpenters, smiths, barrowmen and quarriers'. The Master Mason received 40 pounds yearly while 'everyone of the rest' received 10 pounds. It is said that every carving was first chiselled in wood so that 'the work might be more rare' and so Sir William could approve the designs before they were carved in stone. There were so many craftsmen and masons that 'the town of Rosline' was build to accommodate the workers, all of whom were given a house and lands. Among the young men who set about dressing the rough stone was the legendary apprentice.

The first written account of the legend of the murdered apprentice at Rosslyn dates to approximately 200 years after the building of the chapel. Thomas Kirk, a Yorkshire man, kept a journal of his extensive travels throughout Scotland towards the end of the seventeenth century. Kirk recorded in his journal a brief stop he made at St Catherine's Balm Well at Liberton before heading on to Rosslyn:

> . . . Roslen Chapel, a very pretty design, but was never finished, the choir only and a little vault. The roof is all stone, with good imagery work; there is a better man at exact descriptions of the stories than he at Westminster Abbey: this story he told us that the master builder went abroad to see good patterns, but before his return his apprentice had built one pillar which exceeded all that ever he could do or had seen, therefore he slew him; and he showed us the head of the apprentice on the wall with a gash in the forehead and his master's head opposite to him.

> Thomas Kirk, August 1677

John Slezer wrote about the chapel in 1693 in his book *Theatrum Scotiae*. In a very brief account of the Chapel he makes no direct mention of the legend but merely says: 'The most curious Part of the Building is the Vault of the Quire, and that which is called the Prince's Pillar so much talk'd of.' Interestingly, Slezer does not mention an 'Apprentice Pillar' but rather a 'Prince's Pillar', presumably after Sir William, 'Prince of Orkney'.

In 1700, Father Richard Augustine Hay wrote his *Genealogie of the Saintclaires of Rosslyn*. Hay's mother married Sir James St Clair of Rosslyn after the death of her first husband. Hay, a priest and historian, had unrestricted access to important family manuscripts, source documents that are now all lost or destroyed. Hay collects the various legends associated with the St Clair family, the chapel and the castle, but he makes no mention at all of the legend of the Apprentice Pillar.

Daniel Defoe, the famous author of *Robinson Crusoe*, named it 'the Princess's Pillar' in 1723. Robert Forbes, writing in 1761, recorded the now famous 'Prentice or Apprentice Pillar'. The difference in the names may simply be that writers transcribed what they heard. Perhaps Slezer and Defoe simply misunderstood the local Roslin dialect.

Over the years, many characters have put their mark on the legend. A local guide to the chapel, Annie Wilson, was famed for her rendition of the apprentice legend. Annie was the landlady at the local inn, now College Hill House, next door to the chapel. She acted as a guide to visitors to the ruined chapel for around 50 years from the end of the eighteenth century into the early nineteenth century and became something of a local celebrity. Her 'trademark' pointing stick appeared in an 1809 painting of Rosslyn Chapel by Joseph Michael Gandy, and she was featured in an article written for the *Gentleman's Magazine* in September 1817.

Annie always carried a long stick around the chapel to point out the various carvings to her visitors. It is said that prior to visitors arriving she would apply red ochre to the cut carved in the Apprentice's Head! Annie's account of the legend was recorded in her broad local accent in the *Gentleman's Magazine*:

There ye see it with the lace bands winding sae beautifully roond aboot it. The maister had gane away to Rome to get a plan for it, and while he was away his 'prentice made a plan himself and finished it. And when the maister came back and fand the pillar finished, he was sae enraged that he took a hammer and killed the 'prentice. There you see the prentice's face up there in the corner, wi' a red gash in the brow, and his mother greetin' for him in the corner opposite. And there, in another corner is the maister, as he lookit just before he was hanged; it's him wi' a kind o' ruff roond his neck.

[There you see it with the lace bands winding so beautifully around about it. The master had gone away to Rome to get a plan for it, and while he was away his apprentice made a plan himself and finished it. And when the master came back and found the pillar finished, he was so enraged that he took a hammer and killed the apprentice. There you see the apprentice's face up there in the corner, with a red gash in the brow, and his mother crying for him in the corner opposite. And there, in another corner is the master, as he looked just before he was hanged; it's him with a kind of ruff round his neck.]

Annie and her husband Daniel provided hospitality to all those who visited Roslin. Her celebrity visitors included Dr Samuel Johnson, James Boswell, Dorothy Wordsworth, Sir Walter Scott, Alexander Nasmyth and Robert Burns. Burns, obviously impressed with Annie's hospitality, scratched a couple of verses for her on a pewter plate at the inn:

> My Blessings on you sonsie wife!
> I ne'er was here before;
> You've gi'en us walth for horn and Knife,
> Nae heart could wish for more.

Heaven keep you free from care and strife,
Til far ayont fourscore;
And while I toddle on through life,
I'll ne'er gang by your door.

[My Blessings on you fortunate (or lucky) wife!
I never was here before;
You've given us wealth for horn and Knife, (plenty to
    drink and eat)
No heart could wish for more.

Heaven keep you free from care and strife,
Until far beyond fourscore (eighty years);
And while I walk on through life,
I'll never go by your door.]

The famous writer Sir Walter Scott was not quite so generous. Whilst out at Rosslyn with his friends Gilles and Erskine, Scott noted that 'as habitual visitors, perhaps they would escape the usual endless story of a silly old woman that showed the ruins! There is pleasure in the song which none but the songstress knows. By telling her we know it already, we should make the poor devil unhappy.'

While we will never really know if a young apprentice was murdered within Rosslyn Chapel, we do know that very similar legends are recounted about churches and cathedrals across medieval Europe.

At Rouen Cathedral in Northern France, where Joan of Arc was executed in 1431, there is an apprentice tale associated with two famous rose windows. The master craftsman of Rouen and his apprentice were set to work in competition with each other. The master gave his prodigy one window to work on, whilst he made the other. When the work was completed, the master's window was acknowledged as a fine piece of work, but his apprentice had created an outstanding stained-glass window far superior to that of his master. The master flew into a jealous rage and killed the poor apprentice.

At Melrose Abbey in the Scottish Borders, there is a 'Prentice Window', created by another murdered apprentice. At Lincoln Cathedral, in England, there is a similar tradition. There, an apprentice made a beautiful rose window as in the Rouen story but, just like the Rosslyn tale, the work was carried out in his master's absence. The master in this story was so overcome by his apprentice's superior skill that he took his own life in shame.

Gloucester Cathedral has a 'Prentice Bracket'. This carving is said to depict an apprentice who fell to his death in the fifteenth century while he was working on the south transept. The cathedral custodians e-mailed us the following description:

> The bracket is 'L' shaped like the medieval masons' 'T' square and has led some to suggest that it was the gift of a master mason or more probably a memorial to a mason or mason's apprentice who died after falling from scaffolding in the south transept. The carving depicts an old mason sitting with the tools of his trade in his lap looking thoroughly distraught. In front of him is the splayed body of another workman, possibly an apprentice, lying on an exact miniature of the transept vault. Some people suggest that it is a general memorial to all who died in the Cathedral's construction. Others suggest that it is a record of the life of a mason from youth to old age.

The medieval St Clairs of Rosslyn had close ties with France, so they may well have known the romance associated with the building of Cologne Cathedral. A popular tale in medieval times, the story was known as the 'Four Sons of Aymon'. *The right plesaunt and goodlie historie of the foure sonnes of Aymon* was one of the first books ever printed in England. It was published by William Caxton, famed for his printing of Thomas Malory's *Morte d'Arthur.*

At the time of Charlemagne, the four sons of the Count Aymon of Dordogne – Reynaud, Alard, Guichard and Richard – were attached to the king's court at Paris. The eldest son, Sir Reynaud, was known as a chivalrous and brave knight. He so pleased the king that Charlemagne gifted him a wonderful horse named Bayard. All was well until one day Bertholais, the king's nephew, lost his temper whilst playing Reynaud at chess. Reynaud struck out and killed Bertholais. In fear of what would happen next, he fled the court with his brothers. In time, Reynaud was forgiven and vowed to set off on a pilgrimage. While Reynaud was in the Holy Land, his beloved wife died, and on his return he gave up his wealth and divided his estate between his two sons.

Eventually, Reynaud reached Cologne, where he took work as a stonemason on the construction of the cathedral. He proved to be an excellent craftsman, his work arousing the envy of the other masons. Some workmen slew him as he slept – the ruffians dealt him a deathblow with a mason's mallet.

To hide the evidence of their dastardly crime, they put Reynaud's body in a sack and threw it into the river. As it hit the water, a miracle occurred. Reynaud's corpse was raised to the surface of the waters by fishes whilst angels sang around it. The archbishop had Reynaud's body interred, first at Croym then finally at Cologne, where he was venerated as a Christian martyr.

Sacrifice at the building of holy temples has been suggested as a theme of these various tales. In Scotland at the time of the Celtic Church, there is a strange tale told of St Oran. According to the legend, he was buried alive as a sacrifice to prevent the walls of the first church on Iona from falling down. St Columba had travelled to the Isle of Iona with 12 disciples to found a Christian community on what had previously been an ancient Druid isle. Bizarrely, St Columba is said to have asked for one of his followers to volunteer to be buried alive in the foundations of the new building to somehow sanctify the church. Oran volunteered and with due ceremony was buried alive. After three days, Columba asked that the body of Oran be exhumed. When the grave was opened, Oran was alive and well. Legend says that he exclaimed, 'There is no such great wonder in death, nor is hell what it has been described.' At these remarks, St Columba hastily ordered, 'Earth, earth on Oran's eyes, lest he further blab,' and so the unfortunate Oran was entombed for ever.

It has been suggested that the tale of the murdered apprentice of Rosslyn is somehow related to the third degree in Freemasonry and the Masonic legend of Hiram Abif. The building of Solomon's Temple in Jerusalem is a central theme of Freemasonry. Freemasonic legend tells of a Grand Master named Hiram who was in charge of the building of the Temple of Solomon. Not an apprentice but a Grand Master, Hiram is murdered because he will not share the secrets of his degree with those of an inferior grade. He is attacked by three assailants, fellows of craft less skilled than a master mason. He is killed with a mason's maul.

It is clear that legends of masons and murders in churches and cathedrals were common across medieval Europe, hundreds of years before the founding of Freemasonry. There is no credible evidence that the Apprentice carvings within Rosslyn Chapel depict the Freemasonic legend of Hiram.

Many books have alleged that the dragons carved round the base of the Apprentice Pillar are a depiction of Norse legends. It has been suggested that the Apprentice Pillar represents Yggdrasil, the tree of knowledge at the end of the world. Odin hung suspended upside down from the branches of Yggdrasil to obtain wisdom and knowledge. Odin was the Norse god associated with death, wisdom and magic. He belonged to the mysterious region between life and death. So great was Odin's search for knowledge that he was prepared to sacrifice himself to learn the secret alphabet of the runes. He hung upside down on the great tree for nine days and nights with neither food nor drink.

At the base of Yggdrasil is a well said to hold the deepest wisdom. A dragon called Nidhogg, who lives in Niflheim, the lowest of the nine worlds, protects this wisdom. Round the base of the Apprentice Pillar at Rosslyn we find dragons chewing at the roots of the vines in order to keep this wisdom away from those who are not worthy. Yet again we find the Apprentice Pillar associated with sacrifice.

At the crown of the pillar is a carving depicting Abraham, his son Isaac and the ram in the thicket. In the Old Testament Book of Genesis, Abraham is commanded by God to sacrifice his son on a mountaintop. They climbed the mountain together; Abraham carrying the sacrificial knife and the fire while Isaac brought the wood. Abraham built an altar, bound Isaac and laid him on the wood but as he raised the knife an angel appeared, and told him to stay his hand. Instead, Abraham was to sacrifice a ram that had its horns tangled in a thicket.

Beside the Apprentice Pillar, there are plants carved round the arch of a stained glass window. In recent years, these have been misinterpreted as 'maize' or 'Indian corn'. Pseudo-history writers have let their imaginations run away with them and imagine this carving and another plant they allege is 'aloe cactus' somehow prove that a forebear of the chapel's founder sailed to the New World and back before Columbus.

Again, we find credibility stretched to breaking point. The 'aloe cactus' carvings are clearly wild strawberry leaves, a common medieval motif that represented the Trinity. The 'maize' is actually woven bundles of wheat; both arcs of the window arch are bowing down to a central sheaf. This carving depicts the story of Joseph's first dream in the book of Genesis. Joseph had been given a coat of many colours by his father Jacob. His brothers grew jealous. Their resentment deepened as Joseph told them of two prophetic dreams. In the first, Joseph and his brothers were binding sheaves of wheat in the fields and his brother's sheaves bowed down to his sheaf. In the second dream, the sun, the moon and the stars bowed down to him. His brothers in a fit of jealousy threw Joseph into a well then sold him as a slave. Christian writers have said that Joseph's descent into the pit and drawing back out prefigure the Entombment and Resurrection of Christ.

The Apprentice Pillar has long been associated with murder and death, but it seems that there is a deeper mystery connecting the pillar with sacrifice. The murder of the apprentice, the Norse myth of Odin, the story of Abraham and Isaac, and of Joseph and the pit, all point towards a theme of sacrifice. If Rosslyn Chapel had been completed as its founder intended, the existing chapel would have been the east quire of a vast cruciform building. The Apprentice Pillar would have been the very head of the cross, recalling the sacrifice of Christ.

CHAPTER FIVE

Merlin And The Two Dragons

WIZARDS, DRAGONS, KINGS AND castles are the stuff of legends.

In Dark Age Britain, a treacherous king tried to build a castle. The usurper Vortigern had the true king murdered and stole his throne. He hired foreign Saxon mercenaries to fight his enemies: the Picts of the North, the Scotti from Ireland and the Britons that refused to acknowledge his rule. But the Saxons turned on Vortigern, murdering his commanders and forcing the king to flee.

Vortigern sought refuge in the wilds of North Wales, turning to his druid magicians for advice. They told him that he should build a mighty fortress upon a hilltop amid the mountains of Snowdonia. Vortigern's carpenters and masons dragged stone and timber up the steep hill to begin work, but the following morning all the building materials had vanished. On the second day, they began to build a tower, but after dark it collapsed to a heap of broken rubble. The carpenters and stonemasons spent the third day rebuilding Vortigern's tower, and again that night the tower fell.

King Vortigern grew desperate. Once more, he consulted his magicians. 'Seek a boy who has no father,' they told him. 'Kill the child, mix his blood with the mortar, sprinkle it upon the stone and the tower will stand.' Vortigern's men searched all of Wales till a fatherless boy was found and brought before the king.

As the druids prepared to sacrifice the young boy, the child calmly explained to Vortigern that he alone knew why the tower fell. 'Dig down beneath the stone pavement on the summit of the hill,' the boy told Vortigern. 'You will find a pool of still water. Deep in the pool you will find two dragons fighting ferociously. It is the dragons' battle that shakes the hill and brings your tower crashing down.'

Vortigern had his men raise the stones of the pavement and dig deep into the hill. They unearthed a pool of still water just as the boy had foretold. As the pool was drained, a red and a white dragon were revealed. The dragons fought bitterly, breathing fire and clawing at each other. The battle raged back and forth. The white dragon began to overwhelm the red, but the red dragon fought back ferociously and beat the white dragon down.

Vortigern demanded to know what this could mean. The boy fell into a prophetic trance. With tears in his eyes, he told the king that the red dragon represented the native Britons who were being overrun. The white dragon stood for the Saxon invaders from beyond the sea that Vortigern had brought to Britain. Britain's mountains would be levelled. Her rivers would run with blood. King Vortigern would die and the Britons would unite under a new king to fight the invaders. The hill was known ever after as Dinas Emrys.

The name of the boy with no father was Merlin.

In Rosslyn Chapel, above a doorway in the west wall, is a carving of two dragons: the white and red dragons that Merlin saw, wings unfurled, fighting tooth and claw.

But why are the two dragons from a legend of Merlin in

Wales carved in Rosslyn Chapel and what do the legends of King Arthur and the wizard Merlin have to do with Scotland?

This is the first book among all the published accounts of the chapel to identify Arthurian carving within Rosslyn. There are literally thousands of carved figures in Rosslyn Chapel: angels, green men, magical creatures, wondrous beasts, saints, and flowers. There is a wealth of biblical imagery from the Old and New Testaments and creatures from medieval bestiaries, including griffons, a merman, a camel, an ape, an elephant and many dragons.

Monstrous dragons appear in myths, legends and folktales worldwide. Across the British Isles, local knights rode out to defeat terrible dragons, wyrms and serpents. In the village of Linton, a vile serpent crawled from the dragon hole to eat stray villagers. A stone above the church door is said to depict Lord Somerville slaying the dragon with a fiery lump of peat on the end of his lance. The dragon of Wantley was killed by More of More Hall. More was a far less chivalrous knight. He had a suit of armour custom made – covered in spikes so that he resembled a 'strange outlandish hedgehog'. More proceeded to drink half a dozen pots of ale and a quart or so of aqua vitae. He then hid in the village well and thumped the dragon when it came to drink. Finally, he snuck up behind the dragon and struck a fatal blow . . . a swift kick to its vulnerable rear end.

St Columba is reputed to have rescued a young boy from a fearsome serpent in the River Ness. The account is thought to be the first eyewitness report of the Loch Ness Monster. England's patron saint St George is, of course, a dragon slayer: he is said to have fought the dragon in the Vale of the White Horse. Beneath the Uffington White Horse lies the 'dragon hill', where the dragon fell dead. No grass will grow on the hilltop where the dragon's blood was spilt.

These legendary accounts all share the same basic elements – one dragon and one hero.

Besides the tale of the young Merlin, there are only two other

British tales that have two dragons. In Suffolk in 1449, a black and a red dragon were seen fighting in the field where Boudicca and the Iceni tribe defeated the Roman Ninth Legion centuries earlier. The other legend – the adventure of Lludd and Llefelys – features the same red and white dragons that Merlin revealed. Legend says that Lludd founded the city of London, rebuilding its walls and circling it with innumerable towers. Caer Lludd became Caer Llundein, the Londinium of the Romans.

The Welsh Triads are a collection of short verses that bards and storytellers once used to recall epic tales. The second of the *Three Fortunate Concealments of the Island of Britain* are 'The Dragons in Dinas Emrys, which Lludd son of Beli concealed'.

When Lludd ruled Britain, the land was cursed by three terrible plagues: an unknown enemy who could overhear any plan, a dreadful shriek that left all barren and a giant that stole any food that was prepared.

The second plague, the shriek, sounded on the eve of May each year, blighting the land. Lludd learned that the shriek was made by two fighting dragons. At Oxford, the exact centre of Briton, Lludd laid a trap for the dragons. He dug a pit and concealed a pot of mead within it, covered by a silk cloth. As Lludd watched, the dragons appeared: a red dragon and a white dragon, fighting fiercely. Eventually they grew weary and transformed into two piglets. The piglets fell into the pot and grew drunk on the mead. Lludd tied them up in the cloth and then buried them deep in a hill in the shadow of Mount Snowdon. There the two dragons remained until the boy Merlin revealed them.

The tale of Lludd and Llefelys is one of the Welsh tales preserved in the *White Book of Rhyddererch* and the *Red Book of Hergest*. These two collections of native tales are commonly known as *The Mabinogion*. The *White Book* was written on vellum by an unknown scribe around 1300, but the tale itself and the figures of the two dragons are thought to be far older.

The earliest surviving manuscript containing a version of the tale of the red and white dragons is the *Historia Brittonum*, the

History of the Britons, attributed to a ninth-century monk called Nennius. It tells the story of Vortigern and the two dragons. However, the fatherless boy is not Merlin but Ambrose, the son of a Roman consul. Ambrosius is the Latin form of the Welsh 'Emrys' and the boy is said to have given his name to the hill Dinas Emrys: the 'city' or 'fortress' of Ambrosius. The boy told King Vortigern that he would find a pool within the hill, two vases within the pool and a tent concealing two serpents in the vases. The pool represented the world, the tent was Vortigern's kingdom and the red and white serpents were the dragons that represented the Britons and the Saxons.

Three hundred years after *Historia Brittonum*, a Welsh cleric known as Geoffrey of Monmouth virtually copied Nennius' tale of Vortigern's tower and the two dragons, but in his version the fatherless boy was named Merlin Emrys. Geoffrey of Monmouth's *Historia Regum Britanniae*, the History of the Kings of Britain, was hugely influential. This book and the later *Vita Merlini*, the Life of Merlin, made Arthur, King of the Britons, and the mighty prophet and magician Merlin, immortal.

We imagine King Arthur and the Knights of the Round Table as fairy-tale medieval heroes. We picture them in shining silver armour, riding white warhorses and engaging in romantic adventures to rescue fair maidens. The medieval legends of King Arthur were written and recited to entertain the nobility of Europe. They wanted tales of valiant knights, of chivalry, of romantic courtly love and magical adventure. King Arthur's legendary Camelot was an imaginary castle from which he ruled an idealised Britain that had never really existed.

In reality, Arthur would have been a Dark Age warlord. He was not a king but a 'Dux Bellorum', a leader of battles. Arthur's 'knights' would have been Romano-British cavalry fighting a series of desperate battles against the invading forces that threatened to overrun all Britain.

'Dark Age' is quite misleading. In reality, British culture actually flourished after the Romans abandoned Britain in the fifth century. With the Romans gone, the Saxons, Scots and Picts took the opportunity to attack. The Britons were left to defend themselves from assaults on all sides. Legends say that one leader came forward to unite the fragmented British forces. He led the Britons in a series of decisive battles that saw the invaders defeated and Britain left in peace. His name was Arthur.

The medieval King Arthur ironically became England's greatest hero. In reality, Arthur would have spoken a version of Welsh and fought at least one of his battles in the north in what would eventually become Scotland. The earliest record we have of the name 'Arthur' appears in a Welsh poem entitled *Y Gododdin*.

This poem tells the story of a warband that gathers at Din Eidyn: the Gododdin stronghold that was to become Edinburgh. They feast and get drunk for a year then fight an epic and ultimately tragic battle in the south at Catraeth. The Gododdin were the descendants of a tribe known by the Romans as the Votadini. These were 'P-Celtic' Britons who lived in roughly the area that is now the Lothians of southern Scotland. 'P-Celtic' or, as it is also known, Brythonic, was the ancient root language of the Celtic tribes of Britain that evolved into Cornish, Breton and Welsh. It often comes as a surprise to people that large parts of Scotland were populated by Welsh-speaking 'Celtic' tribes, but fragments of their words still survive in local placenames. 'Pencaitland' and 'Penicuik' (near Rosslyn) both contain the Welsh for 'head'. Arthur Pendragon literally means 'Arthur the head dragon'. In Aneirin's *Y Gododdin* we are told of a warrior named Gwawrddur who attacked three hundred men and fed their corpses to black ravens on the fortress ramparts – 'but he was no Arthur'.

To the Britons who listened to Aneirin recite *Y Gododdin,* this Arthur needed no further introduction. Arthur's name alone was enough to recall his legendary valour. The Britons knew the tales of Arthur and his bloody exploits upon the battlefield.

Hundreds of years after the real Arthur lived, the locations of his battles were listed in Nennius' *Historia Brittonum*. There are twelve battles in all: the battle at the mouth of the river Glein, the four battles beyond the river Dubglas, the battle beyond the river Bassus, the seventh battle in the Wood of Celidon, that is, Cat Coit Celidon, the battle in the stronghold of Guinnon, the battle in the city of the Legion, the battle on the bank of the river Tribruit, the battle on the hill Agned, and the battle at Badon Hill where Arthur slew 960 men in a single charge and 'no one rode down as many as he'.

As placenames changed over the centuries, the battle locations have been lost. Academics and Arthurian enthusiasts have theorised and argued for decades about where these battles took place. Most agree on one thing: the seventh battle took place in what is now Scotland. The seventh battle 'was in the Wood of Celidon, which is, Cat Coit Celidon'. 'Cat Coid Celidon' is the forest of the Caledonians – the huge native woodland that covered much of what would become southern and central Scotland.

The Caledonian Forest was a wild place inhabited by wolves, bear, deer and boar. Its native trees – oak, mountain ash, Scots pine, birch and alder – were home to red squirrels, woodpeckers, owls and pine martins. There, among the native animals and birds, lived the real Merlin.

The real Merlin was not an ancient wizard with a pointy hat and a long white beard. He was a wild man of the woods, a bard driven mad by battle and the 'gift' of prophecy.

He was known as Myrddin Wyllt, Merlin the Wild, Merlin Caledonius, Merlin Sylvestris, Merlin of the Wood, Lailoken or Laloecen. We can piece his life story together from Welsh tales and poems, fragments of manuscripts, saints' lives, local traditions and placenames in Southern Scotland.

In AD 573, the forces of King Rhydderch and Gwenddolau clashed at the dreadful battle of Arderydd, between the Esk and Liddel rivers, at Arthuret near Carlisle. Rhydderch Hael was a Christian king, the patron of St Kentigern. Gwenddolau was a pagan prince and Merlin was his prophet and adviser. Merlin was thought to have the second sight, the ability to see into the future. At Arderydd, Merlin failed to predict that Gwenddolau would fall and his men would be brutally massacred. As Merlin stood upon the battlefield and bore witness to the dreadful slaughter, his heart and his mind broke and he fled into the woods.

Merlin was seized by a 'strange madness'. In the Wood of Celidon, he lived wild with wolves and pigs for company, eating hazel uts, acorns, the roots of herbs and bramble berries. *The Black Book of Carmarthen* contains five poems attributed to Myrddin, including 'The Dialogue of Myrddin and Taliesin' and '*Yr Afallennau*', 'Appletrees':

> Death has taken everyone, why does it not call me?
> . . . The wild man foretells the tidings which will come . . .
> Sweet-apple tree, a red-flowered tree,
> Which grows hidden in the Forest of Celyddon . . .

The forest is an enchanted place. We find dark woods in countless tales from Dante's *Divine Comedy* to the adventures in the Harry Potter books. In the Arthurian legends, the woods are places of mystery and wonder, full of faerie women, magical springs and fabulous creatures.

Legends of Merlin of the Woods are told in Scotland, Wales and France. In the Forest of Brocéliande in Brittany, Merlin met Vivian, the Lady of the Lake. He built her a crystal castle at Comper. The castle was invisible to mortal eyes; people saw only the mirror surface of the lake. Vivian charmed the old wizard, convincing him to teach her all the secrets of magic. She used Merlin's own spells to entrap him and keep him with her in the enchanted forest. In Scotland, Merlin was also entranced by a faerie woman, a mysterious being known simply as 'Hwimleian': the gleam.

A holy man named Kentigern journeyed into the Forest of Celidon to preach. As he tried to bring the message of the gospels to the local people, the wild Merlin shouted him down, throwing stones and insults. Kentigern's prayers were interrupted by Merlin the Wyld, known as Lailoken, who uttered wild prophecies and bitter laments.

The *Vita Kentigerni*, the Life of St Kentigern, was written in the twelfth century by a monk named Jocelyn of Furness, for the See of St Kentigern based at Glasgow Cathedral. To help Jocelyn, the legends of Kentigern and Merlin the Wild, and fragments of early British texts, were brought together by King David I from across his kingdom. These lost tales and the Lailoken fragments were later used by Geoffrey of Monmouth and may also have been the British source material that Chrétien de Troyes used to write *Yvain* and *The Story of the Grail*.

Kentigern's life is in many ways as strange and magical as Merlin's. He was born to the Princess Thaneu, whose father was the pagan King Loth, legendary ruler of the Lothians and Orkney. His stronghold lay on the top of the mighty Traprain Law, a huge hill which rises from the flat plains of East Lothian. Thaneu defied her father, converting to Christianity and falling pregnant. King Loth, or Leudonus, decreed that she must die.

Thaneu, by the king's command, 'was led to the top of a very high hill . . . that, cast down from thence, she might be broken limb by limb, or dashed to pieces'. She was placed in a wooden cart and thrown from the summit of the hill. The fall should have killed her, but miraculously she was unharmed. A freshwater spring appeared in the field where she landed. At nightfall, King Loth had Thaneu set adrift in the treacherous waters of the Firth of Forth in a tiny boat known as a coracle. The tide should have dragged her out to sea, but instead she was safely carried to the far shore. King Loth thought his daughter would be drowned, but as morning dawned Thaneu stepped ashore at Culross in Fife and gave birth to a son, Kentigern.

Kentigern was raised and trained in scripture by Saint Serf. As a boy, Kentigern took a dead robin and brought the little bird back to life. He created fire by blessing and breathing upon a hazel stick. When Kentigern grew into manhood, he became a great Holy Man. King Rhydderch Hael of Strathclyde, the king that defeated Merlin's prince Gwenddolau at the battle of Arderydd, became Kentigern's patron. Kentigern met Lailoken Merlin at the tiny village of Stobo, near Peebles. They talked and Kentigern wept for the old prophet's plight. At a rough-hewn altar stone, the holy man baptised Lailoken Merlin, converting the pagan wizard to Christianity.

Lailoken Merlin had prophesied that he would die a magical three-fold death. That very day as he walked by the banks of the River Tweed, three shepherds attacked him. They clubbed him and threw him into the deep river. He was impaled on fishing spikes and drowned, fulfilling his final prophecy.

At a bend in the Tweed where the river meets the Powsail Burn at Drumelzier is a place known as 'Merlin's Grave', where local tradition claims that Lailoken Merlin lies buried. A local farm is called Merlindale and until the 1890s a cromlech known as 'Arthur's Oven' stood nearby. The cromlech was an ancient Neolithic monument: two huge standing stones with a third flat slab laid across them like a giant stone table. Stobo Kirk is said to be built on the site of an earlier chapel founded by St Kentigern. Its north aisle has Kentigern's altarstone and a huge megalithic standing stone built into its walls. A stained-glass window depicts Kentigern's baptism of Merlin the Wild.

The legendary Merlin has many graves. Marlborough in Wiltshire was once said to derive from 'Merlin's Barrow': an ancient earthwork also known as 'Merlin's Mound' or 'Merlin's Grave'. At the foot of Merlin's Hill near Abergwili village in Wales lies another 'Merlin's Grave', also known as 'Merlin's Cave'. In France, in the heart of the Forest of Brocéliande, is the ruin of a Neolithic gallery grave known as the Tomb of Merlin. It was once partially destroyed in the search for a buried treasure thought to be beneath it. Merlin is also said to rest with King Arthur and the sleeping Knights of the Round Table within hollow hills across Britain, or to wait on the Isle of Avalon for the day that Arthur will return.

Curiously, in 1815, the artist and draughtsman Joseph Michael Gandy completed a watercolour painting entitled *The Tomb of Merlin* which is actually based on Rosslyn Chapel. Gandy had previously painted a large highly detailed watercolour of Rosslyn's Apprentice Pillar and Lady Chapel. The painting was exhibited at the Royal Academy in London in 1807. Gandy was inspired by Rosslyn, filling a sketchbook with meticulous but not entirely accurate ink drawings of the chapel. In *The Tomb of Merlin*, he represents a scene from the sixteenth-century Italian poet Ludovico Ariosto's *Orlando Furioso*, where Merlin's tomb glows with a supernatural light much as Rosslyn is illuminated at the death of a St Clair:

> The very marble was so clear and bright,
> That though the sun no light into it gave,
> The tomb itself did lighten all the cave.

While Gandy's vision of Merlin's tomb is clearly modelled on Rosslyn's architecture, complete with a stylised version of the spirulling Apprentice Pillar, the chapel itself was inspired by an earlier building.

Glasgow Cathedral is dedicated to Saint Kentigern, who is also remembered as Saint Mungo, the patron saint of Glasgow. He is said to have founded 'Glesgu' as the site for his church. By the fifteenth century, Kentigern's humble church had grown into Glasgow Cathedral. The relics of Saint Kentigern rest in his tomb in the Lower Church of this vast gothic cathedral. In 1451, a papal decree declared that a pilgrimage by the faithful to Glasgow Cathedral would be equal in merit to a pilgrimage to Rome.

In the early 1400s, Glasgow Cathedral was struck by lightning and set alight. Fire ripped through the cathedral. Archibald, the fifth Earl of Douglas, helped to fund the reconstruction work.

His coat of arms is carved in stone in a boss in the vault ceiling. Archibald was the brother of Elizabeth Douglas, the first wife of Sir William St Clair, the founder of Rosslyn Chapel. Rosslyn Chapel is modelled closely on Glasgow Cathedral's East Quire.

Elizabeth and Archibald's father was Archibald, fourth Earl of Douglas and first Duke of Touraine, in France. The Scots had long been allied with the French against the English. Elizabeth's father, brother James and first husband John Stewart all died on French soil at the Battle of Verneuill in 1424.

John Stewart, the Earl of Buchan and Constable of France, had led a combined force of Scots and French troops and Italian mercenaries against the English. At first, the English were overwhelmed by the heavily armoured Italian cavalry, but they rallied and slaughtered the Scots and the French in the murderous battle and its brutal aftermath.

In 1432, Elizabeth married William St Clair, her third husband. They wed at St Matthew's Church in Rosslyn. A fragment of this original church remains within the graveyard between the chapel and castle. As William and Elizabeth were cousins, a papal dispensation was sought and granted for them to remain in matrimony. In a century where marriages united powerful families and helped nobles jostle for power, it seems that William and Elizabeth genuinely married for love.

Elizabeth was noted as a devout and godly lady. It may well have been she that inspired her husband to found Rosslyn Chapel. William planned to build a vast cathedral at Rosslyn, but only the East Quire, now known as Rosslyn Chapel, was completed.

Dr Daniel Wilson noted, in his *Prehistoric Annals of Scotland*, that 'many of the most remarkable features of Rosslyn Chapel are derived from the prevailing models of the period, though carried to an exuberant excess' and that parts of Rosslyn are 'nearly a repetition of that of the cathedral of St Mungo at Glasgow'.

Rosslyn Chapel is a scaled-down version of the East Quire of Glasgow Cathedral. It has exactly the same layout: a near identical floor plan of 14 pillars, the same north aisle and south aisle, and a Lady Chapel in the east behind a row of three pillars. Glasgow even has the same arch-vaulted roof; made of oak beams rather than the stone of Rosslyn.

In May 1877, Andrew Kerr published a detailed description of 'The Collegiate Church or Chapel of Rosslyn, its builders, architect and construction', in the *Proceedings of the Society of Antiquaries*. Kerr states that 'comparing the plans of the choir of Rosslyn and the Cathedral of St Mungo at Glasgow, it will be observed that . . . the entire plan is almost a repetition of that of Glasgow'.

As Sir William founded Rosslyn Chapel, the romances of King Arthur and the Knights of the Round Table were being recounted by minstrels, storytellers and scribes. Tales of Arthur were everywhere from the tavern to the king's court.

It may seem surprising that images from an Arthurian legend should appear in a church, but there are other examples across Europe. Most famously the archivolt of the north door of Modena Cathedral has depictions of Arthurian figures. This 'archivolt' (an arched doorway decorated with ornamental mouldings) includes carvings of Sir Gawain, Sir Kay and Arthur. In Ortranto Cathedral in Southern Italy, 'Rex Arturus' appears riding a goat in a spectacular mosaic. Arthurian figures also appear carved in wood in the misericords of English cathedral quires. In Chester Cathedral, Sir Gawain and Sir Yvain appear on either side of Yvain's horse, caught by the falling portcullis. Tristram and Iscult are also shown trysting beneath a tree. At Ripon Minster is a depiction of the two fighting dragons.

As the stonemasons at Rosslyn Chapel carved the two dragons and a knight on horseback, Sir Thomas Malory created *Le Morte d'Arthur* – the death of Arthur. In 1485, as work at Rosslyn drew to a close, William Caxton printed Malory's *Le Morte d'Arthur* on one of the earliest printing presses. At the end of his epic retelling of the Arthurian Matter of Britain, Malory tells us that he could find no more of Arthur 'wrytten in bokis', that three queens bore away the body of Arthur:

> Yet some men say in parts og Inglonde that kynge Arthure ys nat dede, but had by the wyll of oure Lorde Jesu into another place; and men say that he shall come again, and he shall wynne the Holy Crosse. Yet I woll nat say that hit shall be so, but rather I wolde sey: here in thys worlde he chauged hys. Anf many men say that there ys written upon the tumbe thys:

> HIC IACET ARTHURUS, REX QUONDAM REXQUE FUTURUS

> [Yet some men say in parts of England that King Arthur is not dead, but had, by the will of our Lord Jesus into another place; and men say that he shall come again, and he shall win the Holy Cross. Yet I will not say that it shall be so, but rather I would say: here in this world he changed his. And many men say that there is written upon the tomb this:

> Here lies Arthur, the once and future king.]

Sir William St Clair, third earl of Orkney and founder of Rosslyn Chapel, was twice married. In all, Sir William fathered 16 children: William, Katherine, Eleanor, Elizabeth, Margaret, Euphemia, Marjorie, Marietta, Oliver, William, John, David, Alexander, George, Robert . . . and Arthur.

CHAPTER SIX
The Great Fire Of Rosslyn

THE YEAR WAS 1447 and the famous gothic church at Rosslyn, on College Hill, was just one year into its construction. Updating his *Chronicle of the Scottish Nation*, Walter Bower, the Abbot of Inchcolm, noted 'Sir William St Clair is erecting an elegant structure at Rosslyn'.

The sandstone edifice was destined to be a collegiate church. In the fifteenth century, collegiate churches were being built across Scotland. Their purpose was to convey intellectual and spiritual knowledge in an age when the first Scottish universities were founded.

Knowledge and learning were important to Sir William St Clair. In Rosslyn Castle, Sir Gilbert Hay was translating continental books into Scots at Sir William's request. William had a fine manuscript library at a time when books were written by hand on parchment pages. In 1447, Sir William's library was nearly destroyed.

On 2 November 1447, Sir William St Clair of Rosslyn and

Edward St Clair of Draidon were out hunting. For generations, hunting was a favourite pastime of the St Clair family. As usual, the two men set out well enough prepared for the hunt. Edward brought along four greyhounds for the main hunt and also some ratches or slow hounds to start the game.

The tale does not tell us the fortunes of the hunt that day, but we do know that, up to this point in time, life was good for Sir William. He had founded a collegiate church on the hill above his castle, gathering stonemasons from near and far.

In Rosslyn Castle, Sir William, his wife and family were 'royally served in gold and silver vessels, in the most princely manner'. According to Father Hay, 'the Lord Borthwick was his Cup-bearer and Lord Fleming his Carver':

> He had halls and his chambers richly hung with embroidered hangings'. Elizabeth, his 'Princess', was held 'in great reverence, both for her birth, and for the estate she was in; for she had serving her 75 gentlewomen, whereof 53 were daughters to noblemen, all cloathed in velvets and silks, with their chains of gold, and other pertinents; together with 200 rideing gentlemen, who accompanied her in all her journeys.

At 50 years old, Sir William St Clair lived like Arthur in Camelot.

At the end of a long day's hunting, Sir William and Edward turned for home. Nothing remarkable or noteworthy had happened at the hunt. Nearing home, they came to a sudden halt as they encountered a very strange phenomenon. Directly in front of them 'a great company of ratts' appeared scurrying across the path in the woods, heading away from Rosslyn Castle. Sir William and Edward were amazed to see that the rats were led by an old grey-haired rat. The ancient decrepit rodent stood out as it was blind and carried a piece of straw in its mouth.

Rats leaving a house often appear in folklore as omens of

impending doom and harbingers of death and destruction. Francis Bacon noted that, 'It is the wisdom of rats, that will be sure to leave a house, somewhat before it fall.' Rats are also said to forewarn sailors that souls are about to be lost at sea. Superstitions of rats leaving ships before they sail into disaster were at one time very common. The expression 'rats leaving a sinking ship' is still used to describe people leaving a situation that is about to go badly wrong.

Four days after Sir William's strange encounter with the bizarre grey-haired blind rat, disaster struck. It was 6 November 1447, the feast day of St Leonard, patron saint of pregnant women. Although there are no pregnant women in the tale, Lady Elizabeth's little dog was about to give birth to a litter of pups. Sir William's wife Elizabeth was very fond of her dogs and this may suggest why her dog was at home in the castle apartment giving birth under their bed.

A maid, sent to check on the little dog, placed her candle under the bedding without thinking. Immediately, the bedding (probably made of straw, as forewarned by the blind rat) burst into flames. In an instant, the fire engulfed the bed, spread up the walls and set alight the ceiling of the great chamber. From this room, the blaze quickly spread and the alarm was raised.

The castle was quickly evacuated. Only one person remained in the burning building. Sir William's chaplain stayed behind as the fire raged through the chambers and halls, destroying the castle's tapestries and furnishings. The chaplain braved the flames long enough to rescue what he could of the Rosslyn library. Father Hay says that the chamberlain, 'remembering of all his master's writings, passed to the head of the dungeon where they were, and threw out fower great trunks . . .'

Four trunks of precious manuscripts were saved. The chaplain was an educated man. He knew the worth of Sir William's documents and risked his own life to save them. He threw the trunks from the dungeon window, but his own escape was cut off by the flames. The chamberlain grabbed a bell rope, secured it to a wooden beam and, throwing the rope out of the window, climbed out and lowered himself to the ground.

The heroic chamberlain is not named in Father Hay's account of the great fire, but it seems likely that Sir William's manuscripts were saved by Sir Gilbert Hay. This famous knight had returned to Scotland after years spent in the French court and had moved into Rosslyn Castle. Sir Gilbert Hay was engaged in translating the manuscripts into Scots for Sir William, and knowing the library and its contents meant he could identify and save the most treasured books.

As well as the tale of the great fire, there are many descriptions of Rosslyn Castle being the home of valuable manuscripts. In 1837, James Jackson of Penicuik wrote that General Monk's bombardment of the castle in 1650 buried 'an immense collection of rare literary and historical treasures, under a superincumbent mass of rubbish'.

One important document that was allegedly lost in 1447 was the one that pseudo-history writers claim would have 'proved' that Sir William St Clair and his family were appointed hereditary 'Grand Masters' of all the 'Freemasons' in Scotland by King James II. Even if a fifteenth-century document ever did exist, this type of claim is entirely misleading. The stonemasons were craftsmen that built castles and churches. They were not remotely like the 'speculative' bodies termed 'Freemasonic' that exist today. The term 'Grand Master' was not even used in the fifteenth century by those that governed the Incorporated Trade bodies. Deacon Convenor or Master of Works would have been the appropriate terms. These may seem like minor points, but many writers blatantly ignore important distinctions in an attempt to back up their own theories.

Many recent books on Rosslyn base their 'facts' on 'Ancient Masonic documents'. These ancient documents are in fact later seventeenth-century documents commonly referred to as 'the St Clair Charters'.

The charters are actually two letters that are now housed in the museum at Freemasons Hall in Edinburgh. Museum staff state categorically that Freemasonry cannot be traced back to Rosslyn and Sir William St Clair in the fifteenth century. They explain that it would be nice if some evidence existed, but, as it stands, any suggestion that this is the case is historically incorrect.

The first St Clair charter is dated around 1601 and acknowledges hereditary rights that the St Clairs had over the stonemasons:

> Forsomeikle as, from adge to adge, it has been observed amongst us, that the Lairds of Roslin has ever been patrons and protectors of us and our priviledges, like as our predecessors has obeyd and acknowledged them as patrons and protectors . . . we for ourselves, and in the name of our haill brethering and craftsmen, with consent foresaid, agrees and consents that William Saintclair, now of Roslin, for himself and his airs, purchas and obtain, att the hands of our Soveraine Lord, libertie, freedome, and jurisdiction upon us and our succeffors.

> [Forasmuch as, from age to age, it has been observed amongst us, that the Lords of Roslin have ever been patrons and protectors of us and our privileges, like as our predecessors have obeyed and acknowledged them as patrons and protectors . . . we for ourselves, and in the name of our whole brethren and craftsmen, with consent foresaid, agree and consent that William Saintclair, now of Roslin, for himself and his heirs, purchase and obtain, at the hands of our Sovereign Lord, liberty, freedom, and jurisdiction upon us and our successors.]

Unfortunately for the Masons who sent this letter to William Saintclair, he had gone off to live in Ireland and does not seem to have responded to the letter. This Sir William, unlike his ancestors, was said to be a 'lewd man' who 'kept a miller's daughter'. They both left Rosslyn for a new life in self-imposed exile.

A second letter, known as the second St Clair charter, was sent to Saintclair's son William in 1628. It is not known why the Masons issued these letters. Presumably there was a political reason to have an endorsement from patrons in high places, someone to whom they could turn to for protection in difficult times. The second letter was eventually acknowledged. More detailed than the first document, it was sent from both the Masons and the Hammermen, or smiths. This document contains what many suggest is an apocryphal story of a fire, perhaps to give their story more credibility:

> . . . his wreats being consumed in ane flame of fire, within the castle of Rosling anno ...... The consummation and burning thereof being clerly known to us and our predicessoris . . .

> [. . . his writs being consumed in a flame of fire, within the castle of Rosslyn in the year of ...... The consummation and burning thereof being clearly known to us and our predecessors . . .]

A blank space for the date of the fire was left on the document. It was never filled in. It could easily refer to the great fire of 1447, but equally it could refer to a fire at the castle in 1544.

Taking the first date places the 'original' at the time of the founding of Rosslyn Chapel and the great fire of Rosslyn Castle during the reign of King James II. This fits with the timeline and theories of pseudo-historians. There is, however, another twist to the tale concerning the documents and their authenticity.

In 1629, King Charles I appointed Anthony Alexander as his own Master of Work and Warden General. The appointment was challenged by Sir William St Clair, who acknowledged himself as the 'Maister of Work', having been the recipient of the second charter from the Masons a year before.

Why the Masons chose Sir William as the recipient of their letter is not known, but his claim was seen as a pretended one and was passed to the King's Advocate. After inspection, the claim failed to be substantiated and Anthony carried on with this office until his death in August 1637. He was succeeded by his brother and no further appeals were made by the St Clairs.

In the scheme of things, the St Clair charters were of no real historical significance or importance. They would probably have disappeared into obscurity had it not been for a curious quirk of fate.

In 1736, a century after the second charter was signed, Scotland was about to set up its first 'Grand Lodge' of Freemasons. England had already established the world's very first Freemasonic Grand Lodge back in 1717.

Although not the first choice, Sir William St Clair of Rosslyn became the first Grand Master Mason of Scotland. Having no male heirs, history has given him the title of 'the last Rosslyn'. He was the last direct descendant of the chapel's founder. Sir William offered to hand over his family's hereditary rights to the newly formed body. Not a Freemason himself at this point, he was very quickly initiated and offered the chair.

Many historians consider these events as a very clever piece of 'spin'. It is now believed that the newly established Grand Lodge of Scotland wished to give their organisation an ancient pedigree that their English counterparts did not have. The St Clair charters, although meaningless in this context, were made to illustrate an ancient link which didn't really exist.

The introduction to the Grand Lodge of Scotland's translation of Father Hay's *Genealogie of the Saintclaires of Rosslyn* states:

> The high antiquity assigned to the alleged heritable conveyance of the office of Grand Mason in favour

of the ancestor of the last Rosslyn appears somewhat questionable, and there is certainly nothing like legal or even moral evidence to warrant a belief that any grant ever was conferred by King James II.

Thankfully, the story of the great fire has a noble ending that befits the fifteenth-century William. The tale as told by Father Hay records that Sir William, who had been away from Rosslyn all day, was finally told about the disastrous fire at the castle.

Hay says that William's first response was an interesting one that illustrates the importance that he placed on knowledge and learning. We are told that, before asking the fate of his family, he first asked what had become of his library. When he learned that his manuscripts and writings had survived the fire, Sir William 'became chearfull'.

Once at the castle, Sir William comforted his wife and the ladies, asking them 'to put away all sorrow'. Overjoyed with the swift actions of his chaplain, he rewarded him 'very richly'.

Sir William was now faced with having to make substantial repairs to his castle as well as building the Collegiate Church of St Matthew. Father Hay finishes his account by telling us that Sir William was undaunted, knowing that his papers were saved:

> Yet all this stayed him not from the building of the Colledge [Rosslyn Chapel], nether his libertality to the poor; but was more liberall to them than before – applying the safety of his charters and writings to God's particular Providence.

Sir William St Clair, third Earl of Orkney and Lord of Rosslyn, refashioned Rosslyn Castle in fine style, inspired by French architecture, and saw the East Quire of his Collegiate Church, now known as Rosslyn Chapel, created.

CHAPTER SEVEN
The Green Man And The Faeries

❖

THERE ARE FEW PLACES on earth where you can find unicorns and griffons, angels and devils, saints, sinners, gargoyles, elephants, monkeys, knights and dragons all under one roof. At Rosslyn, these magical figures seem to cover every inch of the chapel.

Visitors are often surprised to find out how small Rosslyn Chapel actually is. When you step inside, the first impression can be overwhelming, not because of tales of treasure and secret societies but because of the chapel's amazing carvings. Thousands of medieval figures stare out at you from every wall. Even the ceiling is full of carved stone flowers, angels and stars.

But how many visitors notice the mysterious faces that peer out at them from between the leaves and vines?

Rosslyn Chapel is home to over a hundred Green Men or, as they are alternatively known, 'foliate heads'. Green Men appear carved in either stone or wood in medieval chapels, churches and cathedrals throughout Europe, but to find so many in one building is unique.

The name 'Green Man' was first applied, in this context, to these medieval foliate heads in 1939. Lady Raglan, in an article in *Folklore*, related how the vicar of Llangwm in Monmouthshire, Reverend J. Griffith, showed her a carving in his church. He suggested it was 'the spirit of inspiration', but Lady Raglan decided 'it seemed to me certain that it was man and not a spirit, and moreover that it was a "Green Man". So I named it.'

Lady Raglan's imaginative ideas have been largely disproved by academic folklorists, but they have taken on a life of their own. Today, the Green Man is widely seen as a survival from pagan Britain, an ancient fertility god that somehow survived a thousand years of Christianity to reappear in churches and seasonal festivals.

In reality, the earliest Green Men are found on classical Roman tombs in the Mediterranean. It seems that the Green Man was among the Roman decorative features that were revived during the Romanesque period of church building in the eleventh century. The Green Man moved north along the pilgrim routes from Santiago de Compostella in northern Spain, through France and into Britain.

Foliate heads flourished in medieval churches, carved into roof bosses, wooden misericords, corbels and capitals. They are grotesque figures, often garishly painted and gilded, that vomit leaves and vines.

When the Abbey of Saint-Denis, in Paris, was created *circa* AD 1200, a carver inscribed the word 'Silvan' over a foliate head. Thirty-five years later, the master mason Villard de Honnecourt drew foliate heads among his architectural sketches and named them simply 'Tete de Feuilles', meaning 'head of leaves'.

The pagan gods and goddesses of the ancient Britons may not have survived in the carvings of foliate heads but they did endure in the place names of mountains and rivers, and in legends and tales of giants, giantesses, witches and faeries.

In the twenty-first century, most people think of faeries as tiny fluttering creatures with butterfly wings and pixie dust. The vast majority of people don't believe in fairies, they are too quaint and fanciful to fit into our century.

From a few hundred years' distance, our ancestors' belief in fairies may seem rather naive and pretty amusing. So, were the fairies real? Did they vanish underground or 'diminish and sail into the west', or did we just 'grow out' of our fairy beliefs? It is certainly interesting that today, when most people don't think fairies are real, more than half of all Americans believe in aliens and UFOs. Polls show that an incredible 80 per cent (plus or minus a three per cent margin of error) of Americans think the US Government is hiding knowledge of the existence of extraterrestrial life forms. Every year there are reports of UFO sightings and alien visitations, just as we have a thousand years' worth of tales and eyewitness testament regarding faeries.

In medieval Britain, there were many ways to spell 'fairy' including fairie, pharie, fay, fae and faerie. We are used to pretty little fairies with fluttering wings and tiny feet. These 'diminutive' fairies are the delicate creatures that appear in Victorian nursery picture books and the Cottingley fairy photographs that Sir Arthur Conan Doyle presented to war-torn Britain. The word 'fairy' is now so connected with Tinkerbell from *Peter Pan* and Cicely Mary Barker's *Flower Fairies* that many writers and artists have begun to use an alternative spelling 'faerie'.

A 'faerie' does not flutter. A faerie may be as tall as a human or even larger. It may be ugly and twisted, malevolent and vicious. Faeries may have sharp teeth and vicious tempers. Away from the flowerbeds, there are thousands of strange faerie folk that feast in hollow hills, tread the dark wood and lurk in deep rivers. These are the creatures of legend and folktale that would frighten travellers on lonely roads, steal babies from their cradles and attack cattle in the fields.

Al is bot gaistis and elrich fantasyis
Of brownies and of bogillis ful this buke

[All is but ghosts and eldritch fantasies
Of brownies and of bogles full is this book]

Gavin Douglas, *The Aeneid*, 1513

When Gavin Douglas translated Virgil's *Aeneid* in 1513, he was quick to note the work's strange and fantastical nature. His *Aeneid* is the earliest surviving Scottish manuscript to use the term 'fairfolks' for the faeries.

Quhilk fairfolkis, or elvys, clepyng we

[Which we call fairfolks or elves]

As Gavin Douglas tells us in verse, he was asked to translate Virgil's *Aeneid* by Sir Henry Sinclair of Rosslyn, first lord Sinclair and grandson of the Sir William St Clair who founded Rosslyn Chapel:

At the request of ane lorde of renowne,
Of ancestry maist nobill, and illustir baroun,
Fadir of bukis, protector to science and lair,
My special gude lord Henry lord Sinclare.

[At the request of a lord of renown,
Of ancestry most noble, and illustrious baron,
Father of books, protector to science and law,
My special good lord Henry, lord Sinclair.]

Rosslyn Glen is a wild place, long thought to be haunted by ghosts and faerie folk. Bronze Age rock art is evidence of human activity in the glen dating back approximately 4,000 years. In fields throughout Scotland, Bronze Age burial mounds were left unploughed by generations of farmers who believed they were Sidhe Mounds: the homes of the faeries.

In the course of our research, we have been lucky enough to talk to many people about Rosslyn and their unique experiences in the chapel, castle and glen. We have interviewed eyewitnesses who have seen ghosts at Rosslyn Castle and talked to many people about curious local legends and folklore. One person in particular had a very strange tale to tell.

She was a teenager at the time. She had wandered down into the glen with some friends. They followed the river until they reached a hollow between Rosslyn Chapel and Hawthornden Castle. The hollow is directly opposite Wallace's Cave and ancient Bronze Age rock art depicting spirals, concentric rings, a human figure and a fish. The teenagers sat and talked on a grassy mound close by the path.

Eventually, as it was beginning to get dark and cold, they decided to head back to the village. As they walked towards home, they were met by policemen and worried parents conducting a search. While the teenagers were convinced they had only been away for a few hours they had actually been gone overnight. They had been missing for almost 24 hours when they were found in Rosslyn Glen.

Episodes of 'missing time' are common in faerylore. Faerie legends are full of hapless travellers who find themselves among the faeries. They spend no more than a day in the faerie realm but when they return to their normal lives they discover that they have been away for weeks or even years. After seven days spent in Faerie with the Queen of Elfland, the famous Scottish prophet Thomas the Rhymer was returned to the mortal world to find that seven years had passed.

The nuckelavee, the washer by the ford, bogles, the fuath, booman, the blue men of the minch, brownies, the crodh mara, sheelycoat and a thousand other faeries were very real to our forebears. It was believed that there were two opposing courts of faeries. Those of the Seelie Court were the good faeries that helped with chores and made gentle mischief. The faeries of the Unseelie Court, however, were lethal creatures that killed and maimed without conscience.

The mysterious realm of Elfland is the twilight world of these faeries: the magical otherworld behind a tree, under a green hill or beneath the surface of the water.

On Hallowe'en night, the villagers of the Highlands would light bonfires and carry burning torches around their homes and fields to protect them from attacks by the faeries. Rowan-twig crosses bound with red wool were used to keep homes and cattle safe. The vicious faeries of the Unseelie Court are known as 'the Sluagh'. They were accompanied on their midnight revels by 'the Host': the spirits of the unforgiven human dead. Unwary travellers who walked alone on deserted roads or ventured into faerie rings of moonlit mushrooms could be stolen away. They might find themselves abducted by the Queen of Elfland, dragged into the sky by the Sluagh or lost in the midnight revels of the faerie court.

Thomas the Rhymer or, as he is also known, Thomas of Erceldoune, True Thomas or Thomas Learmont, appears in many Scottish faerie legends. Lowland tales from the Borders of southern Scotland tell of the deeds of True Thomas and recount his prophecies. Borders ballads tell how he spent seven years beneath the Eildon Hills with the enchanting Queen of Elfland. They met beneath the Eildon Tree on Huntlie Bank where she appeared clad all in green, riding a milk-white horse with silver bells jingling in its mane. Thomas was given the magical gift of a tongue that could never lie, a mixed blessing when it came to bartering at market and charming a maiden. From that day forth, as every word he said was true, Thomas could foretell the future.

The Eildon Hills loom over the Borders town of Melrose, south of Rosslyn. Legend tells that their three peaks were formed when Michael Scott the Wizard commanded devils to cleave the hill's original single peak. The Eildons are said to be hollow hills concealing a faerie underworld ruled by the King and Queen of Elfland. Beneath the grassy hilltops are rivers of blood, orchards of apple trees and huge halls full of dancing, feasting and faerie music.

Old maps of the Eildon Hills and detailed Ordnance Survey maps show the thickly wooded Rhymer's Glen, the Huntly Burn and the site of the Eildon Tree. A memorial stone marks the spot where the Eildon Tree once stood. The ruins of a medieval building known as 'Rhymer's Tower' can still be seen in Earlston near Melrose.

Border legend tells of Canobie Dick, a horse trader from Dumfriesshire, who crossed the Eildon Hills late one night. He had attended the fair at Melrose but started the long journey home with his horses unsold. As darkness fell, he started on his way but met a shadowy stranger on the track across the Eildons. The old stranger offered to buy his horses with antique gold. A deal was struck and from then on Canobie Dick's fortunes turned as he continued to sell horses to the mysterious old man. One night, his curiosity got the better of him and he demanded to know where the old man was taking the horses. Reluctantly, the old man showed Canobie Dick a secret entrance into the hollow hills. Deep in an underground cavern, the old man revealed that he was in fact Thomas the Rhymer. He was gathering horses for the knights who slept inside the Eildons. Canobie Dick saw stables full of coal-black horses and knights clad in coal-black armour, and there on a table lay a sword and a hunting horn. Canobie Dick had to choose between them: take the sword first or blow the horn? Trembling, the horse trader took up the horn and gave it a mighty blast. Thomas shook his head as the knights began to wake and a voice proclaimed:

Woe to the coward that ever he was born,
Who did not draw the sword before he blew the horn.

Canobie Dick was dragged from the enchanted cave by a sudden whirlwind. He was found the next morning by local shepherds and died after telling them his tale.

Tales of the 'sleeping hero' are told of Charlemagne, of Frederick Barbarossa and, of course, of King Arthur. Arthur, the once and future king, is said to sleep beneath numerous hills across Wales, Scotland and England, where he waits with his knights to return one day when Britain needs him most. An alternative version of the tale of Canobie Dick and the hollow Eildon Hills was recorded by Dr John Leydon in his *Scenes of Infancy* in 1803. He says that the sleeping warriors within the cave were King Arthur and the Knights of the Round Table.

> Mysterious Rhymer, doomed by fate's decree
> Still to revisit Eildon's fated tree,
> Where oft the swain, at dawn of Hallow-day,
> Hears thy fleet barb with wild impatience neigh,
> Say, who is he, with summons long and high,
> Shall bid the charmed sleep of ages fly,
> Roll the long sound through Eildon's caverns vast,
> While each dark warrior kindles at the blast,
> The horn, the falchion, grasp with mighty hand,
> And peal proud Arthur's march from Fairy-land?

The legends of Thomas the Rhymer, the hollow Eildon Hills and Canobie Dick are closely connected to the legends of Rosslyn. Within the Eildon Hills are the fair Queen of Elfland, True Thomas, the Knights of the Round Table and a sword and hunting horn. Beneath Rosslyn Castle, in a secret underground chamber, are the enchanted White Lady, her Demon Knight and a sword and hunting horn. The task is the same: draw the sword or blow the horn.

Thomas the Rhymer himself seems like an imaginary character – a poet and prophet who lives underground in the faerie court, reads ancient books of magic and battles evil wizards. But Thomas Rhymour was actually very real.

In a thirteenth-century charter, Petrus de Haga agreed to give half a stone of wax to the abbot of Melrose each year. 'Thomas Rhymour of Ercildune' was one of the witnesses who signed the charter. In 1294, Thomas Rhymour's son and heir inherited his father's lands in Earlston and gave them to the medieval hospital at Soutra.

In 1355, Thomas Gray wrote of Thomas Erceldoune and the prophecies of Merlin in his *Scalacronica*. In *The Brus,* John Barbour tells us that Thomas the Rhymer foretold that Robert the Bruce would become the King of Scots. Thomas also appears in Blind Harry's *Wallace,* the epic poem that recounted the deeds of William Wallace. Thomas Rhymour, who had lands in Earlston and who died *circa* 1294, had earned a reputation as a seer during his lifetime or soon after his death. It was a reputation that would be exploited by the Scots and the English to 'prove' that victories, defeats and even kingships were pre-destined.

In the sixteenth century, Sir William Sinclair gathered 'a great many manuscripts' to create an exceptional library at Rosslyn Castle. As Catholic institutions were attacked, Sir William rescued and recovered precious manuscripts and books 'taken by the rabble out of our monasterys [sic] in the time of the reformation'. Many of the surviving books are signed 'Sir William Sinclar of Roslin, Knight'.

Among the books were *The Rosslyn Missal,* a fourteenth-century illuminated manuscript written by Irish monks; Sir Gilbert Hay's *The Buke of the Order of Knyghthood*; the *Lives of the Bishops of Dunkeld*; Bede's *Ecclesiastical History*; Wyntoun's *Chronicle* and a New Testament in English. It should be noted that no less than five of the surviving twenty-one copies of John of Fordun's *Scotichronicon* were part of the Rosslyn library at some point.

John of Fordun was a priest in the Cathedral of Aberdeen in the second half of the fourteenth century. His Latin *Scotichronicon* drew on a multitude of sources, including the Welsh monk Gildas, William of Malmesbury and Geoffrey of Monmouth. Fordun quotes from the prophecies of Merlin and recounts a prophecy of Thomas the Rhymer.

On the night of 19 March 1286, Thomas the Rhymer was entertained in Dunbar Castle by Earl Patrick. Half-jesting and probably the worse for drink, the Earl asked Thomas what tomorrow would bring. The Rhymer bowed his head and prophesied a terrible day of calamity and misery.

As the next day dawned, the Earl of Dunbar was shocked to hear that Alexander, the Scots King, was dead. The king had spent the day meeting with his nobles within Edinburgh's Castle of Maidens. Alexander had been married for barely six months. In a moment of passion, the king decided to ride north through a fierce storm to spend the night with his bride, Yolande of Dreux, at Kinghorn Tower in Fife. He rode to Queensferry and crossed the treacherous waters of the Firth of Forth. Alexander took the ragged clifftop path to Kinghorn, but when his horse took fright the king fell to his death.

Six years before, in September 1280, King Alexander III had granted the barony of Rosslyn to a Sir William St Clair. This William became the first St Clair of Rosslyn. His wife was Agnes, the daughter of Patrick, the Earl of Dunbar: the host of Thomas the Rhymer on that fateful March night.

Sir Walter Scott was fascinated by Thomas the Rhymer. He may have simply felt a sense of kinship to a fellow poet. It is also possible that he secretly desired to experience the magical journey of Thomas into the faerie realm.

Scott's novels were the blockbusters of his day, popular works such as the Waverley novels, *Rob Roy*, *Ivanhoe*, *The Bride of Lammermoor* and *Red Gauntlet*. Scott became a world-famous author and earned a fortune. He could have lived anywhere in the world but chose to buy up a piece of nondescript farmland near Melrose.

He purchased Cartley Hole Farm (known locally as 'Clarty

Hole' – clarty is Scots for dirty or filthy) and promptly renamed it 'Abbotsford'. At Abbotsford, Sir Walter Scott spent a fortune building a lavish baronial manor house, two miles from the Eildon Hills where Thomas the Rhymer met the Queen of Elfland. He purchased a wooded slope in the Eildons known as 'Dick's cleugh' and renamed it 'Rhymer's Glen'. One of Scott's guests at Abbotsford, the famous artist J.M.W. Turner, painted a delicate watercolour of Rhymer's Glen.

Abbotsford is a gothic masterpiece. Among its towers and turrets Scott had his masons create replicas of the stone carvings of Melrose Abbey and Rosslyn Chapel. He filled his fairy-tale castle with suits of armour, antique swords and firearms, fine painting and relics from Scottish history. Among the artefacts Scott collected are Rob Roy's long-barrelled gun and dirk, a lock of Bonnie Prince Charlie's hair and a piece of oatcake from the sporran of a Jacobite slain at the Battle of Culloden. Scott also gathered over 9,000 books in a grand library that included Sir Gilbert Hay's *Buke of the Order of Knyghthood*.

Scott was born in a squalid third-floor flat in Edinburgh's Old Town in August 1771. At the age of two, he developed polio and then, during his childhood, he lost six brothers and sisters. He was sent to his grandfather's farm at Sandyknowe, between Kelso and Melrose. There, the young Scott fell in love with the Border ballads, rural superstitions and local legends. Eventually, Scott returned to Edinburgh and was educated in the High School and the University of Edinburgh. He became an advocate in 1792 and married Charlotte Carpenter in 1797.

In 1798, Walter Scott decided to rent a country cottage, a special place where he could escape from the city. He found a little thatched cottage in the village of Lasswade, three miles north-east of Rosslyn Chapel, and rented it for 30 pounds a year. Scott kept a horse and a cow and grew a garden full of flowers and vegetables. His landlord was Sir John Clerk of Penicuik, son of the Sir John Clerk who had created Hurley's Cove and restored Rosslyn Chapel.

Each year, Scott spent a few months in the cottage in Lasswade walking, fishing, gardening and writing. He dabbled with writing plays before concentrating on poetry. Inspired by the Scottish Border ballads, legends and tales of faeries he heard in his childhood, Walter Scott began to work on *The Minstrelsy of the Scottish Border*.

From his little cottage in Lasswade, he visited Hawthornden Castle, Dalkeith Palace and Woodhouselee, fished in the River Esk and was bewitched by Rosslyn Chapel. At Lasswade, Scott collected Border ballads and local traditions from old people, as well as manuscripts and printed chapbooks. Clearly he also collected, and embellished, the legends of Rosslyn. He had originally intended to include the tale of the fair Rosabelle in the *Minstrelsy*, but his 'romance of Border chivalry and enchantment' grew into a separate work. *The Lay of the Last Minstrel* tells of Rosslyn Castle and wooded glen, of Rosslyn Chapel magically appearing in flame, of knights buried in suits of armour in the crypt and of 'the lordly line of high St Clair':

> Seem'd all on fire that chapel proud,
> Where Roslin's chiefs uncoffin'd lie . . .

Walter Scott's *The Lay of the Last Minstrel* was published in January 1805. It was an unprecedented success, selling tens of thousands of copies, establishing Scott as a renowned poet and bringing sightseers to Scotland to visit Melrose Abbey and Rosslyn Chapel. The chapel was a romantic ruin with shutters on its windows, and green moss and lichens on its carvings. When the poet William Wordsworth and his sister Dorothy visited Walter Scott at Lasswade, Dorothy was charmed by the romantic chapel:

> The stone of both roof and walls is sculptured with
> leaves and flowers, so delicately wrought that I could
> have admired them for hours, and the whole of their

groundwork is stained by time with the softest colours. Some of those leaves and flowers are tinged perfectly green, and at one part the effect was most exquisite – three or four leaves of a small fern, resembling that which we call Adder's Tongue grew round a cluster of them at the top of a pillar, and the natural product and the artificial were so intermingled from the other, they being of an equally determined green, though the fern was of a deeper shade.

Dorothy Wordsworth, *Recollections of a Tour made in Scotland*, AD *1803*, published Edinburgh 1874

In the nineteenth century, Queen Victoria visited Rosslyn Chapel. Extensive and controversial restoration work began and the chapel was rededicated as a place of worship. For 200 years Rosslyn had lain empty; now visitors from around the world came to gaze in wonder at the chapel's incredible carvings. From the shadows, Rosslyn's mysterious Green Men stared back.

CHAPTER EIGHT
The Secret Crypt

BENEATH THE STONE FLOOR of Rosslyn Chapel there is a subterranean crypt, the burial vault of the St Clairs of Rosslyn. Scottish knights and lords, clad in suits of armour, rest in the dark, awaiting the Day of Judgement.

The crypt of the St Clairs has fascinated poets and artists for centuries. In 1805, Sir Walter Scott immortalised the burial vault of the St Clairs of Rosslyn in his epic poem *The Lay of the Last Minstrel*:

> 'Twas seen from Dryden's groves of oak
> And seen from cavern'd Hawthornden.
>
> Seem'd all on fire that chapel proud,
> Where Roslin's chiefs uncoffin'd lie,
> Each Baron, for a sable shroud,
> Sheath'd in his iron panoply.

Seem'd all on fire within, around,
    Deep sacristy and altars pale;
Shone every pillar foliage bound,
    And glimmer'd all the dead men's mail.

In recent years, the vault has become the focus of wild speculation. Is there an ancient secret buried beneath Rosslyn Chapel? Are there booby traps and lost gospels, sacred relics and fabulous treasures? In *The Da Vinci Code*, the novelist Dan Brown took the claims of alternative history writers and spun a fantastical tale. The burial crypt beneath Rosslyn became: an 'astonishing structure', 'a massive subterranean chamber', 'a deep vault' that dwarfed the chapel above it. But what is really buried in Rosslyn's secret crypt?

When William St Clair, the third Earl of Orkney and lord of Rosslyn, first planned a collegiate church at Rosslyn, he decided to begin with the East Quire. If you imagine that the floorplan of the completed collegiate church would have been in the shape of a Christian cross, then the East Quire would be the top or 'head' of that cross. The East Quire was to become the chapel of the St Clairs. It would have housed the High Altar, where the priest said Mass for the souls of the St Clairs and the family received Holy Communion. It was also the chapel where William had his ancestors reburied and where William, his wives, children, and descendants would be buried.

It is thought that Rosslyn Chapel may have been founded on the site of an earlier building. If underground chambers already existed on the site, it would have made sense to reuse them. Substantial foundations were laid, the burial vaults were cut from the solid rock and the sacristy was built.

The sacristy, down a steep flight of stone stairs at the south-east corner of the chapel, is often incorrectly referred to as 'the crypt'. The date of this small chapel is not precisely known but it may be many years older than the main chapel. It has also been suggested that this may have belonged to part of another building, perhaps the original castle of Rosslyn. The exact purpose of the sacristy has been a mystery for centuries:

> The use of this lower building has been a sad puzzling to antiquarian brains. Was it a Chapel as generally asserted? Under the east window there was a stone altar; there is a piscine, and aumbry for the sacramental plate, but what else? . . . a fire place (which has its chimney); a goodly array of closets; a door-way once communicating with the outside; and a second door, leading to an inner room or rooms. Its domestic appurtenances clearly shew it to have been the house of the priestly custodier of the chapel, and the ecclesiastical types first named were for his private meditations. And thus ceases the puzzle.
>
> Robert William Billings, *Baronial and Ecclesiastical Antiquities of Scotland*, 1852

Was the sacristy really a little home for the chapel's priest? It is possible that the priest temporarily took lodgings in the sacristy before he was given separate land and gardens. More likely the fireplace was a practical addition that kept the builders and the congregation warm during the winter months. The chapel took around 40 years to build. Initially, the carpenters, stone masons and carvers would have sheltered within wooden buildings, but the sacristy would have offered a larger space out of the wind, rain and cold where master craftsmen could work on intricate carvings.

When the chapel was completed, the priest stored his vestments down in the sacristy and robed there before saying Mass. It has also been suggested that at various times the sacristy has been used as a hermit's cell, a lady chapel and even a lepers' squint.

The remains of an older church, dedicated to St Matthew, can be found a short distance away in the old churchyard near the castle. It was here that Sir William, the third earl, married Lady Elizabeth Douglas. The St Clair and Douglas coat of arms can be seen on the east wall of the sacristy, suggesting that it may have been dedicated to Lady Elizabeth. The engrailed St Clair cross sits alongside the 'Douglas Heart'. Elizabeth died in 1452, before the chapel was completed. The Douglas arms may have been placed there by William as a memorial to his dead love.

The stairs leading down to the sacristy leave a gaping hole in the south-east corner of the chapel. While all else in the chapel seems perfectly planned and crafted, the area around the stairs appears to have an unfinished quality. Curiously, an altar was built above the stairs to the sacristy. It stands higher than Rosslyn's other altars:

> This altar is raised two steps above the floor; and underneath it is the flight of twenty-two steps leading down to a building erected eastward of the Chapel . . . This building is variously called by the names of chapel, crypt, sacristy, or vestry.
>
> Rev. Edward Bradley, *A Tour in Tartan-Land*, 1863

The burial vaults beneath Rosslyn Chapel and much of the sacristy were cut out of the solid rock of the hilltop. The lands of Roslin are made from sandstone that is easily carved and the surrounding country is dotted with caves and tunnels. Three floors of chambers, stairways, dungeons and passageways lie beneath Rosslyn Castle.

There is a local legend that a tunnel leads from Rosslyn Chapel down to the castle. It is said that a piper once disappeared into the tunnel and was never seen again. Similar legends are told in Edinburgh, where a bagpiper wandered into a secret tunnel running down the Royal Mile between the castle and Holyrood Palace. The citizens of Edinburgh listened intently as the piper played a tune deep underground. Suddenly, he stopped dead.

Groundscans carried out at Roslin seem to support stories of an underground tunnel. They indicate a passageway leading from Rosslyn Chapel, out beneath Gardeners Brae and down towards Rosslyn Castle. This has been leapt on as proof that Rosslyn is built in imitation of King Solomon's Temple of Jerusalem as envisaged in Freemasonic mysteries. In one Masonic ritual, a 14th degree Mason identifies a passageway, deep underground, which leads from Solomon's Temple to his palace. Based on the actual evidence, it seems far more likely that the tunnel leading downhill from under Rosslyn Chapel is, in fact, a medieval drain.

In March 2005, in a farmer's field near Linlithgow, a 700-year-old tunnel was rediscovered. It is thought to have been built by medieval monks. The farmer recalled that his father had once told him that there were secret passageways under the land. The tunnel itself runs for a mile under Park Farm. At Melrose Abbey, large underground drains have been excavated and uncovered. The medieval builders at Rosslyn would have created stone drains beneath the chapel to prevent the burial crypt from flooding.

On the bank of the River Esk, between Rosslyn Castle and Hawthornden, is Wallace's Cave, named because it is said that William Wallace and his men hid inside the cave. Wallace's Camp, a curious crescent-shaped formation, is nearby at Bilston Burn. Wallace's Cave is a cruciform grotto cut from the bare rock.

Further downriver, at Hawthornden Castle, a network of strange man-made caverns is carved from the natural sandstone. In the eighteenth century, the celebrated antiquarian William Stuckely visited the caves of Hawthornden. Stuckely was a close friend of Sir John Clerk of Penicuik and was the founder of the 'Society of Roman Knights'. Their shared interest in early history may account for Stuckely's curious theory about the origin of the caves. In 1724, in his book *Itinerarium Curosum*, Stuckely named the Hawthornden caves 'the King of Pictland's Castle and Palace'.

The origin of the Hawthornden caves is unknown. They are

believed to be at least 700 years old, as Sir Alexander Ramsey, a friend of King Robert the Bruce, is said to have hidden in the caves with his men during the Wars of Independence.

Various writers and historians have romantically named the main caves under Hawthornden 'the King's Gallery', 'Bruce's Bedroom', 'Bruce's Library' and 'Bruce's Wash Basin'. The complex also contains a freshwater well, which could have supplied men hiding underground.

Sir Walter Scott and others name a different cave, away from the rest, as the 'Cypress Grove'. Cypress groves are associated with death and funerals. In an essay entitled 'The Cypress Grove', Sir William Drummond of Hawthornden explores the folly of the fear of death:

> This globe of the earth, which seemeth huge to us in respect of the universe, and compared with that wide pavilion of heaven is less than little, of no sensible quantity, and but as a point.

Drummond noted that there is more to life than mere material wealth and possessions:

> They are like to thorns which, laid on an open hand, are easily blown away and wound the closing and hard-gripping.

Symbolically, caves are places of burial and rebirth, the meeting place of the human and the divine. The body of Christ was laid in the rock-cut tomb of Joseph of Arimathea. There, the miracle of the Resurrection took place. In the ancient mysteries, caves were used for initiation ceremonies. In Celtic culture, caves were seen as an entrance to the magical otherworld.

The crypt beneath Rosslyn Chapel was carved as a burial vault for the St Clairs. Sir William had his father, grandfather and other ancestors re-interred in the vault as the chapel was being built. In November 1456, Alexander Sutherland of Dunbeath, the father of William's second wife, made provision in his will for his body to be buried in the crypt at Rosslyn:

> I gif my soul till Almyte God of Hevyn, and till his blissit modher the glorious Virgin Marie, and till all the haly company of Hevin, my body to be gravyt in the Colledg Kirk of ane hie and mightie Lord, William Earle of Caithnes and Orknay, Lord Sinclare

For the next 200 years, the St Clair earls, lords, knights, squire, ladies and children were buried in the vaults beneath the Rosslyn Chapel. In 1650, the last St Clair to be buried in armour was laid to rest.

In 1693, in one of the earliest accounts of the chapel, John Slezer tells us that the burial vaults are so dry that the bodies of the St Clairs still survived intact 80 years after they were interred:

> Here lies buried George Earl of Caithness, who lived about the Beginning of the Reformation, Alexander Earl of Sutherland, great Grand-Child of King Robert de Bruce, Three Earls of Orkney, and Nine Barons of Roslin.

> The last lay in a Vault, so dry that their bodies have been found intire after Fourscore Years, and as fresh as when they were first buried. There goes a Tradition, That before the Death of any of the Family of Roslin, this Chapel appears all in Fire.

Slezer's account also suggests that the crypt had been opened and inspected in the seventeenth century. Father Hay, the genealogist and historian of the St Clairs of Rosslyn, tells us that he was actually present at the opening of the burial vaults.

He gives an eyewitness account of the state of preservation of the body of Sir William, who had lain in the vault for around 50 years, and of the earls and lords of St Clair who lay in full armour:

> He was lying in his armour, with a red velvet cap on his head, on a flat stone; nothing was spoiled, except a piece of the white furring that went round the cap, and answered to the hinder part of the head. All his predecessors were buried after the same manner in their armour. Late Rosline, my gud father [Hay's father-in-law], was the first to be buried in a coffin, against the sentiments of King James VII.

Slezer's account of Rosslyn Chapel records the famous tradition that before a member of the St Clair family dies the 'Chapel appears all in Fire'. Stories of mysterious 'phantom lights' have been told for thousands of years. In the *Odyssey*, Telemachus, the son of Odysseus, is startled as a hall is illuminated 'as bright as it were with flaming fire'. Phantom lights are commonly said to materialise near a dying person or to appear as 'corpse-candles' or 'tomb-fires' held by ghosts.

A century after Slezer, Sir Walter Scott brought the Rosslyn phantom light tradition to life in *The Lay of the Last Minstrel*:

> Seem'd all on fire within, around,
>   Deep sacristy and altar's pale;
> Shone every pillar foliage bound,
>   And glimmer'd all the dead men's mail.
>
> Blaz'd battlement and pinnet high,
>   Blaz'd every rose-carved buttress fair
> So still they blaze when fate is nigh
>   The lordly line of high St. Clair.

> There are twenty of Roslin's barons bold
> Lie buried within that proud chapelle

It sounds like an apocryphal ghost story, a supernatural tale told late at night, but in 1890 James Francis Harry St Clair Erskine, the fifth Earl of Rosslyn, described the strange phenomena at the death of his father:

> The single bell tolled its dirge, the sun shone through the windows in the Chapel as predicted in Walter Scott's lay of the last Minstrel.

In 1837, James Jackson told a curious story about the lights and buried knights of Rosslyn Chapel. Jackson's book, *Tales of Roslin Castle*, is a bizarre work. It is essentially a history of Scotland that begins with a weird fictional account of the discovery of the secret chamber of the White Lady. Jackson tells us that a mysterious Italian noble 'Count Poli' arrived out of the blue in Roslin, claiming to be the descendant of a local priest. This Count Poli then leads some villagers down to Rosslyn Castle, where they break through a stone wall and uncover the lost library of the St Clairs. At one point, Count Poli picks up an ancient book and reads a very strange description of Rosslyn Chapel:

> But humble as this their final resting place now is, I glory that its original state is preserved in this holy volume of my forefathers which I hold in my hand, the drawing of which I shew you, and the following lines in the description of it, which I shall read:
>
> 'On entering the holy room,
> You'll find this large and stately tomb,
> Covered with rich tapestry,
> Bordered with gold embroidery.
> At head, and feet, and sides there are,

Twenty tapers burning clear;
Of fine gold in the chandeliers,
Of amethyst is the censers,
With which they incense always;
For great honour this tomb each day,
In memory of both young and old,
Of Roslin's dames and barons bold.'

This vision of Rosslyn Chapel seems entirely fantastical. Incense burns in amethyst censers and tapers that are lit every day. Other accounts say that the St Clair knights were 'as fresh as when they were first buried' and note that 'nothing was spoiled'. These depictions of the chapel vaults seem to owe something to legendary descriptions of tombs and burial places.

The legends of the Rosicrucians tell of the tomb of Christian Rosencreutz, the founder of the mystical society. A hundred and twenty years after his death, his tomb was opened and the body of Christian Rosencreutz was found to be intact, with the tomb magically illuminated. An ever-burning lamp still shone brightly, over a century after it was lit.

An ever-burning lamp appears in stories of the tomb of Pallas dating to AD 1401. In that year, the tomb of Pallas was disturbed. Pallas, the son of Evander, lay with a lamp above his head. It was still burning with a steady glow more than 2000 years after Pallas was interred.

The poet Virgil writes of Evander, the father of Pallas, in the *Aeneid*. In 1513, Gavin Douglas translated Virgil's *Aeneid* for Sir Henry Sinclair of Rosslyn, first lord Sinclair, the grandson of Sir William St Clair, the founder of Rosslyn Chapel.

In Book VI of the *Aeneid*, Virgil tells of the finding of the body of Misenus, a great friend of Hector. Aeneas and his companions build a huge funeral pyre, with oak and pine, set in front with 'funereal cypress'. Incense, gifts of food and bowls full of olive oil were heaped upon the fire. Once the flames had died, Aeneas gathered the ashes in a bronze urn and buried them. He raised a great mound over the remains of Misenus. In the hero's tomb were placed his weapons, his trumpet and an oar.

It is striking that this tomb holds a trumpet and weapons, just as the secret chamber of the White Lady and the hollow hills of Arthur's sleeping knights hold a trumpet or a hunting horn, and a sword.

In the medieval age, Virgil was seen as a legendary magician. His works would influence the Arthurian Matter of Britain. Virgil is unique amongst pagan writers in that many Christian writers accepted him because they saw parallels in his writings with their faith. The Christian Emperor Constantine believed that Virgil's fourth Messianic Eclogue contained an early prophecy of the coming of the Christ who would be born of a virgin.

After his death, the historical Virgil's life became mixed with fable. As the legend developed, his own mother Maia was said to have been a virgin when she gave birth to the poet. As he entered the world, there was an earthquake in Rome. The infant Virgil did not cry, he was immediately able to walk and where he trod flowers sprang from the ground in full bloom. He had a golden star on his forehead, a full set of teeth and a full head of hair: all signs of a divine nature.

By the medieval age, Virgil was thought of as a magician and enchanter. In the *Divine Comedy*, Dante is guided through the infernal regions by Virgil. As the two poets journey through the subterranean realm, we find that Virgil has become the personification of human wisdom.

> *Tenebrosa Occultaque Cave*
> which translates as;
> Beware of dark and secret things

This Latin inscription is carved in stone in the darkness of Hurley's Cove. This curious tunnel was built by Sir John Clerk of Penicuik as a replica of the grotto by Virgil's Tomb.

In his journal Clerk wrote, 'This adds a good deal of beauty to the enclosures of Penicuik house as it resembles the grotto of Pauisilipo at Naples.'

It took two years to build Hurley's Cove. It was dug out by hand at an angle through a hill. The mouth of one end of this man-made cave and tunnel opens out onto a landscaped pond.

Work began on Hurley's Cove in 1741, just two years after Sir John Clerk had restored Rosslyn Chapel. In a letter dated 18 August 1739, the distinguished English antiquarian Roger Gale noted:

> . . . we saw Roslin-chapel, a most noble Gothic structure,
> exceeded by few . . . it has lain open to the weather ever
> since the Reformation, but has withstood all its effects,
> by the goodness of the materials, and the excellency of
> its work to a miracle; however, the rain now penetrating
> through the roof, which is vaulted with stone, would in
> a few years have dissolved it entirely, had not that true
> lover of antiquities and the liberal arts, Sir John Clerk,
> persuaded the present Lord Sinclair to put into complete
> repair. The workmen have been upon it all this summer,
> and as Sir John has the whole direction of it, in a year or
> more it will not only be secured from ruin, but be made
> as beautiful and stately as most of that sort of edifices
> in the kingdom . . .

Sir John Clerk feared that the chapel was in danger of being lost for ever. His actions saved it from inevitable ruin. However, it has been suggested that Clerk had another motive for restoring the chapel, a secret motive. It has been said that he was seeking the treasure of Rosslyn and that somehow something he discovered at Rosslyn led him to build Hurley's Cove.

Clerk had another replica built on his family estate at Penicuik: a full size replica of 'Arthur's O'on' (Arthur's Oven). The circular beehive-shaped original, which dated back to the

Roman occupation of ancient Caledonia, once stood at Camelon near Falkirk.

The exact purpose of Arthur's O'on has been debated over the centuries. Most likely it was a Roman or pre-Roman temple. It was said to mark the site where King Arthur was slain in battle, with the inside of it said to have been ornately decorated with scenes of Arthur's battles. Local folklore claimed that its round shape represented the gathering place of Arthur's knights, the famous Round Table.

In AD 1120, the Flemish cleric, Lambert of St Omer, writes a remarkable description of Arthur's O'on in a work entitled *Liber Floridus*:

> There is in Britain, in the land of the Picts, a palace of the warrior Arthur, built with marvellous art and variety, in which the history of all his exploits and wars is to be seen in sculpture. He fought twelve battles against the Saxons who had occupied Britain.

The original Arthur's O'on was thoughtlessly demolished in 1743 by the landowner, who used the stone to build a dam. Enraged, Sir John Clerk publicly damned the man with bell, book and candle for his wilful destruction of the ancient building. This damning was an extreme measure. Its words were taken directly from the Pontificale Romanum formula for 'major excommunication':

> We separate him, together with his accomplices and abettors, from the precious body and blood of the Lord and from the society of all Christians; we exclude him from our holy mother the church in heaven and on earth; we declare him excommunicate and anathema; we judge him damned, with the devil and his angels . . . to eternal fire until he shall recover himself from the toils of the devil and return to amendment and to penitence.

That same year, Sir John Clerk commissioned a copy of Arthur's O'on to be built on his estate. It is thought that Sir John Clerk used his replica of Arthur's O'on and also Hurley's Cove to study astronomy, observing the movement of the heavenly bodies: the stars, the planets and the moon.

So, did Clerk of Penicuik really discover the secret of Rosslyn? Did he uncover something beneath the chapel that led him to build Hurley's Cove? Probably not. This story appears to be nothing more than another conspiracy theory. When the real history of a place is forgotten, it seems that mysteries are created to fill the void.

The truth is that the secret crypt of Rosslyn Chapel is the burial vault of the St Clairs. There is no hidden treasure under the chapel, no lost scrolls or sacred relics. Pseudo-history writers have dreamt these up. Rosslyn Chapel is a fragile building, suffering from centuries of neglect. It is extremely unlikely that any invasive excavation beneath the chapel will be permitted – not because the Rosslyn Chapel Trust has 'something to hide' but because it would do nothing but cause further damage to the chapel.

Carrying out even some very superficial historical research shows that the St Clairs abandoned Rosslyn Chapel to the elements after the Protestant Reformation. A building containing a fabulous treasure would probably have warranted more attention from the family.

The chapel was certainly not viewed as the centre of the Templar or Masonic universe as pseudo-histories and bestselling novels suggest. For 270 years it was a romantic ruin visited by poets, writers, and stone-throwing 'idle boys'! Although admired by many, it took a royal prompt from Queen Victoria to have this 'medieval treasure' restored and rededicated for public worship in the 1860s.

As Rosslyn Chapel lay abandoned, the local villagers lifted the stone slabs in the north aisle. There, at the entrance to the burial vaults of the St Clairs of Rosslyn, they buried their dead children. Over the centuries they became known as 'the Bairns o' Roslin'.

Nowhere in old texts do we find tales of a treasure under Rosslyn Chapel.

The real legends of Rosslyn, dating back hundreds of years, tell of a hidden treasure that lies in a secret chamber under Rosslyn Castle or of a treasure buried somewhere in Rosslyn Glen.

CHAPTER NINE
The Knights Templar

TRUTH WAS VERY IMPORTANT to the St Clairs of Rosslyn. The only words carved into the interior of Rosslyn Chapel translate as:

> Wine is strong. The King is stronger.
> Women are stronger still:
> but truth conquers all.

Truth conquers all. Yet for the last decade successive writers have attempted to rewrite the history of Rosslyn as they see fit, even when the historical evidence proves that their theories are completely wrong.

A series of 'alternative' history writers have taken allegorical Masonic legends, made leaps of faith and guesswork and spun a Templar fantasy that leads from Jerusalem to Rosslyn.

Historical truth is hard to prove. Thorough academics are cautious in their approach to manuscripts and first-hand accounts. Rigorous scholars are extremely careful about their sources and are not prone to sudden flights of fancy or imaginative theories. They investigate who wrote each source and why. What was the writer's agenda and has this document been badly copied or tampered with since it was first written? They are even more cautious with secondary sources and simply dismiss poorly researched 'alternative' pseudo-history books.

Alternative history writers do not feel bound by these constraints. They merrily indulge their fantasies and approach history imaginatively, much as an artist or a songwriter would. They give equal weight to inspiration and unsubstantiated story as to documented history. Some are even guilty of either deliberately ignoring evidence that disproves their theories or of being such poor researchers that they have missed vitally important sources.

Detangling the thicket of theories, claims, counter-claims and conspiracies is a difficult and time-consuming task. The burden of proof lies with alternative history writers, but, because they are producing popular rather than academic books, their theories are not subject to peer review. Their research is simply published and publicised without ever being actively investigated to see if anything they claim actually holds water.

In a bid to make some sense of the bewildering conspiracy theories and bogus alternative histories surrounding Rosslyn, we have investigated as many of the various claims as we have space for and will attempt to separate the facts from the fantasies.

The history of the fall of the Templars is well documented. At dawn on 13 October 1307, the Knights Templar fell into a carefully designed trap. The French King Philip IV had given orders that all Templars across the whole of his kingdom were to be seized and imprisoned.

The 'poor knights' had grown rich and unpopular. The Crusader kingdom of Jerusalem had forged four military orders: the Knights Hospitaller, the Teutonic Knights, the Knights of St Lazarus, and the Knights Templar. They combined the Christian ideals of chivalry and chastity. The Templars were sworn to defend the pilgrim routes to Jerusalem, but now the Holy Land was lost and there was no realistic prospect of another crusade to win it back for Christendom. King Philip IV's attempts to merge the Templar and Hospitaller orders under his control had failed. The French crown was in serious financial difficulty and King Philip coveted the Templars' lands and wealth.

In a single move, he eliminated the Templars and attempted to steal their property. On the evening of 18 March 1314, Jacques de Molay, the last Grand Master of the Templars, was tied to a wooden stake in the shadow of Notre Dame de Paris and burned to death. But were all the Templars destroyed?

Pseudo-histories claim that not all of the Templars were captured, that fugitive knights escaped King Philip's men and fled carrying the fabled Templar Treasure. They claim that the French King searched in vain for the Templars' hidden riches, trying to torture information from the imprisoned knights. But what is the real story?

The Order of the Temple was founded in Jerusalem, the first Military Order founded by the Catholic Church. The fledgling military order was given the site of the Aqsa mosque on the Temple Mount by King Baldwin II; the Crusaders mistakenly believed the mosque was the Temple of Solomon. Within 200 years the Holy Land had been lost and the Templar Order had grown immensely, with properties across Europe. Kings and nobles gave land and wealth to the Templars. The Templars answered to no lord or ruler except the Pope; they were not bound to serve kings and owed no allegiance to any country. With no hope of a new crusade, the reason for the Templar Order's existence was gone. It was only a matter of time until they were brought down.

In 1969, Henry Lincoln, an English writer, was holidaying in France when he picked up a small book at a market stall. The book concerned Bérenger Saunière, the priest of the village of Rennes-le-Château, and a secret treasure he was rumoured to have discovered. Lincoln, with the assistance of Michael Baigent and Richard Leigh, went on to uncover a bizarre tale involving a secret society with an illustrious line of Grand Masters, the Lost Treasure of Jerusalem, the Knights Templar, sacred geometry in the Languedoc region of Southern France and the Holy Bloodline of Jesus and Mary Magdalene. Three BBC documentaries told the story of the priest Saunière and the Prieuré de Sion. Baigent, Leigh and Lincoln's book *The Holy Blood and the Holy Grail* became a controversial international bestseller.

Baigent and Leigh followed their success with *The Temple and the Lodge*. On the bones of this book, a series of alternative history writers including Andrew Sinclair, Tim Wallace-Murphy, Marilyn Hopkins, Robert Lomas, Christopher Knight, Keith Laidler and Laurence Gardner have put forward their own speculative theories about the secrets of the Templars and gradually a modern Templar survival fantasy has evolved.

In essence, it goes something like this:

Not all the Templars were arrested by King Philip's men. Some escaped, bearing the Templar treasure from the Templar Headquarters in Paris. At the port of La Rochelle, the treasure was loaded aboard ships. The Templar fleet was divided in two: half took the short journey to Portugal, the other half made for Scotland, sailing across treacherous seas to either Mull or to the Firth of Forth, or both. Scotland was thought to be a safe haven for the Templars as Robert the Bruce, King of Scots, had been excommunicated by the Pope for the murder of a rival noble within a church.

These fugitive Templars arrived at Rosslyn Castle and were met by the St Clairs, who gave them refuge and became the guardians of their secret treasure. In 1314, the Templars fought valiantly with the Scots at the decisive Battle of Bannockburn. These Templars were led by Sir William St Clair, who was also a Templar Grand Master. Only a Templar cavalry charge saved the Scots, who were floundering against a superior English force.

Over 130 years later, a descendant of this Grand Master Templar William, Sir William St Clair, the third Earl of Orkney, founded Rosslyn Chapel in the image of either Solomon's or Herod's Temple in Jerusalem. It was to be the secret hiding place of the Templar treasure and Sir William left clues and Templar symbols within the carvings in the chapel to prove this.

Most pseudo-history writers agree on this general timeline. Knight and Lomas claim that it was actually twelfth-century Templars that brought the Templar treasure to Scotland during the reign of King David 1.

With each new alternative history book, the fantastical theories of previous books are suddenly accepted by these writers as 'historical fact' and further outlandish claims are added on top like some precarious house of cards.

Most alternative histories agree that Rosslyn Chapel conceals the Templar treasure, but each book disagrees widely on what that treasure is, so that every new book is different from all the others and has an excuse to exist:

> Andrew Sinclair admits that the Chapel itself is a treasure but also claims that it hides the Holy Grail and maybe the Holy Rood, a piece of the True Cross.

> Knight and Lomas claim the treasure is three trunks full of lost sacred texts, like the Dead Sea Scrolls. They call these the 'scrolls of Christ' and claim they were dug up by the Templars in Jerusalem from beneath the Temple.

> Tim Wallace-Murphy and Marilyn Hopkins believe Rosslyn holds scrolls and religious artefacts from the Jerusalem Temple, maybe some lost crown jewels of Holyrood Palace and the Holy Rood, and possibly Rosslyn's lost statues.

Keith Laidler believes the treasure is the embalmed head of Jesus, which had been 'Baphomet', an idol that the Templars were accused of venerating.

Laurence Gardner thinks Rosslyn is the 'likely residence' of the golden plate of the Chartres Cathedral labyrinth, and that the St Clairs were guardians of the 'Rex Deus' kings of Scotland.

Other wild claims and random guesswork from books, magazines, TV documentaries and online articles include: the Ark of the Covenant, the real Stone of Destiny, an alien spacecraft, an astral doorway, forbidden knowledge that came from the devil himself, and the remains of Mary Magdalene.

Academics, the Project Director of the Rosslyn Chapel Trust, and Roslin villagers have noted that all you need is the Loch Ness Monster, the crew of the *Marie Celeste* and the Yeti to have a complete set. As a journalist at *The Scotsman* newspaper once commented, 'If every theory about what lies under Rosslyn Chapel in Midlothian were true, the church would sit on a mound of earth at least 150 feet high.'

Other bizarre theories include: Rosslyn was built on a site of sacred significance 'since the Stone Age', the name 'Roslin' translates as 'ancient knowledge passed down the generations', a Henri de St Clair of Rosslyn 'accompanied Godfroi de Bouillon to the Holy Land in 1096', another Sir Henry St Clair sailed to America and back before Christopher Columbus, the wounded head in the chapel is a carving of Hiram Abif the mythical Grand Master of the Freemasons, Rosslyn was 'the supreme site of initiation in pre-Renaissance Western Europe' and a 'three-dimensional teaching board of Gnostic belief', the St Clairs 'were more powerful than any other family in Scotland', the Templar treasure was taken from Rosslyn to the Oak Island Money

Pit, and the chapel was built as a memorial for the Templar Order.

None of the alternative history writers will acknowledge the possibility that they are utterly wrong. Their theories are built on belief rather than hard evidence. What evidence they do present tends to be previous alternative history writers' theories, their own creative interpretation of medieval symbols, isolated historical facts often from widely disregarded history books, and allegorical Masonic legends from the eighteenth and nineteenth centuries. Some even rely on moments of inspiration when 'they suddenly realise' that they are right and have worked out some startling truth that has evaded more careful researchers and historians for hundreds of years.

Henry Lincoln has a favourite phrase: 'Don't believe a bloody word I say!' Lincoln accepts that new evidence comes to light and discredits old theories. He also encourages everyone to do their own investigation and not to simply accept what they read. The writers who have followed him have tended to lack his wit and his genuine desire to find the truth.

Academics and serious historians have largely avoided addressing the fantastical theories of alternative history. They are busy people with reputations to protect and better things to do than wrangle with writers about poorly researched claims.

'Rosslyn Chapel is the medieval equivalent of a garden gnome. It's a folly.' These words from Dr Juliette Wood of Cardiff University unfortunately show that the nonsense written about Rosslyn can stop academic historians from taking Rosslyn Chapel seriously. When academic historians have commented, they have made their thoughts very clear.

Dr Andrew Roach, Department of Medieval History at the University of Glasgow, is unimpressed by the Templar fantasies. 'I think it's sad. Rosslyn is a fascinating historical artefact, and the fact that people keep analysing it in terms of this nonsense distracts from what is really a fine piece of late medieval art.'

Medieval History reader Dr Gary Dickson of the University

of Edinburgh notes, 'If you have your own agenda, the tendency to impose it and see what you want to see is very great. The danger then is to make connections which do not in fact exist, and cannot be documented. The temptation to connect everything to a great, hidden theme that nobody has perceived before ends up in the sort of history which is a combination of folklore and occultism.'

Helen J. Nicholson Ph.D., Senior Lecturer in History at Cardiff University, is the author of *The Knights Templar: A New History*, and of *Love, War and the Grail: Templars, Hospitallers, and Teutonic Knights in Medieval Epic and Romance 1150–1500*. She also teaches the history of the Military Orders to undergraduates and the history of the Crusades to postgraduates. She warns potential students that 'there are a great many non-historical books, articles and webpages available on the Knights Templar. It is your responsibility as a student to learn how to judge the good from the bad. Past experience indicates that careless reading can seriously damage your final mark for this course.'

Rosslyn Chapel is an incredible medieval treasure. It was built as a Christian place of worship in the fifteenth century by a devout Catholic family. It does not deserve to be treated so poorly and trivialised so widely.

Truth conquers all. It is time that the truth was told.

In order to get at the real facts it is necessary to take apart the Templar fantasies piece by piece to reveal the actual history of Rosslyn Chapel and the St Clair family.

Did a Templar fleet sail from La Rochelle to Scotland?

No. There is nothing but romantic eighteenth- and nineteenth-century allegorical Masonic legends to substantiate the theory, legends that were never intended to be taken seriously as history, legends that did not surface until 500 years after the fall of the Templars.

In reality, it would have been near madness to try to sail to Scotland in October. In Brittany, in the north-west of France, October is known as 'Black Month'. For centuries, the women of La Rochelle in Brittany have looked to the dark winter sea and mourned the dead. In the Black Month, all hope was lost that local fishermen would return alive. Are we really supposed to believe that Templars would have risked a deadly sea voyage to Scotland when they could simply and safely escape the few miles to the Templar strongholds of Portugal?

In their book *The Temple and the Lodge*, the authors Baigent and Leigh tell us they came to Scotland looking for Templar graves. They were following a vague local legend when they 'stumbled across' a series of graves depicting knights, swords and crosses. They leapt to the mistaken conclusion that they were Templar grave slabs.

The Kilmartin and Kilmory graves that Baigent and Leigh describe are definitely not Templar. They are West Highland graves dating from the rule of the Lords of the Isles, whose realm stretched from Knoydart to Kintyre throughout the fourteenth century. The boats which have been mistakenly said to be part of a 'Templar fleet' bear a not terribly surprising resemblance to West Highland boats that appear on other graves and on heraldic crests. West Highland art of the period is characterised by the elaborate graves with combinations of boats, swords, knights, foliage, horses, hounds and sea-monsters. In all, there are over 600 carved stone monuments in the lands that the Lords of the Isles once ruled.

West Highland stone carvings can be found on and in Iona, Harris, Islay, Lorn, Kilmartin, Kilmichael Glassary, Mid-Argyll, Kilmory, Knapdale, Cowal and Saddell Abbey.

Baigent and Leigh went to Argyll looking for Templar graves. They hunted around till they found some stones and decided they were Templar graves. They were simply wrong.

Would Scotland have been a safe haven for the refugee Templars?

No. Pseudo-history writers have claimed that the Templars were never brought to trial in Scotland, that they were given sanctuary by King Robert the Bruce and continued on in secret. This theory hinges on the idea that the excommunication of the Scottish monarch Robert the Bruce meant that Scotland somehow became a 'safe haven'.

In 1306, Bruce and his men murdered John 'the Red' Comyn at the high altar of a sanctuary of the Grey Friars, in Dumfries. While Bruce was excommunicated, Scotland was not. The Papacy did not act against the Scots until 1319, five years after Bannockburn, prompting the famous 'Declaration of Arbroath': a letter addressed to 'the most holy father and lord in Christ' Pope John XXII.

Masonic legends claim that the refugee Templars who fled to Scotland became members of either the Royal Order of Scotland or the Order of St Andrew of the Thistle. But even Victorian Masonic historians stated definitively that these were allegorical 'esoteric' legends. As Albert Mackey comments in his *History of Freemasonry* in 1898, 'none of these statements are susceptible of historical proof'.

The Papal Bull against the Templars was acted on in Scotland in 1309. On 19 December at the Abbey of Holyrood in Edinburgh, the Knights Templar were brought to trial. The proceedings were led by the Bishop of St Andrews, and by Master John of Solerius, clerk to Pope Clement V. Over forty witnesses gave evidence against two Templars: Walter de Clifton, Grand Preceptor of Scotland, and William de Middleton.

Did the Templars fight at the Battle of Bannockburn?

No. 'We may safely conclude that the Bruce and Bannockburn legend of Scottish Templarism is to be deemed a pure myth, without the slightest historical clement to sustain it.' In 1898,

Masonic historian Albert Mackey noted in *The History of Freemasonry* that Masonic legends of refugee Templars fighting at Bannockburn were entirely untrue. Pseudo-history writers have attempted to revive these tales because they suit their own Templar survival fantasies. The Scots army under Robert the Bruce was perfectly capable of defeating the English under Edward II at Bannockburn without the aid of a fairy-tale Templar cavalry. The implication that the Scots would have lost the battle without the help of these imaginary Templars is deeply insulting.

Not one contemporary chronicle even suggests the presence of any Templars at the battle. English chroniclers lamented their defeat at the hands of Scottish peasants. If there had been any hint of Templars at Bannockburn, these embedded chroniclers would have leapt at the chance to blame the humiliating defeat on a Templar force and accuse the Scots of harbouring fugitive knights.

The decisive Battle of Bannockburn was won by the Scots. In 1314, five years after the Templar trial in Scotland, Robert the Bruce led his knights and his men to victory over a larger English force. It was the common men of Scotland formed into 'schiltrons' that truly won the battle. The schiltron was a well-disciplined formation of pikemen that resembled a hedgehog. In two bloody days, hundreds of English knights and over thirty English lords fell. Their defeat would ultimately lead to the independence of Scotland.

Was Sir William St Clair a Grand Master of the Templars and did he shelter Templar fugitives?

No. The accusation that William St Clair was a Templar is probably the worst slur that this Scottish knight could suffer.

Andrew Sinclair seems to think that this is some lost secret he is revealing, some great honour to bestow on the St Clair family. In reality, it is an insult to the memory of a Scots knight who has been dead for almost 700 years and cannot defend his honour. If William had actually been a Templar, he would have been a traitor to the order: a man without honour who broke his most sacred vows.

The Templar Rule, the sacred oath that every Templar swore at their initiation, states: 'the company of women is a dangerous thing', 'none of you may presume to kiss a woman', knights 'should avoid at all costs the embraces of women' and 'scorn the temptations of your body'.

It is important to note that Templar Knights took the three monastic vows of poverty, obedience and chastity. Templars made a vow of celibacy. William St Clair was married. His wife Isabel bore him three sons, Henry, William and David, and a daughter Margaret. His eldest son survived him by many years and became Sir Henry St Clair, first Earl of Orkney.

A Templar Knight's life was devoted to Christ. He would never fight against a fellow Christian. William fought and killed fellow Christians. He joined the Scot's army and faced the English during the Wars of Independence.

If William had been a Templar, his lands would have been given to the order and would have passed to the Hospitallers with the other Templar properties in Scotland.

It is clear from these facts alone that Sir William was never a Templar, but the fatal blow for the Templar lie is that William and his father Henry testified against the Knights Templar when the order was brought to trial in Edinburgh in 1309.

Records of the Templar trial survived the Wars of Independence, but, until now, they have never been translated into English from the original Latin. At Holyrood, Sir William gave evidence that the Templars 'were not willing to offer hospitality to the poor', were 'very anxious to acquire the property of others for their Order, by fair means or foul' and said that 'if the Templars had been faithful Christians they would in no way have lost the Holy Land'.

To accuse Sir William St Clair of even being a Templar sympathiser, let alone a Templar Grand Master, is a dreadful insult. William died on the field of battle at Teba in Spain nearly 700 years ago. He cannot speak out against the lies that have been written about him. Sir William St Clair was a Scots knight, a man of honour who fought and died for his country and for his king.

Is Sir William's gravestone 'Templar'?

No. There has never been any historical evidence that William was a Templar, so why did anyone ever think he was? The mistake was made by the writer Andrew Sinclair in 1992. The foundation of Andrew Sinclair's erroneous theory is a small grave slab carved with a sword and a cross. The decorative head of the cross is a 'floriated' eight-spoked wheel, ornamented to resemble a flower. It bears the inscription 'WILLHM DE SINNCLER'. Andrew Sinclair believes that this was the grave of a Templar and that the St Clairs discovered America before Columbus. 'This story is history,' he claims.

'This discovery is the cornerstone of this book,' Sinclair says, referring to William's grave slab in his book *The Sword and the Grail*. These are fateful words. His entire thesis falls apart because this 'cornerstone' proves to be utterly false. With no sensible historical evidence, Andrew Sinclair leapt to the conclusion that the sword and eight-spoked head of the cross somehow showed that William was a Templar Master.

Nothing could be further from the truth.

Andrew Sinclair's theory is based partly on Baigent and Leigh's misidentification of Scottish graves in *The Temple and the Lodge*. But just because a grave has a sword carved on it does not remotely prove it is a Templar grave.

Even more incredible is that the truth was under Andrew Sinclair's nose all along. He notes the legend of the Royal Hunt: when William's life hung in the balance he called on Christ, the blessed Virgin, and St Catherine to save him. After the white stag fell, William vowed to build a chapel to St Catherine in thanks. Though the legend may be fantasy, the chapel of St Katherine of the Hopes was real enough. It was dedicated to St Catherine of Alexandria.

St Catherine of Alexandria was the family saint of the St Clairs. The two symbols of the martyrdom of St Catherine are the sword and the eight-spoked wheel, the exact symbols carved into Sir William's grave slab.

St Catherine was fated to die on a terrible wheeled torture machine, but angels sent by Jesus destroyed it with lightning, so she was beheaded with a sword. St Catherine, her wheel and her sword are found carved in medieval sculptures, painted in devotional art and depicted in stained-glass windows. Though this hugely popular medieval saint is largely forgotten today, we still light the blue touch-paper on 'Catherine wheel' fireworks.

The form of William's grave slab was popular in the fourteenth century. The three steps at the base of the cross-shaft do not represent the 'steps to the Temple of Solomon'. This type of cross is known as a 'graded' cross; the three steps symbolise faith, hope and love. The style of the lettering cut into the slab dates the carving to roughly the thirteenth or fourteenth century. It is even in no way certain that this is the gravestone of the Sir William who accompanied the Good Sir James Douglas with Robert the Bruce's heart. It may be one of his many ancestors or descendants.

Was Rosslyn Chapel built by the Templars and is it based on either Solomon's or Herod's Temple?

No. Rosslyn Chapel bears no more resemblance to Solomon's or Herod's Temple than a house brick does to a paperback book. If you superimpose the floor plans of Rosslyn Chapel and either Solomon's or Herod's Temple, you will actually find they are not even remotely similar. Writers admit that the chapel is far smaller than either of the temples. They freely scale the plans up or down in an attempt to fit them together. What they actually find are no significant similarities at all.

The famed pillars of the Temple of Jerusalem are not replicated in Rosslyn. There are actually three pillars at the Lady Choir, not two. In the temple, 'Jachin and Boaz' were the two pillars at the east entrance. In Rosslyn, the three pillars are as far as you can get from the doorways to the chapel, by the only wall that doesn't have an entrance at all.

It is unclear precisely where Knight and Lomas found their floorplan and measurements for Herod's Temple. There are no reliable measurements for Herod's Temple. The Urban Simulation Team at UCLA have created a digital reconstruction of Jerusalem's Herodian Temple Mount: a real-time simulation model that 'represents the most accurate reconstruction possible given the information available'. They note that the 'wealth of conflicting reconstructions are based solely on historic written descriptions'. Their own virtual Temple is based on the research of the late Professor Michael Avi-Yonah of the Hebrew University. They decided to create a very simple computer model of the Temple which will be updated if any excavation ever provides more accurate dimensions.

Suggestions that the west exterior wall of Rosslyn Chapel was deliberately built to resemble the Wailing Wall in Jerusalem are simply wishful thinking. The walls of Rosslyn have been rebuilt, crudely repaired and robbed numerous times over the centuries. Unsurprisingly, they also resemble the walls of cathedrals, collegiate churches and castles throughout Scotland.

If you superimpose the floor plans of Rosslyn Chapel and the East Quire of Glasgow Cathedral you will find a startling match: the four walls of both buildings fit precisely. The East Quire of Glasgow is larger than Rosslyn, but the designs of these two medieval Scottish buildings are virtually identical. They both have the same number of windows and the same number of pillars in the same configuration. The six easternmost pillars are spaced differently, as Rosslyn has a proportionally larger Lady

Choir. Glasgow even has an arched ceiling like Rosslyn's but made of wood rather than stone. The similarity between Rosslyn Chapel and Glasgow's East Quire is well established. Andrew Kemp noted that 'the entire plan of this Chapel corresponds to a large extent with the choir of Glasgow Cathedral' as far back as 1877 in the Proceedings of the Society of Antiquaries. Many alternative history writers are well aware of this but fail to mention it in their books.

The close connection between Glasgow's East Quire and Rosslyn Chapel is hardly surprising. Vital repairs and reconstruction work on Glasgow Cathedral was funded by Archibald, fifth Earl of Douglas, the brother of Elizabeth Douglas. Elizabeth was the first wife of Sir William, the third Earl, the founder of Rosslyn Chapel. As the coat of arms of Archibald Douglas is carved in stone in Glasgow Cathedral, so the Douglas heart is found carved in Rosslyn Chapel in memory of Elizabeth.

Are there really Templar symbols carved within Rosslyn Chapel?

No. There are thousands of carvings within Rosslyn Chapel, but alternative historians claim to have found only a handful of 'Templar symbols'. Various alternative historians have alleged that the following carvings are 'Templar'. All have far more rational explanations.

Two knights on one horse

One image that commonly appears on Templar seals is two knights on one horse.

The carving in Rosslyn actually shows only one knight on horseback, holding a lance. The figure behind him is either a woman or an angel holding a cross. She is not a knight and is not even on the horse! She is actually behind the horse. It has also been claimed that this carving shows William 'the Seemly' or the knight Leslyn and the future queen Margaret bearing the Holy Rood to Scotland. It is rather more likely that this is simply a representation of a knight as a faithful Christian. The laws of chivalry dictated that a knight should be true to God and the Church.

The dove
The Templars, like other religious orders, used common sacred symbols but this does not mean they are even remotely 'Templar' symbols. The dove appears amid the field of stars in the chapel's ceiling. This may be the dove that brought the olive branch to Noah after the flood or simply a carving of the Holy Ghost. The Gospel of Luke speaks of the Holy Spirit descending in bodily form like a dove. The dove appears in cathedrals, chapels and paintings across Europe representing the Holy Spirit.

The Lamb of God
The Lamb of the Apocalypse bearing the cross and banner also appears in countless medieval and renaissance buildings, and artworks. Within Rosslyn, its position is significant. It is placed in the north aisle within the Seventh Seal. Angels are breaking the seal unleashing the Apocalypse as foretold in the Book of Revelation. Again, this is a Biblical rather than Templar symbol.

The Cross of the five wounds
Andrew Sinclair mistakenly says this is a Templar cross. In reality, it is simply a symbol of the five wounds that Christ received on the cross. It is used in medieval ecclesiastical buildings as a consecration mark.

The five-pointed star
There is a field of five-pointed stars at the west end of the ceiling. Five-pointed stars are a Templar symbol. So are six-pointed stars, eight-pointed stars, octagonal crosses, etc. In all, there are dozens of symbols linked with Solomon and by proxy with the Templars. In reality, over a century after the fall of

the Templars, five-pointed stars were a 'symbol of troth' that denoted a pledge of loyalty. In *Sir Gawain and the Green Knight*, the courteous Gawain bears the pentangle on his shield. The anonymous Gawain poet tells us that in England it is known as 'the endless knot'; it also symbolised the five wounds of Christ, the four nails to his hands and feet, and the spear to his side.

The 'Templar' gravestone
We have already shown that Andrew Sinclair has leapt to the wrong conclusion about William St Clair's grave slab.

Does the heraldic Engrailed Cross of the St Clair family contain a Templar cross?

No. Unsurprisingly this is yet another spurious claim. In Scotland, a coat of arms belongs to an individual person, a family does not have a coat of arms. Descendants have to make sure their own Arms differ from those of their forebears by using marks of difference known as 'cadency marks'.

There are many different designs for edges in heraldry. These include: indented (small zigzags), rayonné (like indented but with curved lines), nebuly (stylized clouds), embattled (small squares like a castle battlement) and engrailed (a ragged line of half-circles).

'Engrailed' does not imply that the bearer of the arms is the 'guardian of a Rex Deus bloodline' or protector of the Holy Grail. It is simply a common heraldic term and numerous coats of arms include engrailed crosses.

It should be noted that the Sinclair clan crest is not actually the engrailed cross. It is a cock proper, armed and crested, surrounded by a strap-and-buckle bearing the family motto 'Commit thy work to God'. In Scotland, the governing body for heraldry is the Lyon office, headed by Lord Lyon King of Arms. It is illegal to bear another man's coat of arms or to invent a coat of arms.

'The initiation'

Knight and Lomas have leapt on a single carving as conclusive proof of all their theories, misleadingly naming it 'the initiation'. The carving is on the outside of the south wall, a little to the west of the Ladies' Door. It shows two figures. One is standing and bearded. The other is kneeling with a rope about his neck, apparently blindfolded, and possibly holding a book in one hand (though the carving is badly eroded). They claim that this shows a Templar initiation rite and that this ritual has many points of correspondence with Freemasonic initiation, thus 'proving' a connection. Bizarrely, they try to use statistics to 'prove' their theory. Their method and their conclusions are fatally flawed.

The carving itself is now quite badly worn. Earlier photographs appear to show a cross on the clothing of the standing figure. Knight and Lomas claim this shows he is a Templar Knight. It shows nothing of the sort. The Knights Hospitaller, who were granted the Templars' lands including Balantrodoch, had a cross on the front of their mantles. Countless Scottish knights also had a cross in their family coat of arms and would also have worn it on their mantles to identify them in battle. Finally, Knight and Lomas seem to have forgotten another famous cross: the English flag, the cross of St George.

If we do stretch credibility to imagine for a moment that the figure is a Templar, there is another more sinister explanation for the carving. In 1298, the infamous Templar Master Brian le Jay led a section of King Edward's army through Scotland to face William Wallace. A local widow's son, Richard Cook, was forced by Brian le Jay to lead the troops between Balantrodoch and Temple Liston. The following day, Richard was murdered. Another Templar, Thomas Tocci, stated that Brian le Jay asserted that a single hair of a Saracen's head was worth more than Christ's whole body. It is highly unlikely that the carving at Rosslyn depicts a Templar at all. If it does, it may depict the murder of Richard Cook by Brian le Jay.

Alternative history writers like to claim that the Templars

fought during the Wars of Independence. Templars did fight, but not on the side of the Scots. At the Battle of Falkirk in 1298, the Templar Grand Master Brian le Jay fought in the service of the English King. Le Jay was dragged from his horse and drowned by the Scots.

Is the Templar Treasure hidden in a secret vault beneath Rosslyn Chapel?

No. Andrew Sinclair went so far as to dig beneath the floor at Rosslyn looking for the Holy Grail. A borehole was cut in an attempt to 'find the grail' in the vaults beside the Apprentice Pillar. A small video camera was pushed down the hole but infill prevented any further investigation. Andrew Sinclair did find a small wooden object which he removed from the chapel. He was pictured with it in national newspapers professing his belief that he had almost found the Grail. Considering that Rosslyn is an active place of worship and that generations of the St Clair family are buried beneath the chapel, Mr Sinclair was very lucky not to be accused of grave robbing. Scotland's Rite of Sepulchre laws legislate against the disturbance of burial places. It is unclear what has become of the wooden object. In all probability, it is not a stonemason's wooden bowl but actually a headrest from one of the burials.

The Templar fantasies are illusions, tricks done with smoke and mirrors. When you examine them closely, every alternative history theory falls apart. Pseudo-history writers have trivialised Rosslyn and made false accusations against the medieval St Clairs. The real Rosslyn Chapel has nothing to do with Templars, their legendary treasure or their lost secrets. There has never been any credible evidence linking Rosslyn and the Templars, so the revelation that a Templar artefact had been uncovered at Roslin came as quite a surprise.

What appears to be a genuine Templar seal was found just a mile or so from Rosslyn Chapel at the village of Roslin. If the seal dates to the 1300s, when the Templars were active in Scotland, then it may have lain undiscovered for almost 700 years. It may have been lost over 100 years before Rosslyn Chapel was founded.

The seal is circular, badly worn, blackened with age, and broken into two halves. It is approximately 43mm in diameter. The front of the seal shows two knights on one horse, with shields and lances. An inscription encircles the two Templar knights.

+ SIGILLVM MILITVM XPISTI

+ Seal of the knighthood of Christ

The majority of the inscription is Latin, the XP is the Greek equivalent of CHR. A very rough equal-armed cross pattée, the Templar cross was cut into the reverse of the seal before it was fired.

There are no other datable finds to provide a context for the seal but it certainly appears to be genuine and we have no reason at all to doubt its authenticity. It is possible that it is a twentieth-century fake but this seems unlikely. It may be a nineteenth-century Freemasonic token of some kind or it may have been made at any time using a genuine Templar seal matrix. The question is, how did the Knights Templar seal end up at Roslin?

The Templar Preceptory at Balantrodoch was only a few miles south-east of Rosslyn. It was founded in the twelfth century under King David I and survived until the order was brought to trial at Holyrood in 1309. The seal may have been sent to the Templars in Scotland or it may have been the seal of a Master at the Balantrodoch Preceptory. In the Middle Ages, a seal was the common way to show that a document was genuine.

The seal may have been lost at the Battle of Roslin. We certainly know that Templars were fighting alongside King Edward's English army during the Wars of Independence.

Human bones from the battle were ploughed up at Roslin for centuries.

The seal may have been taken by local villagers from Balantrodoch when the Templars were arrested or after their trial. The cross on its back may suggest that the seal was created as some kind of 'good luck token'. It is even possible that the seal was accidentally lost or deliberately hidden at Roslin by someone, perhaps a mischievous local or a Victorian Freemason, at any time in the last few hundred years.

After centuries of Templar myths and Masonic legends, the Templar seal has emerged as a solid piece of historical evidence. It takes the story of the Knights Templar in Scotland out of the realm of fantasy and into history, where it belongs.

CHAPTER TEN
The White Lady

Ghosts yell'd out frae 'mang the trees,
And Roslin Castle seem'd a' in a bleeze . . .

John Rigby, *Traditionary Tales of Roslin Castle*, 1860

IF YOU BELIEVE THE old tales, somewhere beneath Rosslyn Castle lies the key to a treasure worth many millions of pounds. Deep within the haunted ruin a mysterious White Lady waits to reveal the treasure's hiding place. For hundreds of years she has kept her secret.

The White Lady is said to be a maiden of the St Clair line, bewitched by an evil spell and doomed to sleep in an enchanted chamber until a knight comes to her rescue. Upon a table, at the lady's side, lie a magical sword and a golden hunting horn. A dark demonic creature watches over her. Only a brave knight can wield the sword, blow the horn and defeat the dark creature. Then finally the enchantment will be broken, the White Lady will be free and the brave knight will win the treasure.

Throughout the eighteenth and nineteenth centuries, the tales of Rosslyn's riches brought fortune hunters from all across Scotland. It was thought by some that only a blind man could find the treasure, as 'the angel lady' who guarded it was 'of such dazzling purity, that mortal eye could not look long upon her and live'. Others said that only a man named Wilson was destined to win the treasure. The foolhardy laughed at the stories and ventured down into the castle dungeons seeking the Rosslyn treasure. None returned.

'In the days of old,' it is said, 'a Highlander came from the Highlands with the intention of breaking the enchantment of Rosslyn Castle.' The villagers of Roslin followed the brave Highlander and his loyal dog down the winding road by the chapel. They cheered him on as he approached the castle and took up his bagpipes to play a merry tune. They watched as the Highlander and his wee dog stepped through the castle's doorway. They listened to the sound of his bagpipes fade as he descended the great stair down into the vaults. Then they heard nothing. The piping stopped dead. The villagers waited in fearful silence. Suddenly there came a single blast from the hunting horn. Moments later a strange voice echoed from the ruins:

> Woe be unto you, man,
> That ever you were born!
> You haven't drawn the sword,
> Before you blew the horn.

As the villagers looked on, the piper's dog ran out from the castle towards them. The dog ran wild, its eyes wide. The poor creature was frightened half to death but what was worse – it had no skin. The villagers bowed their heads and turned for home. The Highlander was never seen again.

But who is the White Lady of Rosslyn Castle? Is she a ghost or an angel? Is she a maiden in an enchanted sleep or is she of the faerie race?

It is often said that Scotland is the most haunted country in the world. Shadowy armies clash on ancient battlefields; phantom coaches hurtle down cobbled streets and hanged men swing from ancient trees. Ghost tours will take you through poltergeist-infested graveyards and down into spooky underground vaults. Scotland's castles, cathedrals and churches sometimes seem to have more dead inhabitants than live ones.

At Saddell Castle, near Campbeltown in Kintyre, a phantom White Lady walks the battlements. Meldrum House, in Aberdeenshire, is haunted by a kindly White Lady who looks after lost children. During a thunderstorm, this White Lady gave one male guest an icy cold kiss. A White Lady wanders the ruins of St Andrews Cathedral in a flowing dress, staring out from beneath a veil. Sometimes White Ladies are said to be the spirits of servant girls who fell pregnant by young noblemen and threw themselves to their deaths from the battlements. Others are thought to be maidens who vanished mysteriously and whose broken skeletons were discovered years later in shallow graves.

Many White Ladies are anonymous but some are reputed to be particular real people. The White Lady of Old Woodhouselee Castle was said to be Lady Hamilton. Her awful fate was remembered for generations. One frozen winter's night, an enemy of James Hamilton of Bothwellheugh, her husband, appeared at Woodhouselee Castle. The cruel man threw Lady Hamilton and her infant son out into the cold in only their nightclothes. The pair were abandoned to die in the snow and ice. Lady Hamilton went mad as she cradled her dead child and is said to have wept herself to death. Her mournful ghost searched the castle and its grounds for her baby until the castle was eventually demolished. Old Woodhouselee Castle was not far from Rosslyn, near Penicuik in Midlothian. When the castle's stones were used to build Fulford Tower, it seems Lady Hamilton moved in as well until this tower was also torn down.

At Edzell Castle, near Brechin in Angus, the White Lady is a fearful apparition. In 1578, Catherine Campbell was thought to have died and was duly interred within the family vault. The poor lady was buried alive. She was awakened by a thief cutting off her fingers to steal her rings. She rose from her tomb but died at the castle gates of exposure and was later laid in her grave – for a second time. Lady Campbell's spirit haunts the castle to this day, dressed in a white dress and with a blur where her face should be.

Hermitage Castle, near Newcastleton in the Borders, is one of the darkest, most haunted places in all Scotland. Here the dread Lord Soulis practised the forbidden arts and trafficked with the devil. The White Lady of Hermitage Castle is, however, a much gentler spirit: Mary Queen of Scots herself is said to appear at the ruined fortress. Mary once rode across country to Hermitage Castle without a thought for her own welfare to tend her wounded lover the Earl of Bothwell. Her ghost still walks the walls in a fine white dress. It should be noted that Mary Queen of Scots' ghost is rather busy, as she seems to flit around to haunt multiple castles and palaces.

A Sinclair White Lady is said to haunt Brims Castle, a few miles west of Thurso in Caithness. Legend says that she is the ghost of the daughter of James Sinclair of Uttersquoy. The girl became the lover of the notorious Patrick Sinclair. She disappeared in suspicious circumstances and it was rumoured that Patrick murdered the girl and hid her body. Her restless spirit still haunts the castle. Locals also recalled that a serving girl vanished from the castle: a joiner in Thurso was hired in secret to make a coffin and in the dead of night a body was removed. Ghost or not, the local fishermen still dug around Brims Castle searching for a legendary buried treasure.

In all, there are over 30 ghostly White Ladies haunting the castles, towers, palaces, cathedrals, houses and rivers of

Scotland. There are almost as many phantom Grey Ladies in residence, a half dozen spectral Ladies in Black, and a handful of Blue and even Pink Ladies. However, by far the most popular colour for Scots ghosts is green. There are over 40 Green Ladies haunting castles, hotels, theatres and hospitals from the Castle of Mey near John O'Groats to Comlongon Castle a few miles from the border with England.

It should be said in passing that the Green Lady of the Castle of Mey was also a Sinclair maiden: the daughter of the fifth Sinclair Earl of Caithness. The Earl was a proud man who was horrified to discover his daughter had fallen in love with a humble ploughman. The unfortunate girl was imprisoned high in an attic room by her disapproving father. She stared down, broken-hearted, at her true love from her attic window until the Earl had it boarded up. In despair, she threw herself from the roof down to the courtyard far below. Her ghost, clad all in green, still haunts her father's castle. A virtually identical tale is told concerning the White Lady who haunts Castle Huntly near Dundee.

Is the White Lady of Rosslyn Castle really an 'angel lady'?

There are dozens of carvings of angels within Rosslyn Chapel: angels with scrolls, angels with books, angels playing medieval instruments – even angels playing the bagpipes. A heavenly choir of angels plays to Mary and the Baby Jesus in the nativity carving in the Lady Chapel. On a gothic arch over a window on the south wall are the nine choirs of angels: the Cherubim, Seraphim and Thrones, the Dominations, Virtues and Powers, and the Principalities, Archangels and Angels.

The word 'angel' is derived from the Greek word 'aggelos', which was a translation of the Hebrew for messenger, 'mal'akh'. The angels of the Bible are neither male nor female, and are unable to reproduce. God made the angels with his own hands. It has been said that the angels in the Bible 'do God's dirty work'; they level cities, slay armies and kill without mercy. They are also God's messengers on earth:

> Then I saw another mighty angel coming down from
> heaven. He was robed in a cloud, with a rainbow above
> his head; his face was like the sun, and his legs were
> like fiery pillars. He was holding a little book, which
> lay open in his hand.

Revelation 10

Despite their androgyny, angels were initially depicted in Christian art as young males. The Greek 'aggelos' is a masculine noun. The archangel Michael is a warrior angel. Michael is dressed in armour and wields a sword as he leads the host of heaven against the forces of Satan.

The image of the beautiful winged angel in flowing robes we are so familiar with today has evolved over the centuries. By the Victorian era the vision of feminine guardian angels was established. This was the gentle nurturing angel that protected and healed. She was dressed in pure white robes and bathed in divine light. In the graveyard that lies between Rosslyn Chapel and Castle, there is a Victorian stone angel. Her face is beautiful. Her robes are knotted with ivy and briars. She is the perfect vision of the romantic view of angels – a radiant white angel lady. The tales of Rosslyn's White Lady may well be influenced by the romantic Victorian view of angels as bright, shining and magical beings but there is certainly no mention of wings or halos in her legends.

The White Lady of Rosslyn is often described as an Enchanted or a Sleeping Lady. Tales of enchanted ladies clad in white are popular across Europe. They are not the spirits of the dead or faerie women – these are real maidens who have fallen victim to evil spells.

On the Castle Hill at Biesenthal in Brandenburg, Germany, a beautiful princess in white is seen holding a golden spinning-wheel. Late one night a gardener heard a voice calling him into the castle garden. There he saw the White Lady. She asked him to carry her from the castle grounds to the nearby church. The gardener was too frightened at first and ran away. At midnight some days later, he again came to the garden and the White Lady appeared before him. She asked for his help as before and this time the gardener agreed. He carried the lady on his back out of the castle garden and up the hill to the churchyard. But the moment he passed through the churchyard gate a dark carriage drawn by black horses, vomiting fire, appeared. The gardener screamed out in horror a few feet from the church door, the carriage vanished and the enchanted princess fled into the night, wailing, 'For ever lost.'

The Chateau d'Usse, also known as the castle of dreams, lies in the Loire Valley in Northern France. Its gothic towers and Renaissance galleries were built in the fifteenth and sixteenth centuries on the foundations of an earlier fortress. Usse's high white walls, pointed turrets and immaculate ornamental gardens lend it a magical air. The chateau and its chapel lie at the edge of the Forest of Chinon: a dark enchanted forest that is said to hide a fortune in buried treasure. Usse is simply the perfect fairy-tale castle. In the late seventeenth century, Charles Perrault wrote a series of classic fairy tales, including Cinderella, Little Red Riding Hood and Puss in Boots. As Perrault was writing his great book of fairy tales *Contes du temps passé*, he took the Chateau d'Usse as the inspiration for the enchanted castle of Sleeping Beauty – *La Belle au Bois Dormant*:

> . . . in this castle lies a princess, the most beautiful that
> has ever been seen. It is her doom to sleep there for a
> hundred years, and then to be awakened by a king's
> son, for whose coming she waits.

Could Perrault's famous fairy story of Sleeping Beauty and her handsome young prince have inspired the tales of the White Lady of Rosslyn Castle? Both maidens fall victim to an evil spell, both lie in an enchanted sleep deep within their castles, both await a brave hero who will rescue them. Perrault's fairy tales, including the story of Sleeping Beauty, certainly became hugely popular in Britain when they were translated into English by Robert Samber in 1729, long before the tales of Rosslyn's White Lady were recorded and published.

There are also White Ladies among the strange inhabitants of Faerie.

The primary colour of Scots faerie folk is green. Green is therefore thought to be unlucky and should never be worn as part of a wedding dress. It may be that at least some of the Green Ladies thought to be ghosts are in fact faeries. Scottish faeries are, however, nothing if not contrary beings that are happy to appear in brown, grey, red and, of course, white.

Faerie White Ladies should always be approached with caution. In France, the White Ladies of Normandy are known as Les Dames Blanches. These fair ladies wait at river fords, bridges and in ravines for passing travellers. They will ask mortal men to dance with them and if they are refused they seize the discourteous man and throw him into a ditch full of briars and thorn bushes to teach him good manners. In Ireland, at Lough Gur, in County Limerick, the locals fear the White Lady. The lake is an enchanted place. Once every seven years, a mortal is drowned by the Beann Fhionn, the White Lady, in the icy waters of the lake. The Irish Banshees, whose baleful wailing foretells death, are said to be clad all in white as are The Gentry, an aristocratic clan of Irish trooping faeries.

The Welsh faerie folk of South Caernarvonshire are known as the Tylwyth Teg, the 'Fair Family'. These are diminutive faeries, small in stature, noted for their beauty and the fineness of their white clothes. By day they make mischief and even steal children in exchange for hunchbacked changelings. By night they sing and dance in faerie rings and, like the French Dames Blanche, will try to lure unwary passers-by into their faerie revels then torment them with tricks.

The Greek Nereids have much in common with the faeries

There are over 100 Green Men within Rosslyn Chapel.

Angel bearing an open book, marking the beginning of the story of Rosslyn Chapel.
(CAROLINE DAVIES © 2005)

Rosslyn's Green Men 'age' as you move clockwise around the building, beginning with young boy Green Men in the north-east corner.

Engraving (*c.*1700) showing a garden
with a well in the courtyard of Rosslyn Castle

The 'Lady Choir' or 'Lady Chapel', with a carving of the Nativity showing the manger, the three wise men and the Virgin Mary holding the infant Jesus. (CAROLINE DAVIES © 2005)

Sir William St.Clair of Roslin wins his wager with King Rob. Bruce that his two dogs "Help" & "Hold" would kill the deer before she could cross March Burn

R.P. Phillimore postcard depicting the Royal Hunt of
King Robert the Bruce, William St Clair and the White Deer.

Two battling dragons, from the legend of Merlin
and the red and white dragons. (CAROLINE DAVIES © 2005)

Bearded Green Man facing south, carved
above a pillar in the south aisle.

Engraving of Rosslyn Chapel above the ruins of the castle.
(1797, J KOOPER, FRANCIS GROSE'S *ANTIQUITIES OF SCOTLAND*)

Carving described for over 200 years
as 'the head of the apprentice'.

Damaged carving of the Crucifixion of Christ.

The Prentice Pillar or Apprentice Pillar has also been
known as 'the Prince's Pillar' and 'the Princess's Pillar'.
(CAROLINE DAVIES © 2005)

Dead Green Man facing north, on
the external north wall of Rosslyn Chapel.

The last angel, in the north aisle, cradles a closed book in its arms.

of Britain and Ireland. They dance by moonlight, cast spells, steal babies and fall in love with mortal men. They are thought to be half-divine and appear ever young though they are not immortal. Their faces are fair and their lithe bodies are draped in flowing white dresses.

Faeries and ghosts have a long and deep connection. Sidhe mounds, or faerie hills as they are popularly known, can be found across the British Isles. Churches were often built near these sidhe mounds. They were often known as 'the mounds of the dead'. Villagers would not disturb or destroy a sidhe mound for fear of bringing down the wrath of the faeries upon themselves. In parts of the Scottish Highlands, it was believed that the spirits of the dead would live with the faeries in their sidhe mounds until the Day of Judgement finally came. Sidhe mounds are often ancient burial mounds. The ancestral spirits of earlier ages became the faerie creatures of local folklore.

King Arthur's wife 'Guinevere' is named 'Gwenhwyfar' in the Welsh Triads and the Welsh legends known as *The Mabinogion*. Gwenhwyfar has been translated as 'White Phantom' or 'White Sprite'. 'Gwenn' is 'White' while 'hwyvar' is thought to be derived from a word for a ghost or a faerie. We are used to the idea that Arthur's sister Morgan le Fay is Morgan the Faery. The Lady of the Lake is a faerie woman, dressed in shimmering white and silver, who bears the sword Excalibur. It seems that Arthur's wife was thought to be an otherworldly White Lady too.

Rosslyn's White Lady may in reality be more symbolic than supernatural. Ultimately the fall of the Sinclair family came about because they refused to give up their Catholic faith.

At one time, all of the noble families of Scotland had been Catholic. With the Protestant Reformation in Scotland, the tide turned and by the time that Mary Queen of Scots came to the throne she was a Catholic Queen in a Protestant country. In AD 1560, the Scots parliament formally abolished the authority of the Pope in Scotland and the celebration of the Catholic Mass was forbidden. Mary herself had to celebrate Mass in a small private chapel, and suffered verbal assaults from the Protestant preacher John Knox. As Catholicism was attacked and Catholics themselves were persecuted, the nobility of Scotland embraced the new religion. The Sinclairs of Rosslyn refused to give up the Catholic faith. They were loyal Catholics whose commitment to their faith would ultimately be their undoing.

On 29 July 1565, at Holyrood in Edinburgh, Mary Queen of Scots was married to Henry Lord Darnley. The marriage was a Catholic ceremony performed by John St Clair, Bishop of Brechin, fourth son of Oliver St Clair of Rosslyn.

Rosslyn had already suffered greatly on account of Mary. In 1544, Rosslyn Castle was attacked and virtually destroyed by Henry VIII's troops during the 'Rough Wooing', when the English king tried to force the marriage of his young son Edward and the infant Mary Queen of Scots.

Rosslyn Chapel ceased to be a place of worship in 1592. The St Clairs of Rosslyn had stubbornly held on to their Catholic faith for fifty years after the Protestant Reformation in Scotland. The provost and prebendaries of Rosslyn Chapel resigned in 1571, when their endowments were taken 'by force and violence'. The homes and gardens they had been given were attacked by a Protestant mob. In 1589, William Knox, the brother of John Knox and minister of Cockpen, was censured for baptising the child of 'the Laird of Rosling'. The baptism was performed in Rosslyn Chapel, which was described in the Dalkeith Presbytery records as a 'monument of idolatrie'. The end finally came in 1592, when the St Clairs were threatened with excommunication if they failed to have the altars within Rosslyn Chapel destroyed. By the end of August it was recorded that the altars had been demolished and Rosslyn Chapel was abandoned as a House of God.

In 1650, another English army came north and attacked Rosslyn. Oliver Cromwell had led the Parliamentarians to victory and overseen the execution of King Charles I. The monarchy was abolished but a year after his father's beheading Charles II landed in Scotland and was proclaimed King. Cromwell's forces moved north and Rosslyn Castle was bombarded with cannon and grandeles (an early form of grenade) by a Parliamentarian force under the command of the English General Monk. His troops stabled their horses within Rosslyn Chapel, fired their muskets at the west wall and may have taken hammers to some of the carvings. Rosslyn Castle and Chapel lay in ruins.

Further degradation occurred when in 1688 a Protestant mob attacked and damaged the chapel. Carved figures had their heads broken off and faces were mutilated with hammers and iron spikes. The figure of Christ on the cross was beheaded. A figure of a devout Catholic at prayer with a book of psalms was defaced. To the Protestants of Midlothian, Rosslyn was a place haunted by the Old Religion, a place of idolatry and superstition.

A central figure of Catholic worship is 'Our Lady': the Blessed Virgin, Mary the mother of Jesus Christ. The divine Lady appeared in Lady Chapels, Lady Wells, devotional paintings, illuminations and church sculpture. At the east end of Rosslyn Chapel, beyond the Apprentice Pillar, lies the 'Lady Chapel'.

The light of the sun rises through the windows of the Lady Chapel each dawn. One of Rosslyn's four altars was dedicated to the Blessed Virgin and she is depicted cradling the infant Christ on one of the pendant bosses of the Lady Chapel, along with the Star of Bethlehem and the manger, in a nativity scene. Over the centuries there have been many visions of the Blessed Virgin – most famously the Lady of Lourdes. She radiates pure light and appears in white or pale blue. The Protestants recalled Catholicism with fear and suspicion. To the Protestant Scots the phantom White Lady of Rosslyn may have been the Blessed Lady of the Catholic faith or simply a remembrance of Rosslyn's Catholic past. Perhaps her treasure represented the lost wealth of the Catholic St Clairs. In time, the religious association was forgotten and only the legend remained.

In 1860, John Rigby of Rumbletyne Cottage, Hawthornden, saw his *Traditionary Tales of Roslin Castle* appear in print. The volume also includes 'the History of Margaret Hawthorn, more generally known as Camp Meg' and 'poems and songs of the Glens'. An imperfect copy of this very rare book is bound within a miscellaneous volume at the National Library of Scotland in Edinburgh. Some of the pages are missing, others are duplicated and some appear in the wrong order, but with a little work most of Mr Rigby's book can be read. It contains the most detailed surviving version of the legend of Rosslyn's White Lady.

According to the *Traditionary Tales of Roslin Castle*, the White Lady was once a maiden who attracted the attention of the dread Lord Soulis, the Wizard of Hermitage Castle. The notorious Lord tried to woo the lady but she was already in love with a young knight. This 'young chevalier . . . was in every respect worthy of her love, and he also loved her with equal ardour'.

Lord Soulis fell into a jealous rage and sought revenge on the young couple. 'He threw the cantrips of his witchcraft . . . and conjured her to dreary vault in the lower recesses of the Castle.'

So, in Rigby's version of the legend at least, it is the dark magic of Lord Soulis that enchants the White Lady of Rosslyn. Soulis is widely regarded in Scottish legend as an evil necromancer. In the early 1800s, John Leyden reported in Scott's *Border Minstrelsy* that Lord Soulis' stronghold, Hermitage Castle, had 'partly sunk beneath the ground' as it was 'unable to support the load of iniquity which had been long accumulating within its walls'. Lord Soulis had made a pact with the devil, it was said. He stole children, kept them captive in his dungeons then murdered them to use their blood in his spells. Leyden tells us that, even hundreds of years after Soulis died in the fourteenth century, the ruins of his castle were 'still regarded by the peasants with peculiar aversion and terror'.

Legend says that Lord Soulis had a vicious goblin known as Redcap as his wizard's familiar. This creature was short and stocky. It had large fiery red eyes, long teeth and sharp talons for fingernails. He wore huge iron boots and a red cap stained with the blood of unwary travellers. As long as Redcap remained the familiar of Lord Soulis the dark wizard would be protected from harm. Neither 'Forged steel nor hempen band' could kill him – Lord Soulis was safe from sword and the hangman's noose. Deep within Hermitage Castle was a secret locked dungeon where he spoke with evil spirits. He had an ancient chest with rusted padlocks which, if he struck it three times, summoned Redcap or the devil himself. It seemed that nothing could be done to get rid of the wizard of Hermitage Castle.

The White Lady of Rosslyn was doomed to spend eternity trapped in an enchanted chamber. Rigby tells us that her 'song can be heard at midnight at the top of the stair that leads to the lower vaults':

> A lady lonely – ha! ha! ha!
> Where foot ha'e never trod that's free;
> A lady lonely – ha! ha! ha!
> Who shall dare to set me free?
>
> Carena for the three ahas!
> Let nae fear your courage ding;
> But frae the horn, wi' three blows;
> Freedom to the lady bring.
>
> Between the Lee and the roarin' Linn,
> There it is lies millions three
> For him who ventures – when it's win,
> Me and my true love is free.
>
> Woe be to the man that ever was born
> If timid the sword he ever draws,
> And daurna blaw the warlock horn
> To silence the three ahas!

All that the White Lady could do was wait for a knight to come to her rescue. In the chamber are three figures: the spellbound lady, her young chevalier and the 'spirit of darkness'. The spirit was a 'fearful looking' creature, 'more like a demon from the deep than anything else'. The White Lady remains seated in a chair. She wears golden slippers on her feet, a golden necklace about her neck and her head is 'adorned with a beautiful diadem, set with jewels and gems of the richest hue'. Her feet rest upon a footstool. Her hand holds a white handkerchief and rests against her cheek. She has gold rings upon her fingers and gold bracelets on her wrists.

A golden horn lies on a stone table that stands in the middle of the chamber. Beside it sits a magical sword sheathed in a golden scabbard. The legend says that one day a knight will find the enchanted chamber. The knight will stand before the White Lady, her beloved chevalier and the spirit of darkness and he will have to choose between drawing the sword and blowing the horn. At the first blow of the horn, the dark creature will leap up and attack the knight with 'a great broadsword' as it shouts 'aha!' three times. The knight who does not draw the sword or is not brave enough will be defeated by the 'demon' and is doomed to suffer 'all the horrors of the enchanted vault'. A brave and courageous knight will beat the creature and watch as it vanishes with a 'horrid cry', exclaiming, 'All is lost! Farewell!'

The knight will next blow the golden horn for a second time, which wakes the bewitched young chevalier. Finally, the third blow will release the White Lady:

> At the third blast it grew dark, and a storm arose.
> Flashes of lightning glanced through the vaults, and a
> noise was heard like that of thunder.

The warlock's spell will finally be broken and the White Lady will rise from her chair and be reunited with her lover. The grateful lady will lead the brave knight to the secret hiding place of the treasure of Rosslyn and reward her rescuer with a fortune worth millions of pounds.

There was to be no happy ending for the evil Lord Soulis. Tales of his dark deeds spread through the Border country and reached the ears of the king. When fearful locals went to him for justice, the king is said to have exclaimed, 'Boil him if you please! But let me hear no more of him.' The locals took him at his word. They sought out the great prophet Thomas the Rhymer to find a way to defeat Soulis. Thomas led the men to the ruins of Melrose Abbey. There, by moonlight, they dug up the grave of Michael Scott the Wizard. Clutched in the wizard's arms was his book of magic that explained how Lord Soulis could be killed. A trap was set at the Nine Stane Rig – a field named after an ancient stone circle. Soulis could not be bound with ropes nor stabbed with swords or daggers. Traditional Border tales tell that Thomas and the men wrapped the evil Lord in a lead sheet and boiled him in a huge cauldron:

> They rolled him up in a sheet of lead,
>   A sheet of lead for a funeral pall;
> They plunged him in the cauldron red,
>   And melted him, lead, and bones, and all.

Many men have sought the enchanted chamber of White Lady of Rosslyn and found the sword and the golden hunting horn. They have tried to free the lady and win the treasure. All have died in the attempt. The legends say that a knight named 'Wilson' is destined to succeed where all others have failed:

> Wilson gotten, and Wilson born,
> Shall draw the sword and blow the horn.

He will arrive at Rosslyn Castle in a full suit of shining armour accompanied by a group of knights. A 1920s newspaper article 'Local Myths: The Enchanted Lady of Roslin Castle' tells the story of Wilson's adventure. They will break into the haunted chamber with a pick-axe but Wilson alone will step 'cautiously into the darkness'. From the shadows he will hear the White Lady's song:

A lady lonely, ha! ha!! ha!!!
  Welcomes a Wilson born,
To break for her a demon spell,
  If he first blow the horn.   But,

Woe be unto that man,
  That ever he was born;
If he draw the sword,
  Before he blows the horn.

A lady lonely, ha! ha!! ha!!!
  Welcomes a Wilson born,
To claim her for his lawful bride,
  If he can blow the horn.   But,

Woe be unto that man,
  That ever he was born;
If he draw the sword,
  And cannot blow the horn.

A lady lonely; ha! ha!! ha!!!
  Welcomes a Wilson born,
To share with her the St Clair wealth,
  If he dare blow the horn.   But,

Woe be unto that man,
  That ever you were born;
If he draw the sword,
  And dare not blow the horn.

According to the article, the knight Wilson's blast on the horn 'shall awaken all the echoes in Roslin Glen'. He will slay the demon guardian 'with the charmed "Excalibur" in his hand' and free the lady. Wilson will claim the lady as his bride and with the 'untold wealth' of the Rosslyn treasure they will restore the castle and 'reside in . . . princely grandeur'.

These two versions of the legend have marked differences. The young chevalier is lost from the later version as Wilson himself becomes the White Lady's true love. There is also confusion about whether a brave knight should first draw the sword or blow the golden horn. The earlier version blames the dread Lord Soulis while the newspaper article simply mentions 'a demon spell'.

However, the most interesting difference between the two texts is the attitude of the author to the legend. Rigby is inspired by the tale; his writing is full of warmth and magic, he composes his own original poems to accompany it. The newspaper article recounts the main elements then ends with this statement, 'Such, then, is the romantic story of the "Enchanted Lady" of Roslin Castle. It was originally the creation of a superstition long dead but, during the greater part of eighteenth century, it was one of those weird tales which our great-grandmothers believed to have its foundation in fact. However, it is simply a myth, which even now the most pronounced credulity is loath to accept, indeed cannot accept.'

Does it matter if the White Lady of Rosslyn really exists? Strange sounds and unexplained footfalls are still heard in the castle but you don't have to believe in ghosts, angels or faeries to appreciate the legend. It is at once a tale of knights, castles and adventure, of evil spells and fairy-tale villainy, a ghost story, a gothic romance, and a mystery of secret treasures still to be revealed.

CHAPTER ELEVEN
The Rosslyn Treasure

THE LEGEND OF THE White Lady of Rosslyn Castle claims that she guards a treasure worth many millions. But what could the treasure of Rosslyn actually be?

Buried treasure hidden in castles or churches may seem like the stuff of legend and fairy tale but, considering the religious upheavals and continual threat from wars that ravaged Scotland, it actually made very good sense.

Within Edinburgh Castle, hidden treasures were lost for over a hundred years. 'The Honours of Scotland' were the Crown Jewels of the Kings and Queens of Scotland. The Crown of Scotland, Sword of State and Sceptre of Scotland were first used together for the coronation of Mary Queen of Scots in 1543. They were then used at the coronations of Mary's son King James VI in 1567, King Charles I in 1633, and King Charles II in 1651. They are the oldest crown jewels in Europe.

In 1707, the Union of the Parliaments saw the seat of power move to London. Before they became redundant the Earl of

Seafield, then Lord Chancellor, performed the last public duty with them. He took the royal sceptre and placed it on the Treaty in an act that dissolved the Scottish parliament. This final duty completed, the Honours were locked in a large oak chest and returned to the Crown Room in Edinburgh Castle.

Bizarrely, the Honours of Scotland were then simply forgotten about for over a century. The crown, said to date back to King Robert the Bruce, sat in a wooden chest.

In 1818, Sir Walter Scott set about researching the jewels. He persuaded the Prince Regent to allow him to carry out a thorough investigation into the last known whereabouts of the Crown Jewels within the castle. Given full access to the Crown Room, Scott eventually found the locked chest. Scott later wrote:

> . . . the ponderous lid of the chest being forced open, at the expense of time and labour, the Regalia was discovered lying in the bottom covered with linen cloths, exactly as they had been left in the year 1707.

Could there be a real historical treasure lost at Rosslyn? One fantastical tale suggests that the treasure has already been discovered.

In 1837, James Jackson wrote *Tales of Roslin Castle*. The opening chapter, entitled 'Discovery of the Roslin Manuscripts', tells of a mysterious 'Count Poli' who visited the Rosslyn Inn by the chapel a few years before.

The tale begins towards the end of June 1834, when some local men pay their annual visit to the chapel. On the way, they come across a coach with a Continental gentleman on board. In excellent English, with a slight accent, he asks for directions to the chapel.

He explains to them that his ancestor had been a priest at the chapel up until the time of the Reformation. Escaping to the Continent, the priest told a strange story that was passed down through his family. The tale spoke of a wonderful treasure, manuscripts of accumulated learning and knowledge, hidden within Rosslyn Castle.

The stranger carried with him a volume describing the chapel, the castle and the library. His mission to Scotland was to retrieve the manuscripts in order to save them from oblivion. Once the introductions had taken place and he had given his name as General Count Poli, Old John, the curator, commented, 'O aye, Sir . . . the Polys' graves are down in St. Matthew's kirk-yard.'

At the Count's invitation the party accompanied him into the chapel where they spent the afternoon. As the day wore on, Poli asked the men if they wished to join him on his quest. He would enter the castle at midnight and find the White Lady

Rosslyn residents had often commented that 'at witching time of night', the guardian spirit of the castle was seen 'skipping with light and airy gaiety through its ancient halls, or walking in its garden under the fruit trees, in the bright moonlight, reclining on the walls of the draw-bridge . . . '

Joining the Count in the early evening, the party headed down to the castle. On viewing the glen for the first time, Count Poli commented: 'It has been my lot to travel in many a country; but I must say, that I have never seen such a magnificent view as this; such an eminence, commanding such a glorious prospect, is worthy of having such a chapel built upon it.'

Down at the castle they waited until nightfall. As midnight approached a flash of lightning startled the party as they searched for the treasure. Count Poli's book led them to a part of the castle where the secret library was hidden behind a stone wall.

Setting to work on knocking through the wall, the events are given in verse:

> By dint of passing strength,
> We moved the massy stones at length.
> They heard a voice in Roslin Hall,
> And saw a sight not seen by all,

That dreadful voice was heard to sound,
Now Roslin treasure's found – found – found.

John saw a head with golden crown,
Bob saw the waving of a gown,
John saw a hand and Bob an arm,
And both fell down in dread alarm,
Their blood did freeze, their brain did burn,
'Twas feared their mind would near return.

Count Poli and the men had discovered the lost library!

Come along boys, the good old lady is now gone,
The prize is here, 'tis all our own.

Jackson's story ends as the Count takes the manuscripts away with him to the Continent. In a footnote the author mentions that:

Mr Chambers in his Gazetteer of Scotland, vol ii. pg 600, states that the History of the Scottish Nation, from the beginning of the world till the year 1535, entitled Rota Temporum, was lost at Rosslyn among its other literary treasures.

Jackson's tale of Count Poli is clearly fiction but there certainly was a notable library at Rosslyn before the Reformation. Many volumes were sold, others were taken by General Monk's troops or by Protestant looters. Some of these manuscripts are today preserved in the Bodleian Library.

Rosslyn Chapel has been described as a 'Masonic treasure'. Writers have claimed that Oliver Cromwell, who was renowned for destroying pre-Reformation churches, spared the chapel because he recognised its Masonic significance. They further claim that Cromwell was himself a Freemason. Some even suggest he was the Grand Master.

There is no proof whatsoever that Cromwell was a Freemason. One book entitled *The Freemasons Crushed* by the Abbé Larudan suggested that Cromwell actually organised the society. All serious researchers and historians agree that this claim is highly imaginative and 'unsupported by reason or evidence'.

As Cromwell's General Monk bombarded Rosslyn Castle his troops stabled their horses in the chapel, defaced carvings and fired their muskets at the chapel's west wall. These are hardly acts of reverence.

The medieval St Clairs were closely associated with the kings and queens of Scotland. As devoted Roman Catholics, they would become trusted friends to the Catholic monarchy as the Protestant Reformation took hold.

In the National Library in Edinburgh there is a letter dated 1546 from Marie of Guise, the Queen Regent, to Lord William St Clair. She swears to be a 'true mistress' to him and protect him and his servants for the rest of her life in gratitude for being shown 'a secret' within Rosslyn:

> herfor we bind and oblifs us to the faid Sir William, in likwis that we fall be leill and true maiftres to him, his counfell and fecret fhewen to us we fall keip fecret . . .

> [herefore we bind and oblige ourselves to the said Sir William, and likewise we shall be a loyal true mistress to him, his counsel and secret shown to us we shall keep secret . . .]

William is similarly bound to her as a trusted councillor and ally. Marie also gives William a pension of 'three hundredth markis, ufual moneu of Scotland, to be payit to him yeirlie' – [three hundred marks, usual money of Scotland, to be paid to him yearly]. This was a substantial amount of money.

But does this really suggest a 'secret' at Rosslyn, or was Marie of Guise simply stating that she will be a true friend to Sir

William, that she would not betray him or repeat any secrets or confidences they shared?

Catholic allies were plentiful on the Continent but in Scotland they were becoming very rare. Marie was clearly keen to ensure the continued allegiance of a staunchly Catholic ally, and rewarded his loyalty and devotion.

A year before Marie's letter, two passages within the 'acts of The Lords of Council in public affairs' may suggest that another kind of treasure was once at Rosslyn:

> the lords ordain William St Clair of Roslin to produce within three days all jewels, vestments and ornaments of 'the abbay and place of Halyrudhous . . . put and ressavit within his place' so that the Cardinal and administrator may see them and that they may be 'usit in this solempnyt tyme now approchand, to the honour of god and halykirk and upoun the expens of the commendatar and administrator thai payand to the gentill men of the said place . . . the somme of xx lib. for thair labouris maid in keeping . . .

The Laird of Craigmillar later protested that the laird of Rosslyn had still not returned the Holyrood jewels.

It has been speculated 'the jewels, vestments and ornaments of the Abbey and Palace of Holyroodhouse' would have included the Holy Rood of Scotland. This relic, also known as 'the Black Rood', had belonged to Queen Margaret of Scotland. It was said to be a piece of the True Cross. It has been further claimed that the Holy Rood, the jewels and treasures of Holyrood were not returned by the St Clairs and are still hidden at Rosslyn. This seems highly unlikely.

If William St Clair had attempted to keep the jewels, vestments and ornaments permanently then the protests and actions against him would have escalated. The Lords of the Privy Council of Scotland would not have simply 'given up' and allowed William to keep the items. The fact that William is to be paid twenty pounds for keeping the jewels, vestments and ornaments may imply that he was awaiting payment before he returned them.

The fate of the Black Rood is well documented. Just as the Monymusk Reliquary that is said to hold the relics of St Columba was carried to battle at Bannockburn in 1314, so the Black Rood was taken by the Scots to the Battle of Neville's Cross in 1346. The Scots were defeated and the Black Rood fell into English hands. It was last recorded upon the Shrine of St Cuthbert in the Cathedral of Durham. It vanished from history during the Reformation.

James Jackson mentions another local tradition about the Rosslyn treasure:

> Historical tradition has likewise insinuated that the treasure of the unfortunate Darnley was secreted in the castle, and lost among its ruins. And ever since its demolition, there has been a traditionary prediction through Scotland, that these immured treasures would ultimately be discovered . . .

The reference to Lord Darnley's treasure is particularly interesting. While there is no record of the exact nature of Darnley's treasure, there is reliable historical evidence that Darnley knew the St Clairs of Rosslyn.

If legends of a secret treasure at Rosslyn are true, then it is probably the lost treasure of Lord Darnley, the murdered husband of Mary Queen of Scots.

Lord Darnley was the second husband of Mary Queen of Scots. Mary was a Catholic monarch who reigned during the Protestant Reformation, a time of violent religious upheaval across Europe. The Reformation was to bring about the downfall of the staunchly Catholic St Clairs.

In 1565, Mary Queen of Scots married Lord Darnley at

Holyrood Palace. She wore the black dress of a widow. The marriage ceremony was performed by Sir John St Clair, the Bishop of Brechin and great-grandson of the founder of Rosslyn Chapel. It would be the last Roman Catholic wedding ceremony for a reigning Scottish monarch.

Darnley, a cousin of Queen Elizabeth, was not a popular choice. His marriage to Mary was short and unhappy. Two years after he was wed, Lord Darnley lay in his sick bed in lodgings at Kirk o' Field on the outskirts of Edinburgh. On the night of 9 February 1567, Darnley was assassinated. Conspirators had hidden barrels of gunpowder beneath his bedchamber. After Mary had visited her husband the gunpowder exploded. Lord Darnley was found dead the following morning.

The main suspect was James Hepburn, Earl of Bothwell. He was promptly brought to trial but was acquitted. He then abducted and married Mary. It is interesting to note that George St Clair, the fourth Earl of Caithness and Justiciar of Caithness, sat at the 1567 trial that acquitted James of the murder. James's sister was married to George's son.

Mary was imprisoned and was eventually executed in England. She went to the scaffold and was beheaded in the red dress of a Catholic martyr. Her son, fathered by Lord Darnley, would eventually become King James the VI of Scotland and I of England. King James was paranoid that he would be assassinated like his father before him. His fears were well founded as he was the target of the famous gunpowder plot of Guy Fawkes.

Throughout her reign and her imprisonment, Mary Queen of Scots was supported by a small group of fiercely loyal Catholic families. Is it possible that her dead husband's treasure was hidden at Rosslyn under the safe keeping of the Catholic St Clairs?

There is one final twist in the tale. Amid all the legends and theories regarding the secret treasure hidden under Rosslyn Chapel or Rosslyn Castle there is a local tale that was passed down by word of mouth. An old local worthy recalled that the lost treasure was not buried beneath the chapel or the castle; it was hidden in the woods of Roslin Glen. A Penicuik man named Eckie Pendleton passed on a story to the author's father of a buried treasure. He said that if you walked from Rosslyn Castle and Old Woodhouselee Castle, you'd find the treasure buried between an oak and an ash tree.

CHAPTER TWELVE
The Holy Grail

A YOUNG KNIGHT NAMED Percival sits in the Castle of the Fisher King. As he dines with his courteous host, a strange ritual procession passes before him. Percival looks on in wonder as three handsome youths appear bearing, in turn, a lance that drips blood and two golden candlesticks inlaid with black enamel. A fair damsel enters the room, beautifully adorned and radiant. She bears a grail. As the grail appears, the candles seem to lose their brightness. The grail illuminates the room like the sun or the moon. Finally, another damsel steps by carrying a silver carving-dish.

In the late twelfth century a cleric in the Champagne region of Northern France sat at a table with blank pages of vellum and began to write a story. His patron was the Count Philip of Flanders, a powerful noble who was courting Marie de Champagne. The cleric, Chrétien de Troyes, was already famed for his Arthurian romances *Yvain* and *Lancelot*.

Chrétien began by singing the praises of Count Philip, 'whose merit exceeds that of Alexander'. In marked contrast to the overblown magnificence of Chrétien's portrait of his patron, he courteously understates his own talent. He says simply that this is a humble translation, his reworking in rhyme of an earlier tale from a 'British Book' which Philip has given to him.

With inky fingers, Chrétien sat scratching the story of the Grail upon the pages with a quill pen, 'Sow little and you reap little.' The Grail that Chrétien describes is not a cup or a chalice; it is a serving platter, a dish carried in a magical procession in the castle of the mysterious Fisher King. Chrétien makes no mention of Christ or the crucifixion, though the grail does hold a single consecrated wafer that sustains the ailing father of the Fisher King. He does not call the platter 'the Holy Grail'; to Chrétien it is simply 'the grail'.

He would never finish the Conte du Graal – the Story of the Grail. It is said that 'death took him' and it fell to a series of 'continuators' to add to and complete his story. Chrétien's unfinished Story of the Grail has fascinated writers, poets, artists, theologians, adventurers and mystics ever since. What is the Grail? Where does it come from, what does it symbolise, and where is it hidden? Whom does it serve?

It fell to Robert de Boron to truly turn Chrétien's serving platter into a Christian symbol. In his romance *Joseph of Arimathea*, Robert explains that the Grail was the chalice used at the Last Supper. Joseph of Arimathea, the uncle of Jesus, persuaded Pontius Pilate to let him have the body of Christ. Joseph had Jesus laid to rest in his own rock-cut tomb. After the resurrection Joseph, accompanied by his brother-in-law Bron, and Bron's 12 sons, sailed from the Holy Land bearing the Grail.

Other continuators said that the Grail bore a bleeding decapitated human head or one hundred boars' heads. In time, the Holy Grail was said to have been not only the cup of Christ at the Last Supper but also the cup that caught the blood of Christ as he was crucified at Golgotha.

In Germany, a writer named Wolfram Von Eschenbach penned his own version of the Grail story entitled *Parzival*. He tells us that Chrétien has told the wrong tale, that he has the genuine story and that the Grail is in fact a magical stone. Wolfram's Grail is borne by a Princess whose name is Bringer of Joy. She was radiant and luminous as the light of dawn. She wears Arabian silks. The Grail is described as 'the innermost essence of Paradise'. Wolfram calls it 'Lapsit exillis', an invented term that probably alludes to the Philosopher's Stone of the Alchemists, made famous in the first Harry Potter novel.

In recent years alternative history writers have theorised that the Holy Grail is actually the 'Holy Blood': a sacred bloodline of direct descendants, a union between Jesus and Mary Magdalene. Through an unconvincing play on words, 'San graal' was said to conceal 'Sang raal' or 'Sang real': literally 'blood royal'. From the wordplay of Baigent, Lincoln and Leigh it was a small step for Dan Brown to say that the Holy Grail was the remains and bloodline of Mary Magdalene:

The Holy Grail 'neath ancient Roslin waits.

In *The Da Vinci Code* this clue leads Professor Langdon and Sophie Neveu to Rosslyn Chapel in search of the Grail. Each year tens of thousands of visitors visit Rosslyn to gaze in awe and to wonder if the chapel conceals some fabulous secret treasure. Millions believe that the Holy Grail lies hidden at Rosslyn, but could they be right?

Alternative history writers will try to convince you that they know not only what the Grail is but also where it is hidden . . . *If we could just dig under the chapel we would find the Holy Grail!* To them the Grail is another physical relic that the Knights Templar somehow dug out from underneath Jerusalem's Temple Mount and smuggled to Scotland.

In reality there is absolutely no proof whatsoever that the Templars ever looked for or found any artefacts in Jerusalem.

There is actually no archaeological evidence of Solomon's Temple in Jerusalem at all, let alone a treasure beneath it. The Templars were not supported by the St Clairs and the Templars' legendary treasure was not secretly hidden in vaults under the chapel, nor inside the Apprentice Pillar: so where did the story that the Holy Grail is at Rosslyn actually come from?

Of all the many legends of Rosslyn, the story that the Holy Grail is hidden in the chapel is actually one of the newest. Some recent writers have claimed that it is a 'local tradition' yet no collections of local folk tales and legends ever mention the Grail. Not one of the old books about Rosslyn Chapel and Castle that are packed with stories of ghosts, knights and secret treasure has anything at all to say about the Grail.

The first mention of the Grail in relation to Rosslyn appears in 1952, in an article entitled 'Mystical Rosslyn' by Lewis Spence. He simply says that Rosslyn is 'indeed the Chapel of the Grail'. Spence, a prolific historian and esoteric writer, admits that 'nothing can shake me from my conviction that Roslin was built according to the pattern of the Chapel of the Grail . . . and that William St Clair had in his poet's mind a vision of the Chapel Perilous when he set hand to the work'.

In the last few years, it has emerged that the Nazis seem to have had an interest in Rosslyn. In May 1930, a Dr Karl Hans Fuchs visited Rosslyn Chapel with a party of Germans, signing the visitor book. Fuchs is said to have been a member of the Thule Society, a Munich-based esoteric and occult group which has been linked to the rise of Nazism. Fuchs visited the Theosophical Society in Edinburgh, where he was said to have confided that Rudolph Hess, who would later become Hitler's Deputy Führer, believed that Rosslyn was the chapel of the Grail, 'where the black hand snuffed out the candle'. This story has led some alternative history writers to try to connect Rosslyn with the Grail of Wolfram Von Eschenbach's Parzival.

If this was all there was to the story of Rosslyn and the Grail it would barely be a footnote in history. But all the alternative history writers and the esoteric grail-seekers have missed virtually everything that links Rosslyn Chapel to King Arthur and the quest for the Holy Grail.

Rosslyn is surrounded by places associated with Arthur and the Knights of the Round Table. To the north-east is Traprain Law, the legendary fortress of King Loth, father of Sir Gawain. To the south-east is Wedale, the site of one of Arthur's battles, the ruins of Torsonce Chapel that was said to hold King Arthur's shield, and Melrose, where Arthur and his knights are said to sleep in the hollow Eildon Hills. Sixteen miles south is Stobo Kirk with its stained glass window commemorating the baptism of Merlin and the altar stone where St Kentigern converted the old wizard to Christianity. South too was once the vast Forest of Celidon where Merlin wandered mad and lived with the wolves and wild pigs. To the south-west was the land of Fergus of Galloway, knight of King Arthur, while the realm of King Urien and Yvain lay to the west, as did an ancient building known as 'Arthur's O'on', (Arthur's Oven). Finally, north of Rosslyn lies Edinburgh, built upon seven hills including Arthur's Seat and the Castle Rock. In the twelfth century, Edinburgh Castle was known as 'Castellum Puellarum', the Castle of Maidens. Arthurian romance speaks of chivalric tournaments and jousts in the shadow of the Castle of Maidens, the castle of Morgan Le Fay.

Sir William St Clair, third Earl of Orkney and founder of Rosslyn Chapel, grew up completely surrounded by the romances of Arthur, Merlin and the Knights of the Round Table. Sir William even named one of his children 'Arthur', the first time the name appears in the St Clair family tree. For three hundred years the Arthurian romances had been the tales of the nobility; told in winter halls, sung by firelight in banqueting halls and inscribed in Latin and French in illuminated books. Arthur was not thought of as some fairy-tale king, he was believed in as firmly as Alexander the Great and Charlemagne. The romances of Arthur influenced the behaviour and morals of the age. Courtly love and the laws of chivalry attempted to civilise the warrior knight. A knight was to be a protector of women and children, a courteous and noble man, and above all a good Christian.

By 1450, as Rosslyn Chapel was being built, Sir William St Clair was one of the leading nobles of Scotland. He had married well and his wife Elizabeth Douglas had borne him two children, William and Katherine. He had travelled to France to the court of the king as ambassador and escort to the Scots Princess Margaret, who went to marry the Dauphin. On his return, William began an ambitious building programme, remodelling Rosslyn Castle in the continental French style. It is said that 'he had his halls and his chambers richly hung with embroidered hangings, and he was royally served from gold and silver vessels'.

It is likely that William and Elizabeth met with Sir Gilbert Hay, William's friend and tutor, while they were in France. Sir Gilbert was one of the finest scholars in all Europe. He was educated at the University of St Andrews then headed to the Continent, probably to the University of Paris, then into the service of the French monarch in the Garde Ecosse – the Scots Guard of Archers. The Scots had long been allied to the French against the English. During the Hundred Years War, the Scots fought and died alongside the French. William's wife Elizabeth had lost her father, her first husband and one of her brothers on French soil at the Battle of Verneuill.

It is probable that Sir Gilbert Hay knew Joan of Arc. The Scots were instrumental in Joan's war against the English. When the city of Orléans was besieged, it was the Scottish Bishop John Carmichael 'and a great number of Scottes' who fortified the town and held it against attack. The soldiers of the Garde Ecosse were among Joan's most valued troops. One archer in the Scots Guard who would later became a monk in Dunfermline wrote about Joan, 'The marvellous maid who brought about the recovery of France – whom I saw and knew and in whose company I was present during her endeavours for the said recovery to her life's end.' Bishop Carmichael was one of the clergy who officiated

at the coronation of Joan's royal patron Charles, at Rheims
Cathedral. There the Garde Ecosse appeared as the first regiment
of the French army while Joan of Arc and Gilbert Hay watched
the dauphin they had fought for become king.

It is likely that Sir Gilbert Hay also knew one of Joan's
captains, René d'Anjou, who joined the Maid at the siege of
Paris. Good King René was a poet, an artist and a dreamer who
saw himself as a chivalrous knight: by title he was King of
Jerusalem. Among René's works were the *Traictié de la forme et
devis d'ung tournoy*, a treatise on devising chivalric tournaments,
and *Le Cueur d'Amours Espris*, the Book of the Heart Possessed
by Love. René, Sir Gilbert Hay and Sir William St Clair shared a
devotion to chivalry.

Sir Gilbert spent over 20 years in France. On his return to
his native Scotland, Sir Gilbert was given a commission by Sir
William St Clair to translate *L'Arbre des Bataille*, *L'Ordre de
Chevalerie* and *Le Governement des Princes* into Scots. This work
was collected into a single unique folio, the earliest literary prose
in the Scots language:

> . . . at the request of ane hye and mychty Prince and
> worthy lord. William erle of Orknay   and of Cathnes,
> lord Synclere and chancclare of Scotland, in his castell
> of Rosselyn.

At the beginning of the *Buke of the Law of Armys*, Sir Gilbert
tells us that the book was 'translatit be me Gilbert of the Hayc
Knycht. maister in arte and bachilere in decreis' [Translated
by me Gilbert of the Hay, Knight. Master in Art and Bachelor
in Degree], Chamberlain to the most worthy King Charles of
France. Sir Gilbert is clearly proud of his elevation to knighthood
and of his university education.

The Hay manuscript is a medieval treasure. The binding is
brown leather ornamented with flowers, leaves, unicorns, lions
rampant, the Agnus Dei, images of 12 of the Apostles, and the

names 'Ihesus', 'Maria' and 'Johannes' stamped into the leather using 33 separate stamps. The paper bears four watermarks: two unicorns, a heraldic shield of the arms of France and a small heart with a cross rising from it. Hay notes that battles are not won by strength of arms but by strength of spirit:

> Certainly nocht force na strength corporal maikis a man
> to win the batail. Bot force spiritual, that is to say, hardy
> curage, maikis victory.

> [Certainly not force nor strength of arms makes a man to
> win the battle. But force spiritual, that is to say, hardy
> courage, makes victory.]

The *Buke of the Law of Armys*, *Buke of the Ordre of Knychthede* and *Buke of the Gouernaunce of Princis* are a celebration of chivalry and knighthood, written in Rosslyn Castle at Sir William's request as his chapel was being built. Sir Gilbert explains that a knight defends widows, maidens and motherless bairns, the weak and the poor. The knight fights wickedness, cruelty and tyranny, and maintains faith in Jesus Christ, his lord, and the rights of the people:

> God him self ordanyt knychthese
> and honourit jt
> and honouris jy

In 1451, Lady Elizabeth died at Rosslyn. If you step down the stone stairs into the sacristy beneath Rosslyn Chapel, you will find painted figures of saints and angels: their robes are sky blue, their hair golden. The carvings were probably painted in the time of Queen Victoria, possibly for a royal visit. In the sacristy, an angel holds a set of wooden rosary beads that match her ten perfect little toes, St Peter holds the key to the Gates of Heaven, and a mysterious figure holds two children. This carving is probably unique within Rosslyn as the only figure which faces into the wall. We see only the back of the figure, dressed in a shapely medieval gown with long flowing sleeves. She cradles two small children, their heads looking out over their mother's shoulders. It is pure speculation but this carving may depict William's dead wife, Elizabeth Douglas, holding their son and daughter. The figure vanishes into the south, by the side of St Peter who guards the way to Heaven.

We are told by Father Hay that when William found 'his age creeping on him . . . it came in his minde to build a house for God's service, of most curious worke'. In reality, it is far more likely that the impetus to create the Collegiate Church of St Matthew came from Elizabeth Douglas and Sir Gilbert Hay.

The University of Glasgow was founded in 1451 at Glasgow Cathedral, where Elizabeth's brother funded repair work. Its first classes were held in the Cathedral's Chapter House. Sir Gilbert Hay had been taught at St Andrews, Scotland's first university. It seems likely that there was a grander plan for Rosslyn. If the Collegiate Church of St Matthew at Rosslyn had been completed it would have been a huge cruciform church, almost a cathedral. The plan seems out of all proportion to Roslin village but not if the intention was to create a new centre of learning: a university.

As work continued at Rosslyn on the East Quire of the Collegiate Church of St Matthew, three renowned books were being translated into Scots by Sir Gilbert Hay in Rosslyn Castle. Sir Gilbert's translations, collectively known as *The Hay Manuscript*, were once thought lost. They were rediscovered in Sir Walter Scott's vast library at Abbotsford in 1838.

Sir Gilbert Hay, knight, scholar, chamberlain, soldier and poet, was remembered in the sixteenth-century poem, *The Lament for the Makaris*. In this poem, William Dunbar recalls some of the finest writers, poets and chroniclers of the medieval age: Chaucer, Wyntoun, Barbour, Henryson, Kennedy, Blind Harry and Sir Hew of Eglinton.

In one verse, Dunbar notes the passing of Sir Gilbert Hay and another Makar: Clerk of Tranent:

> Clerk of Tranent eik he has tane,
> That maid the Anteris of Gawane;
> Schir Gilbert Hay endit has he;
> Timor Mortis conturbit me.

> [Clerk of Tranent in addition he has been taken,
> That made the Adventures of Gawain;
> Sir Gilbert Hay ended has he;
> The fear of death worries me.]

We know virtually nothing of Clerk of Tranent. The village of Tranent is ten miles north-east of Rosslyn. There, the mysterious Clerk wrote *The Adventures of Gawain*, thought to be the Scots alliterative poem *The Knightly Tale of Gologras and Gawain*.

Sir Gawain, in this and countless Arthurian romances, was a courteous and chivalrous knight without equal. He was Gawain of Lothian and Orkney, the son of the legendary King Loth.

Twenty miles north-east of Rosslyn, the huge volcanic hill known as Traprain Law rises amid the fields of East Lothian. Legend says that this was the site of King Loth's fortress. Archaeological excavations on Traprain Law have shown it was a stronghold of the Votadini. The Votadini were a 'Brythonic' Welsh-speaking British tribe that traded with the Romans and may have acted as a 'buffer zone' north of Hadrian's Wall between the Romano-Britons and the warrior Picts.

When the Princess Thaneu was pregnant with St Kentigern, her father King Loth had her thrown from the summit of Traprain Law. As Castle Rock in Edinburgh is associated with the sorceress Morgan le Fay, Traprain Law was the legendary home of Anna (also known as Morgause), the sister of King Arthur and Morgan le Fay. She was King Loth's wife and Sir Gawain's mother:

'Tell me now, though, about King Lot: how many sons did he have by his wife?' – 'Four, my lady' – 'Name them for me.' – 'My lady, Gawain was the eldest, and then came Agravain, the arrogant one with strong hands. The names of the last two are Gaheriet and Guerrehet.'

Chrétien's Conte du Graal tells the story of two knights who quest for the Grail: Sir Percival and Sir Gawain. Some have speculated that if Chrétien had finished his tale it would have been Gawain who would have attained the Grail. Curiously, in Chrétien's story of the Grail, Sir Gawain carries Arthur's famous sword Excalibur: 'Escalibor, the best sword ever, that cuts through iron like wood.'

There is something rather strange about the tales of Sir Gawain and the legends of Rosslyn.

Gawain was 'of the Orkney Clan', he was Sir Gawain of Lothian and Orkney. The St Clair estate of Rosslyn reached all the way to the Pentland Hills and as far as Bruntsfield in Edinburgh. They were lords of extensive lands across the Lothians. In 1379, Sir Henry St Clair became the first St Clair Earl of Orkney, inheriting the title through his mother Isabella de Strathearn, daughter of Malise, Earl of Caithness, Strathearn and Orkney. Sir William St Clair, the founder of Rosslyn Chapel, was the third and final St Clair Earl of Orkney. In 1471, Sir William was given Ravenscraig by King James III in exchange for the Earldom of Orkney.

Descriptions of Sir Gawain and his son, the Fair Unknown, note their stature, their courtesy and their blonde hair. Sir Henry St Clair, second Earl of Orkney, was likewise described as 'a valiant Prince, well proportioned, of middle stature, broad bodied, fair of face' and 'yellow haired'. Sir William St Clair, third Earl of Orkney, was said to be 'a very fair man, of great stature, broad bodied, yellow haired' and 'courteous'.

Many of the legends of Rosslyn are startlingly similar to the legends of Sir Gawain. Just as Sir William St Clair's two hounds,

Help and Hold, hunted the white deer on Pentland Moor so Sir Gawain's hounds hunted the white hind in Malory's *Morte d'Arthur*. In *Sir Gawain and the Green Knight*, Gawain has a pentangle on his shield: the same five-pointed star that appears in Rosslyn's ceiling.

Sir Gawain was slain by a wound to the head strangely similar to the legendary blow that killed the Apprentice of Rosslyn Chapel. In a vengeful fury, Gawain fought with Sir Lancelot and suffered a grievous head wound. Gawain dies in Arthur's arms, blaming his own hastiness and wilfulness. The Apprentice of Rosslyn bears a deep gash to his temple and curiously the carving clearly once had a beard; at some point it has been chiselled away.

When a St Clair died, it is said that Rosslyn 'seem'd all on fire'. Once, on a late autumn evening, we watched as Rosslyn Castle seemed to burn in fiery orange and deep scarlet as the sunset illuminated the red stone. It is said that when Gawain died he was laid to rest in Dover Castle and so many candles were lit that the castle appeared in flame.

Is there actually some relationship between the legends of Sir Gawain and the St Clairs or are these similarities purely coincidental? If there is a 'prime suspect' who could have linked Rosslyn with the legends of Sir Gawain, it has to be Sir Walter Scott.

The famous novelist and poet was also a keen collector of stories. Scott knew the legends of King Arthur and the Knights of the Round Table, the balladry and traditional tales of the Borders, and he was also fascinated by the romantic ruins of Rosslyn Chapel and Castle. It was Scott who wrote a lament for the Lordly line of High St Clair in *The Lay of the Last Minstrel*:

> O'er Roslin all that dreary night
> A wondrous blaze was seen to gleam;
> 'Twas broader than the watch-fire's light,
> and redder than the bright moon-beam.

So, could the Holy Grail really be hidden somewhere beneath Rosslyn Chapel? The evidence isn't exactly overwhelming. Legends of hidden treasure seem to naturally attach themselves to ancient ruined castles and churches, but no one ever seems to find them. It is said that Merlin left a fortune in gold beneath Dina Emrys hill in Wales, and that a secret treasure lies somewhere in the woods near the Chateau d'Usse. It appears that the story of Rosslyn Chapel and the Holy Grail is just another fanciful romantic tale. Or maybe it isn't. Sometimes secret treasures really do exist.

On Monday, 12 May 1919, an archaeological dig was underway on Traprain Law in East Lothian. The dig foreman George Pringle had spent the summers of 1914 and 1915 digging on the hill during the first serious excavations. The summer digs had stopped with the advent of the First World War. George had barely survived the war, after suffering grievous wounds. That May morning, Alexander Curle, Director of the National Museum of Antiquities of Scotland, sat at his desk on what he expected would be an ordinary day. Then the telephone began to ring.

The dig had unearthed a real buried treasure: a fabulous hoard of Roman silver dating to AD 395–423. The Traprain Treasure consists of over a hundred silver objects including cups, flagons, bowls, spoons and coins. It is thought that the silver hoard was some form of payment made by the Romans to the Votadini tribe in return for their cooperation.

Among the treasures are silver cups and wine goblets, a Pictish silver chain, and a silver flagon decorated with an image of the Christ child and the Virgin Mary — one of the earliest surviving pieces of Christian metalwork in the world.

The Traprain Treasure is on permanent display in the Museum of Scotland in Edinburgh. Less than a mile away the Hay Manuscript, Sir Gilbert Hay's *Buke of the Ordre of Knychthede*, is preserved by the Manuscripts Department of the National Library of Scotland.

As Sir Gilbert Hay translated books of knighthood and chivalry, Sir William built a realm fit for King Arthur and the Knights of the Round Table. Medieval Rosslyn was home to writers, poets, minstrels, stonemasons, carpenters, craftsmen and artisans. Sir William was patron and friend to one of Europe's finest scholars. Rosslyn Castle sat amid woods and fields, deer parks and orchards. The lands of Rosslyn included the mills and town of Roslin, and the 'Colledge of Roslyne'.

When Sir William St Clair died, his son 'Schir Oliver Santcler, Knycht' abandoned his father's ambitious plans for the 'College Kirk'. He had the arched stone ceiling completed and floored the East Quire that we now know as Rosslyn Chapel. The town of Roslin had grown from a village for masons and craftsmen to a medieval 'Burgh in Barony' with an annual market.

The world of the St Clairs of Rosslyn was a world of knights, lords and kings; a world of battle and bloodshed but also a world of poetry, story and romance. Minstrels sang of fair maidens and courtly love, of the chivalrous and courtly Sir Gawain, and the quest for the Holy Grail:

> And thus a knight has in his heart a noble dwelling place
> for the virtues and nobleness of courage
> that should govern and maintain knighthood.
> Keep well that castle place and dwelling.

Sir Gilbert Hay, *The Buke of the Ordre of Knychthede*

CHAPTER THIRTEEN
The Da Vinci Code

'EVERYONE LOVES A GOOD conspiracy.' *The Da Vinci Code* by Dan Brown hit number one in the *New York Times* bestseller list and rapidly became a multimillion-selling blockbuster. Its mix of breathless thriller and historical mystery has proved highly profitable and extremely controversial.

The Da Vinci Code is an intricate tale full of murder, secret societies and puzzles that eventually lead the reader to Scotland, to Rosslyn Chapel and the quest for the Holy Grail.

In the novel, Harvard Professor Robert Langdon and French cryptographer Sophie Neveu evade the police and an Opus Dei assassin as they try to unravel a series of cryptic clues left by the deceased museum curator Jacques Saunière. When Saunière is found murdered in the Grand Gallery of the Louvre in Paris, Langdon is soon the prime suspect, hunted across France, in a desperate race to find the Holy Grail before the sinister 'Teacher'. As Langdon and Sophie, with the aid of Grail historian Sir Leigh Teabing, decipher Saunière's clues, their quest leads them first to London then on to Rosslyn Chapel. There they uncover an earth-shattering revelation about the secret truth behind the legend of the Grail.

In 2005, at the book's second anniversary, there were 25 million copies in print in 44 languages. Oscar-winning director Ron Howard began production of a Hollywood movie adaptation starring Tom Hanks, Audrey Tatou, Jean Reno, Alfred Molina and Sir Ian McKellan. Dan Brown had gone into hiding to write the next Robert Langdon novel, *The Solomon Key*.

Theologians, art historians and academics felt compelled to counter the book's theories. An unprecedented 'trial' took place in Italy in an attempt to set the record straight, and in Vatican City an Archbishop spoke out against the book's 'untruths':

> The book is everywhere. There is a very real risk that many people who read it will believe that the fables it contains are true . . . It astonishes and worries me that so many people believe these lies . . .

The Vatican had remained silent until Cardinal Tarcisio Bertone, Archbishop of Genoa, railed against the novel. In a bid to undermine the 'absurd and vulgar falsifications' within the novel, Cardinal Bertone hosted a seminar entitled 'Storia Senza Storia' – Story Without History. The 70-year-old Cardinal Bertone was deputy to Cardinal Joseph Ratzinger, then known as 'the Pope's enforcer' under Pope John Paul II. In April 2005, Cardinal Ratzinger was the chief celebrant at the funeral Mass of Pope John Paul II. In the conclave that followed, 115 cardinals gathered in secret to appoint the 265th pontiff, spiritual leader to over a billion Catholics. On 19 April, Cardinal Joseph Ratzinger emerged from the Sistine Chapel to greet the crowds in St Peter's Square as Pope Benedict XVI.

Father Raniero Cantalamessa, Preacher of the Papal Household, spoke out indirectly against *The Da Vinci Code* during a 'Passion of the Lord' service that commemorated Christ's death. In the

Good Friday sermon in St Peter's Basilica, Vatican City, he hit back at the 'unending stream of novels, films and plays' in which 'writers manipulate the figure of Christ under cover of imaginary and non-existent new documents and discoveries'.

In Leonardo's hometown of Vinci, just outside Florence in Italy, a gathering of art experts and clerics led by Alessandro Vezzosi, director of an Italian Leonardo museum, conducted a 'trial' of Dan Brown's novel to investigate its various claims.

Dozens of books have set about 'cracking', 'revealing', 'unlocking', 'breaking', 'decoding' and 'debunking' *The Da Vinci Code*. Evangelical Christians have preached against it, newspapers, TV and DVD documentaries have explored the facts behind the fiction, and academics and theologians have publicly debated the theories at the core of the novel. No book in living memory has provoked such a reaction.

But for all the conspiracy theories and controversial ideas that *The Da Vinci Code* discusses, one statement has proved to be particularly provocative:

> Fact . . . All descriptions of artwork, architecture, documents and secret rituals in this novel are accurate.

At the start of his novel, Dan Brown makes the bold claim that his fictional book is factually accurate. But how accurate are these 'facts' and how much of *The Da Vinci Code* is actually true?

Dan Brown built his fictional novel *The Da Vinci Code* on the fanciful theories originally aired in a series of bestselling pseudo-history books.

In the last 20 years, books about the Knights Templar have become highly popular. These range from the scholarly works of Helen J. Nicholson and Richard Barber to the publishing sub-genre of 'alternative history'. But it was the unprecedented success of *The Da Vinci Code* that introduced the Knights Templar to millions of readers and popularised a series of esoteric theories.

For years, alternative history writers have blamed the French King Philip IV and Pope Clement V equally for the destruction of the Templars. In these pseudo-history books, Pope Clement V has been branded as King Philip's puppet. Academic historians have stated that Clement V was certainly weak and indecisive but have stopped short of accusing him of conspiring with King Philip 'the Fair' against the Templars. In *The Da Vinci Code*, Dan Brown condemns Pope Clement as the architect of the Templars' downfall, claiming that the Pope imprisoned and killed hundreds of Knights Templar, having many burned at the stake and 'tossed unceremoniously into the Tiber' – the suggestion being that Templars were executed in Rome and their ashes were thrown into the River Tiber.

In reality, historical documents that have been recently unearthed in the Vatican Library prove that Pope Clement V acted against the French king's persecution and tried to save the Templars. Barbara Frale, a researcher at the Vatican School of Palaeontology, noted that the Pope had acted 'with skill and determination', ensuring that his own emissaries questioned Jacques de Molay and other captive Templars in 1308 in the dungeons of Chinon Castle in the Loire.

In effect, the Knights Templar received a secret Papal trial. Accusations of heresy, idolatry, blasphemy and sodomy were examined and in the end the knights were exonerated by the Pope. When the Templar Grand Master Jacques de Molay and his brother knights asked for the Pope's pardon, Pope Clement V absolved them:

> We hereby decree that they are absolved by the church
> and may again receive Christian sacraments.

However, the details of the trial were never made public. Pope Clement's bid to save the Templars failed and in 1314 Jacques de Molay, the last Grand Master of the Knights Templar, was burned to death, not in Rome but in the shadow of Notre Dame Cathedral in Paris. It was thought that the record of the Papal investigation had been lost during Napoleon's invasion of Italy in the eighteenth century when he looted the Vatican. The rediscovery of the record has been described as 'an exceptional event'. It is now clear that Pope Clement V and the Catholic Church did not set out to destroy the Templars. The Templar order was the victim of King Philip IV.

Brown also claims that the Church burned 'an astonishing five million women' during the witch hunts. Academic researchers put the figure of men and women executed closer to tens of thousands: less than a hundredth of the figure Brown suggests.

As Dan Brown's novel grew from a publishing hit to an international media phenomena, enterprising travel companies began *The Da Vinci Code* tours. The Louvre found itself full of tourists clutching copies of the novel and wondering where the curator Saunière had been murdered. At Saint Sulpice Church in Paris, a polite notice in French and English was put on display: 'Contrary to fanciful allegations in a recent best-selling novel this is not the vestige of a pagan temple. Please also note that the letters "P" and "S" in the small round windows at both ends of the transept refer to Peter and Sulpice, the patron saints of the church, not an imaginary Priory of Sion.'

Since the publication of *The Da Vinci Code*, visitor numbers at Rosslyn Chapel have increased by 56 per cent. Seventy thousand people visited the tiny chapel in 2004, prompting fears for the fragile stonework. Suddenly millions of people around the world read completely bizarre and utterly bogus 'facts' about Rosslyn Chapel. Meanwhile, the majority of pseudo-history writers cursed Brown's massive success and were bitterly disappointed that they hadn't written his novel.

Dan Brown clearly read quite a few alternative history books as he researched his novel. He mentions specifically *Holy Blood Holy Grail* and *The Templar Revelation* in the novel and names one of his major characters after Richard Leigh and Michael

Baigent. Brown also borrows theories from other pseudo-history books but drops their 'maybes' and 'possiblies' to present Templar fantasies as 'fact'.

In *The Da Vinci Code*, Brown states that Rosslyn Chapel was 'built by the Knights Templar'. While alternative history writers have theorised that the Knights Templar may have somehow influenced the St Clairs in the design of the chapel, Dan Brown drops the speculation and simply claims that the Templars built it themselves! Professor Langdon also tells Sophie Neveu that the chapel is a copy of Solomon's Temple, that it is full of secret Templar symbols and that the Rosslyn Trust 'has something to hide', prohibiting excavations despite calls from archaeologists. Later revelations include a six-pointed Star of David worn into the chapel floor, symbolising the union of male and female, and the bombshell that Rosslyn once housed the mortal remains of Mary Magdalene and her lost gospels.

But is any of it true? The simple answer is 'no'.

Dan Brown simply invented the 'Rose Line' linking Rosslyn and Glastonbury. The name 'Roslin' definitely does not derive from any 'hallowed Rose Line'. It has nothing to do with a 'Rose Bloodline' or a 'Rose Line meridian'. There are many medieval spellings of 'Rosslyn'. 'Roslin' is certainly not the 'original spelling'; it is now the most common spelling for the village. The root of the name 'Rosslyn' is simply in two Scots words: 'Ross' is hill, while 'Lynn' is waterfall. Rosslyn is 'the hill by the waterfall', named after the stone hill at a bend in the River Esk where Rosslyn Castle is built.

The Knights Templar did not build Rosslyn Chapel. The order of the Knights Templar was proscribed and destroyed over a century before the foundation stone of Rosslyn Chapel was laid. Jacques de Molay, the last Templar Grand Master, was burned at the stake in AD 1314. Rosslyn Chapel was founded by Sir William St Clair, third Earl of Orkney and Lord of Rosslyn, in AD 1446. The Poor Knights of the Temple of Solomon have absolutely no connection to the building of Rosslyn Chapel whatsoever. There is also no connection or similarity between Rosslyn Chapel and King Solomon's Jerusalem temple.

One 'code' that may actually exist within Rosslyn is the mysterious carved cubes that ornament some of the arches in the chapel. They have been studied by amateur cryptographers but nobody has yet come close to 'deciphering' the cubes. If they are a secret code then the message definitely has nothing to do with the entrance to the chapel's underground vault. The entrance to Rosslyn's burial vaults is well known: there are two black slabs in the north aisle. The cubes may simply be abstract designs or possibly they may be an ornamental form of musical notation. There is a 'heavenly choir' of stone angels playing a medieval instrument at the end of each arch of cubes.

Is there a 'massive subterranean chamber' beneath Rosslyn Chapel?

The secret crypt beneath Rosslyn Chapel is the burial vault of the St Clairs. For hundreds of years St Clair earls, lords, knights, ladies and children were laid to rest in the family burial vault.

Rosslyn Chapel is still a working church with a congregation. An excavation of the vaults would only damage the chapel and disturb a burial place. There is no proof of any 'secret treasure' in the vaults of the chapel. It is misleading to say that the Rosslyn Chapel Trust 'has something to hide'; the trust was set up to conserve and protect the fragile building, not to dig up the chapel hunting for hidden treasure!

What about the Priory of Sion?

The St Clair name within the Prieure de Sion Dossiers Secrets appears to have only become connected with the St Clairs of Rosslyn after the publication of *The Holy Blood and the Holy Grail*. 'Marie' and 'Jean' de Saint-Clair are entirely fictional: fake names within the Priory's fantastical foundation documents.

They do not exist in the historical record. The 'Dossiers Secrets' actually date to the mid-twentieth century. They were invented, along with the Priory of Sion, by Pierre Plantard and a few fellow hoaxers as some kind of surrealist joke. 'Catherine de St Clair' also seems to be entirely fictitious. Knight and Lomas claim that she married Hugh de Payns, the first Templar Grand Master, and that the Templars were given land at Balantrodoch near Rosslyn by her relatives. The only problem is that they appear to have completely invented the whole thing! No evidence whatsoever that this 'Catherine de St Clair' ever existed has been brought to light, and the St Clairs did not own any land at Rosslyn until the thirteenth century: over a hundred years after the Templars were granted lands at Balantrodoch by the Scots king. Knight and Lomas give no references for their claims.

Is there a six-pointed Star of David worn into the floor of the chapel?

No. If you look under the red carpet that now covers much of the chapel's floor and examine the aisles, you will find no sign whatsoever of any path worn into the stone floor. Dan Brown invented it. There are many five-pointed stars in the vaulted stone ceiling of the chapel and an eight-pointed star beneath the Nativity scene in the Lady Choir. This octagonal star is the Star of Bethlehem: the bright star that guided the three kings and the shepherds who surround the holy family in the carving.

The notion of a six-pointed star design in the floor plan of Rosslyn Chapel was invented by Knight and Lomas. In *The Hiram Key*, they claim that the chapel is a scaled-down copy of Herod's Temple in Jerusalem. They try to show an 'invisible Seal of Solomon' between some of the pillars in a bid to create a wholly bogus 'X marks the spot' where they believe the Templar Treasure is buried. Their central spot corresponds with a carved arrow and St Clair shield held by two hands in the ceiling but this does not mark the burial vaults. It is merely the midpoint between the west end of the chapel and the near side of the Lady Choir.

The perspective diagram that Knight and Lomas use to show their Star of David is a thing of smoke and mirrors. When you actually examine a straightforward plan drawing, you find that their alleged points are in fact totally random. Four points of their six-pointed star join the north wall to the south wall, forming a rectangle. One point is the centre of a pillar and the last point marks absolutely nothing at all! It's just a random spot on the floor of no significance whatsoever. Two out of the six lines cut through the centre of pillars, two meet at one pillar, and the last two lines miss all the pillars completely!

Just as anyone at all can draw a straight line between two fixed points with a ruler, anyone can invent a five-, six-, seven-, eight- or nine-pointed star on any floor plan as long as your design doesn't have to join up any significant points! What this game of join-the-dots proves is that Knight and Lomas needed to concoct some 'proof' to back up their flimsy theories.

Interestingly, there have been six-pointed stars in the chapel in the past. Early twentieth-century black-and-white photographs show the chapel decked out with winter greenery at Christmastide. Woven vines spiralled down all the pillars in imitation of the Apprentice Pillar and decorative six-pointed stars made with holly and ivy were hung from the walls. It is unknown whether these were deliberate representations of the Seal of Solomon or a practical way to make a star using two coat hangers or six sticks.

In short, Rosslyn Chapel was not built by the Templars. It is not connected in any way to the Priory of Sion. It is not a copy of any Temple of Jerusalem. It does not have a six-pointed star worn into the floor. It has nothing whatsoever to do with any 'Rose Lines', 'Rose Meridians' or 'Rose Bloodlines', and it has never ever held any remains or relics of Mary Magdalene.

Umberto Eco is probably most famous as the author of *The Name of the Rose*, which was made into a Hollywood movie starring Sean Connery and Christian Slater. Eco is an Italian author of academic texts, essays, fiction and even children's books. He is also Professor of Semiotics at the University of Bologna. In another of Eco's novels, *Foucault's Pendulum,* an Italian Colonel tells three book editors in a Milan publishing house of a grandiose Templar conspiracy. When the Colonel disappears, the three are drawn into a paranoid downward spiral involving Templars, Rosicrucians, hermeticism, a secret history of the world, and the occult. It is now described as 'the thinking man's *The Da Vinci Code'.*

Among Umberto Eco's works is a list of ten classifications of a variety of re-inventions of the Middle Ages. This list was reproduced with practical examples in *Strange Landscape: A Journey Through the Middle Ages* by Professor Christopher Frayling, formerly Professor of Cultural History and Head of the School of Humanities at London's Royal College of Art, and Pro-Rector since 1992. Umberto Eco's ninth classification nicely sums up the *The Da Vinci Code* and the pseudo-history fantasies about Rosslyn Chapel:

> The Middle Ages of so called Tradition – a ramshackle assemblage of loosely translated texts and over-hasty conclusions which brings into its ragbag everything from the Druids, force-fields and earth-power to Solomon's Temple, Knights Templar, Rosicrucians, Hermetic philosophy, the Holy Blood and the Holy Grail, runic stones, buried treasure . . .

The cover of *The Da Vinci Code* says it is 'a novel'. Dan Brown has written a highly successful work of fiction. But it is a work of fiction – not a work of fact. As Stuart Beattie, Project Director of the Rosslyn Chapel Trust, once said, 'My favourite book is *The Lord of the Rings* but it doesn't make it true.'

CHAPTER FOURTEEN
The Earthly Paradise

ROSSLYN CASTLE ECHOED WITH the sound of medieval music and song. A 'dwelling for the bards of the house of Roslin' was built overlooking the river. 'Harper's Hall' was home to musicians, singers and storytellers. A pathway known as 'Minstrel Wynd' was made between the Hall and Rosslyn Castle. It is said that two hundred years ago, workmen building a new road across Minstrel Wynd discovered ancient silver coins and silver buckles ornamented with green enamel.

Beneath the shade of oak and beech trees, musicians and minstrels would wander to William's court as, up on the hill, Rosslyn Chapel took shape. Songs of courtly love were sung by firelight, heroic romances of King Arthur and his knights were told, and the adventures of King Alexander were recounted.

In our age, the figure of Alexander the Great conjures up images of ancient journeys and epic desert battles. In the medieval age, Alexander was a chivalric hero: a king, a knight and a conqueror who fought and defeated fabulous mythical beasts and voyaged to the Earthly Paradise:

> It was sa huge, mervellus and hie,
> And eik it was sa plesand and sa fare
>
> [It was so huge, marvellous and high,
> And also it was so pleasant and so fair]

In 1456, as carpenters and stonemasons worked on Rosslyn Chapel, Sir Gilbert Hay embarked on what would become the first prose work in the Scots language: *The Buik of King Alexander the Conqueror*, which has survived in two manuscripts. As Sir Gilbert sat and spoke, a scribe carefully wrote down his every word. Among the medieval Scots is a line or two of French as Hay thought aloud and his scribe automatically transcribed what he heard.

Within Sir Gilbert's *Buik of King Alexander the Conqueror* is a poetic vision of Paradise on Earth:

> It was so huge, marvellous and high,
> And also it was so pleasant and so fair,
> So temperate and sober was the air,
> And where before was woods and wilderness,
> Nothing but fruits and flowers and spices was;
> The crags all along the river's sides,
> The trees of balm they glittered gold overhead.

Alexander's Journey to Paradise was an epic adventure across mountains, crags and forests, beset with lions, dragons, griffons and wild beasts. The Earthly Paradise was an enchanted place of flowers, fruit and trees. There fountains gently flowed with fresh water and the warm air carried the scent of roses and lilies. There was no war, no pain, no disease or plague or hunger. There was no death. This was a Heaven on Earth.

As William's family grew, it seems likely that Sir Gilbert

would have tutored his children. He would have taught them the liberal arts: grammar, rhetoric, dialectic, arithmetic, geometry, astronomy and music. He would also have taught them about chivalry and courtesy and told them of King Arthur, Alexander, and of his own adventures in France. William even named two of his children 'Arthur' and 'Alexander'.

William's children would have learned that Paradise was not some magical never-never land. In the Middle Ages, it was widely believed that the Earthly Paradise was a real place, that it actually existed. It appeared on maps as a remote island at the edge of the known world. To the people of medieval Europe, the Earthly Paradise was the Garden of Eden:

> And the LORD God planted a garden eastward in Eden;
> and there he put the man whom he had formed.
>   And out of the ground made the LORD God to grow
> every tree that is pleasant to the sight, and good for
> food; the tree of life also in the midst of the garden, and
> the tree of knowledge of good and evil.
>
> Genesis 2:8-9

The biblical story of Adam and Eve describes how the first man and the first woman were tempted by the serpent, tasted the forbidden fruit and were cast out of Paradise:

> So he drove out the man; and he placed at the east of the
> garden of Eden Cherubim, and a flaming sword which
> turned every way, to keep the way of the tree of life.
>
> Genesis 3:24

In the fifteenth century, the story of Adam and Eve and the expulsion from Eden was depicted in church murals, stone carvings and even Christmas Carols:

Adam lay ybounden,
   Bounden in a bond;
Four thousand winter
   Thought he not too long.

And all was for an apple,
   An apple that he took,
As clerk`es finden
   Written in their book.

Adam lay ybounden.

Edith Rickert, *'Ancient English Christmas Carols,
1400-1700'*, London 1914

Artists and poets also found inspiration for their images of the Garden of Eden from the biblical 'Song of Solomon'. Here a bride and bridegroom engage in an intimate dialogue. Each uses the garden as a metaphor to compliment their lover. To the bridegroom his bride is an orchard full of rare fruits:

Thy plants are an orchard of pomegranates, with pleasant fruits; camphire, with spikenard,
   Spikenard and saffron; calamus and cinnamon, with all trees of frankincense; myrrh and aloes, with all the chief spices:
   A fountain of gardens, a well of living waters, and streams from Lebanon.

Song of Solomon 4:13-16

The bridegroom says of his love that she is a 'garden enclosed', a 'spring shut up', a 'fountain sealed'. His virginal bride is a secret garden. The garden is an enclosed space: an Earthly Paradise enclosed by high walls. The Song of Solomon was seen as a spiritual allegory in which the enclosed garden symbolised the Virgin Mary:

> My beloved is gone down into his garden, to the beds of spices, to feed in the gardens, and to gather lilies.
> I am my beloved's, and my beloved is mine: he feedeth among the lilies.

Song of Solomon 6:2-3

In medieval paintings and tapestries, the walled garden symbolises the purity of the Virgin Mary. Around 1410, an unknown German master painted *The Garden of Eden*. The garden has medieval castellated walls. The Virgin Mary and her companions sit in a beautiful garden surrounded by flowers, herbs, trees, birds and butterflies. Like medieval nobles they sit and read books, play musical instruments, and pick fruit.

Paradise is depicted as an extraordinary garden with an ornate fountain at its heart in the *Garden of Earthly Delights*, the famous triptych created by Hieronymous Bosch *circa* 1500. Adam and Eve are joined by a host of exotic and fantastical animals including an elephant, a giraffe and a unicorn.

The fourteenth and fifteenth centuries were dominated by plague, famine and war. The Black Death decimated medieval Europe. Millions died, their bodies buried in makeshift mass graves or heaped and burned. Approximately one third of the population of Scotland died: some 300,000 men, women and children in all. In the early 1400s, Scotland was struck by a series of dreadful famines. In France, the Hundred Years War seemed to be a war without end, and the Wars of Independence saw Scotland and England locked in horrific conflict. Many thought that the Four Horsemen of the Apocalypse had been loosed upon the world, that the end of the world had come.

The Earthly Paradise was a marvellous vision of peace amid a world full of death and horror. Its appeal is obvious; it was a

Heaven on Earth when medieval Europe more closely resembled a vision of Hell. Inevitably, monastic communities and the nobility were inspired to create their own Earthly Paradises: medieval gardens.

The earliest medieval gardens were monastic gardens, devoted to the day-to-day needs of the monastery and the wider community. Vegetables and herbs were grown for the kitchens, ponds were stocked with fish, and medicinal plants were used to tend the sick and wounded.

The largest medieval hospital in Scotland was located at Soutra, twelve miles from Rosslyn. The House of the Holy Trinity at Soutra was a monastic community at the cutting edge of medicine. The monks cultivated and worked with medicinal herbs, plants and fungi including St John's wort, watercress, juniper, bilberries, hemp, opium poppy, hemlock, ergot, tormentil and black henbane. Archaeological excavations have shown that they carried out sophisticated surgical procedures using early anaesthetics. The monks also administered antiseptic salves, sleeping draughts and hangover cures.

In time, the monastic gardens became at once functional working gardens, symbolic enclosed spaces and sanctuaries of peace.

The garden of a Scottish monastery would have been a *hortus conclusus*, an enclosed garden that symbolised the beloved Virgin Mary. A cloister was a great court surrounded by high walls: an outdoor room with a garden of flowers, trees and paths open to the sky and the stars. At Melrose Abbey, two walls of the Great Cloister have survived with stone seating and ornately carved arcades. Here the monks would have sat beneath carved leaves, flowers, berries and buds to read from the Lives of the Fathers and contemplate their formal gardens. In time, the skills of monastic gardeners helped to create fantastical gardens for lords and ladies.

To the nobility, the walled garden became the Earthly Paradise. It was at once a peaceful haven, a pleasure garden dedicated to courtly love, and a symbolic landscape where flowers and trees were planted as much for their meaning as for beauty and fragrance.

Medieval gardens were usually rectangular, their lawns and flower beds laid out geometrically in squares and rectangles separated by narrow pathways, often with a central fountain, well or pool. Scottish nobles embraced the fashionable garden designs of Continental Europe. The Scots nobility brought plants, flowers and even gardeners from France. Despite the harsh northern climate, the medieval gardens of Scotland would have been beautiful and sophisticated allegorical creations.

To the lords and ladies of Scotland the garden also became a symbol of romantic courtly love. The thirteenth-century poem *Le Roman de la Rose* was one of the most popular works of literature in the medieval age. It survives in some 300 manuscripts and in numerous printed editions. Nothing is known about the poem's writer Guillaume de Lorris. *Le Roman de la Rose* is the story of a dream set in the allegorical Garden of Delight. The dreamer Amant gazes into the Fountain of Love and begins to fall in love with an exquisite rosebud. As Amant studies the rose directly, Cupid shoots five arrows of love through his eyes into his heart.

We can only guess at the design of the medieval gardens of Rosslyn. Sir William St Clair and his wife Elizabeth were profoundly influenced by their time in France. Rosslyn Castle was remodelled in Continental style and it seems likely that the gardens of Rosslyn would have been based on French enclosed gardens inspired by the Earthly Paradise and dedicated to courtly love.

In engravings of Rosslyn Castle dating to 1700, the castle courtyard has a well at its centre surrounded by four square beds. When the engravings were made, the castle courtyard was almost certainly covered in a heap of rubble – the aftermath of General Monk's bombardment. This castle garden may be a figment of the artist's imagination, but equally it may be based on descriptions passed down by villagers who remembered Rosslyn before its ruin.

In the 1480s, as the building of Rosslyn Chapel was nearing its end, it stood amid a carefully constructed landscape of fields, woods, orchards and deer parks. The remains of Rosslyn's parks, hedges and orchards can still be found if you explore Roslin Glen:

> The Chapel of Roslin . . . is situated on a rising ground charmingly beautified with wood, water and rocks . . . some trees below rustling their boughs across the purling stream . . . A place formed by Nature for heavenly contemplation.

> Robert Forbes, Episcopalian Bishop of Caithness, 1761

To the north-east of the chapel is the 'great yew hedge' planted by Sir William St Clair. The hedge has grown wild over its five hundred years. Tall yew trees arch over the path, their roots pulling apart the medieval stone wall. In the shadow of the castle, an ancient yew tree still flourishes, and down towards the bend in the river a single old apple tree still bears fruit and blossom every year, marking the site of Rosslyn's fruit orchard.

The St Clairs' medieval gardens may have all but vanished, but Rosslyn Chapel is itself an Earthly Paradise. 'The Chapel amidst the Woods' is the Garden of Eden carved in stone, a Heaven on Earth:

> It is strangely and beautifully decorated in pillars and arches, with sumptuous rare carvings, a very garden of stone flowers, the poetry of sacred architecture.

> Francis Watt, *Edinburgh and the Lothians*, 1912

The St Clairs were a staunchly Catholic family. Rosslyn Chapel is the ultimate expression of their faith: a building devoted to their God, full of biblical stories and medieval allegory. The flowers and plants carved in stone within Rosslyn Chapel were grown in medieval gardens and monastic cloisters. Every flower had its own story and meaning. Every plant could be 'read' by medieval worshippers.

Rosslyn Chapel is a rectangular building. Its four walls enclose a stone garden full of carved trees, fruit, leaves and flowers: the enclosed garden that symbolises the blessed Virgin. Dozens of pinnacles grow from above the walls like sculpted trees. By the north door, a single badly worn figure stands guard: an angel with a raised sword, like the cherubim of the Garden of Eden.

The interior of Rosslyn Chapel is full of stylised flowers and foliage. Walls and arches are covered in curly kale, a native form of cabbage. Vines bearing grapes and exotic fruit weave over the aisles. Roses, lilies, daisies, wheat and oak leaves adorn the walls and window arches. Like all the Earthly Paradises of medieval art, Rosslyn is an abundant garden bursting with fruit, flowers, vegetables and trees.

In Eden, 'every tree that is pleasant to the sight, and good for food' grew as well as 'the tree of life also in the midst of the garden, and the tree of knowledge of good and evil'.

The Apprentice Pillar is widely thought to symbolise the Tree of Knowledge. The 'Mason's Pillar' may well represent the Tree of Life. Facing these two pillars is a central pillar; carved at the head of this pillar is the expulsion of Adam and Eve from the Garden of Eden. Two figures try to cover their nakedness in shame as they are cast from the garden, their backs turned to a tree.

Jewish legend says that Abraham planted trees across Canaan but only one grew tall and flourished. This tree would offer shade and protection to believers but turn its branches away from idolaters.

Medieval legend told that Christ's cross was made with wood from the Tree of Knowledge. The Apprentice Pillar seems inextricably connected with sacrifice: the murder of the apprentice, the sacrifice of Isaac, and the crucifixion of Christ. Abraham is depicted with his son Isaac and the sacrificial ram in the carvings above it.

In total, Rosslyn Chapel has 14 pillars, marking out the lines of the north and south aisles like the trees planted along a path. Rosslyn's aisles are like the covered alleys that encircled monastic cloisters. The aisles have stone benches like the arcades at Melrose Abbey. It is only when you step out from under the low arches of the aisles into the choir that you discover the high stone ceiling with its flowers and stars: like the open sky above a medieval walled garden.

The arched ceiling itself is divided into five sections, each full of symbolic flowers and five-pointed stars. From east to west there are: daisies, lilies, flowers which are possibly marigolds or violets, roses, and a field of stars. This design, with its rectangular boxes divided by arched ribs, is like the layout of a medieval garden. Each flower bed is planted out with stone flowers that carry allegorical meanings.

Daisies appear in the east field of the chapel's stone ceiling. The name 'daisy' means 'day's eye' as the daisy opens with the first rays of the morning sun. Chaucer says, 'Love I most those flowers white and rede such as men callen daysies.' In Chaucer's time, knights would wear daisies as a token of their lady's love. Legend says that when Mary Magdalene wept in repentance each tear became a daisy when it fell to earth.

Lilies symbolised the Blessed Virgin Mary. Mary, the Mother of Christ, was known as 'the flower of flowers'. The lily appears in the Song of Solomon: 'As the lily among thorns, so is my love among the daughters (Song of Solomon 2:2). Marigolds were known as 'Marygolds'. They were associated with the blessed Virgin, as were violets which symbolised purity and innocence.

Roses also symbolised purity and the Virgin. It was said that Mary was *rosa sine spina* – the rose without thorns. St Ambrose said that before the fall the rose had no thorns, that the wonderful scent and the beauty of the rose were reminders of the lost paradise, and that the thorns remind mankind of the suffering we must now endure.

The field of stars is full of five-pointed stars, symbolising the five wounds of Christ: the four nail wounds to his hands and feet and the spear wound to his side. They were also symbolic of 'the Five Joys of our Lady': the Annunciation, the Nativity, the Resurrection, the Ascension, and the Assumption, and also the Five Sorrows that centred on the Passion of Christ. Amid the stars are carvings of the sun, the moon, the dove, four angels including the archangel Michael, and an image of Christ.

The sun, which is sometimes a symbol of Jesus, lies directly above the figure of Christ. The moon, emerging from behind clouds, is beneath the dove. The dove symbolises the Holy Spirit. It also appears in the story of Noah and the Ark, bearing an olive branch. The archangel Michael bears a raised sword while Christ is depicted with a simple halo, his right hand raised in blessing.

The life of Christ is shown throughout Rosslyn; the positioning of each carving is one clue to understanding the chapel. Another piece of the puzzle is Rosslyn's famous Green Men. By carefully studying all the carvings within Rosslyn it is finally possible to 'read' the chapel, to understand at least some of Rosslyn's secrets.

Many believe that the Green Man is an ancient figure. They see him as the wild spirit of nature, the laughter in the woods. He is a supernatural being that is young each spring, fertile and bountiful in summer, autumnal and overgrown as the leaves fall, old and dying in winter then reborn with the new growth of the following spring. The Green Man has become an eternal figure representing the cycle of life, death and rebirth.

Within Rosslyn Chapel there is some evidence to support the theory that the Green Man is the spirit of nature or the spirit of life in nature. If you walk around the chapel clockwise, you will find that the Green Men become older as you move from east to south, west to north.

The east, where each day dawns with the rising of the sun,

is marked by young boyish Green Men. Each young face has a single vine emerging from the corner of its mouth. In the south, the Green Men are bearded and in the prime of life; their overgrown faces surrounded by leaves and wild foliage. But it is the Green Men on the north side of Rosslyn Chapel that are particularly startling: they are dead and dying. On the north wall, the foliate heads include a peg-toothed decaying face and a skull with vines twisting from between its teeth and out of its empty eye sockets.

From the darkness and death of the north, you turn back to the east, to the new growth of spring, the dawn of the year and the reborn Green Men.

The cycle of nature, the four seasons of the year, was part of the cosmology of the medieval age. As you faced the sunrise, the new day dawned in the east. The east symbolised spring, new growth and the beginning of life. To your right or 'dexter' side was the south, the bountiful summer half of the year with its fruit, flowers and harvest. The south symbolised the prime of life. In the west, the sun would set and night would fall. The north was to your left or 'sinister' side. North was associated with death and winter.

Rosslyn Chapel has been called 'a book in stone'. That book can be read. Beginning in the north-east corner of the chapel, the carvings tell a story as you move clockwise around the four walls. Just as the Green Men grow older as you move around the chapel, the carvings on the east, south, west and north walls can be read as 'the beginning, middle and end': a reflection of nature's seasons in an Earthly Paradise.

In the north-east corner of the chapel are three angels. One angel bears a scroll, another unrolls a parchment while a third angel crowned with a cross holds an open book. This is the beginning of Rosslyn's story. This open book is the first page.

Rosslyn's Lady Chapel is full of beginnings. High on a ceiling boss is a carving of the Nativity. The Virgin and Child sit by the manger, surrounded by the three shepherds and the three kings.

Here, too, is the Star of Bethlehem: an eight-pointed star. The octagonal geometry of the star and the eightfold arches in the Lady Choir show that this is a sacred space halfway between the fourfold realm of the Earth and the perfect circle of Heaven.

Eleven Angels playing medieval musical instruments face the rising sun as each day dawns. This Heavenly Host sings and plays lutes, a rebec, a pipe and tabor, a psaltery, cornets and bagpipes for the Holy Family. Until their destruction in 1592, the Lady Choir had four altars, dedicated to the Blessed Virgin, St Matthew, St Peter and St Andrew.

The south aisle is full of scenes of medieval life. Fifteenth-century Scots would have instantly recognised the figures carved in the Seven Deadly Sins and the Seven Works of Mercy as men and women from their daily lives. The lovers are dressed in flowing medieval robes, courage is a knight in armour. The Seven Deadly Sins literally lead to hell as the devil leers out from a monstrous mouth. This is the devil of medieval folk plays. The device he carries is not a triple hook, a fiery torch or a pitchfork but a pyrotechnic firework on a staff. The Mouth of Hell was a piece of stagecraft: a theatrical set where devils and demons emerged during Corpus Christi plays.

The south door was known as the Ladies' Door, where women entered the chapel. Outside it, in the south porch, is a small, badly worn figure of a female saint: a virgin martyr with a palm leaf in her right hand. Inside, there is a stoup for holy water, where ladies dipped their fingers as they entered the church to spiritually cleanse themselves. Above the door is carved a woman's act of kindness to Christ: a depiction of the Veil of Veronica from the Stations of the Cross. As Christ bore the Cross, a woman from the crowd handed him a piece of cloth to wipe his brow. Miraculously the image of Christ's face appeared upon the cloth.

Further along the south aisle are two carvings at the base of a window. One shows a knight on horseback with a lance in his hand and an angel bearing a cross at his back. This is the knight as the flower of chivalry. Across from the knight is a carving of an angel with a scroll and a figure kneeling at prayer. Of all Rosslyn's carvings. this figure is probably the most overlooked and one of the most important. Among all the biblical figures and saints, the kings and queens, the fabulous beasts and monstrous creatures, this is a simple carving of a Catholic at prayer, a small devotional book held in his clasped hands. This is not a public act of worship, it is a personal moment between a faithful Catholic and his God.

These two carvings define the St Clairs of Rosslyn. The chivalrous knights who fought and died for what they believed and the devoted Christians whose unswerving devotion to the Catholic faith would ultimately lead to their downfall.

In recent years, a carving on the west wall has been identified as Sir William St Clair, the third earl, the founder of the chapel. The bearded figure bears a sword in his right hand and wears a crown. To his left is a scallop shell, the coquille of St James, pilgrim badge of Santiago de Compostella, suggesting the figure had made the long pilgrimage to Spain. Father Hay claims that William was 'a Knight of the Cockle'. This may be a depiction of the founder but equally it may be a historical or biblical king or possibly King Alexander or King Arthur.

Across the west doorway are the two dragons associated with Merlin and Vortigern's tower. Beneath the dragons is a single angel, bearing a scroll, staring into the north. There, under a window in the north aisle, the devil stares back.

The north aisle of Rosslyn is the dark half of the chapel. The devil greets you as you approach from the choir. This is the folk devil, with ass's ears and goat's horns, the devil of the medieval plays. A mother and child turn their backs on the devil to face a carving of the Crucifixion.

At some point in Rosslyn's history, the figure of Christ on the Cross has been attacked and badly damaged. The head of Jesus is broken, the image literally defaced, possibly by General Monk's troops as they stabled their horses in the chapel or by the Protestant mob that attacked the 'monument of idolatrie'.

Three now unidentifiable figures (possibly Mary Magdalene, Simon Peter and another disciple) watch the Crucifixion from the opposite pillar, and a carving thought to be the Crown of Thorns tops a pillar on the other side of the 'Bachelor's door'. This was the traditional entrance for men. Across from the door, angels are rolling back the stone from the door to the tomb of Christ.

In the middle of the north aisle is another depiction of Christ, in the figure of the Lamb of God, the Agnus Dei. The Lamb with the flag appears upon a seal held by two angels. This is the Seventh Seal from the Book of Revelation; as the Lamb breaks the Seventh Seal, it ushers in the apocalypse.

Just as a carving of Adam and Eve from the Book of Genesis, the first book of the Old Testament of the Bible, appears in the east of the chapel, so the last book of the New Testament of the Bible, the Book of Revelation, is depicted in the north aisle.

To the north-east, at the other side of a window, is Rosslyn's only angel with a beard. In one hand, this angel holds an open book. With the other he points to a single page:

> I could see the dead, great and small, standing before
> the throne: and books were opened. Then another
> book was opened, the roll of the living. From what was
> written in these books the dead were judged upon the
> record of their deeds.

> Revelation 20:12

Beneath this depiction of the Last Judgement are two black slabs, the only black stones in the paving of the chapel. This is the entrance to the burial vaults of the St Clairs. When the Day of Judgement arrived, the St Clairs of Rosslyn, as devout Catholics, believed that their tomb would open wide and they would take their place among the blessed.

To the north-east is a stone carving of the Danse Macabre. A king, a farmer, an abbot, a carpenter, a courtier, a ploughman, a cardinal and a lady gazing in a mirror; each figure is joined by a grinning skeleton in the dance of death. These carvings have also been interpreted as the dead rising from their graves on the Day of Judgement.

Above the black slabs, carved into the architrave, is a vision of Christ in glory. Seven kings lie horizontally before Christ as 'all kings shall fall down before him: all nations shall serve him' (Psalm 72).

One final carving closes the circle. From Rosslyn's north-east corner the stories within the chapel are read clockwise around all four walls. The story begins with an angel holding an open book. At the end of the north aisle is one last angel, an angel that cradles a closed book in its arms.

One of the earliest maps of the Lothians of Scotland was created by Timothy Pont in the sixteenth century. It survives in Hendrik Hondius' *A new description of the shyres Lothian and Linlitquo*. Edinburgh is recorded as 'Edenborough' and Rosslyn Castle and Chapel appear as 'Roflyin' and its 'Colledge'. Immediately above 'Roflyin', by Loanhead, about a mile from Rosslyn Chapel is a tiny place called 'Paradife'.

Thousands of words have been written about Rosslyn Chapel. For hundreds of years artists, musicians, poets and writers have found inspiration in the chapel, castle and glen. There are books of Rosslyn legends, tales and ghost stories, and guides to the carvings in the chapel. The imaginations of some writers have run wild, dreaming up bizarre theories and fictional histories. Thousands of visitors come to Rosslyn Chapel each year drawn by stories of secret treasures, medieval knights and the Holy Grail.

The Holy Grail may or may not be a real artefact, but in essence it symbolises the quest for purity, perfection and divinity. It is said that the Holy Grail has the power to restore life: to heal the wounded Fisher King. Once upon a time, Rosslyn Chapel lay abandoned and lost, left to fall into ruin. In the twenty-first century, the chapel is a living place of worship with an active congregation who fill the chapel with flowers, song and prayer, as an ambitious conservation project seeks to restore this medieval wonder.

At one time, Rosslyn Chapel was all but forgotten. Now, it is world famous. Over 500 years after its creation, Rosslyn, like the Grail, still has the magical ability to inspire and enchant.

APPENDICES

APPENDIX ONE
A Rosslyn Timeline

*c.*2000 BC	Bronze Age rock art carved in stone cliff face at Rosslyn.
c. AD 203	Alleged founding of Rosslyn by 'Asterius'. His daughter Panthioria was said to have married King Donaldus, the first Christian king of the Scots.
756	Battle of Athelstaneford. Angus mac Fergus, the King of the Picts, defeats the Northumbrian army of King Athelstane. A vision of the Saltire, destined to become the flag of Scotland, is seen in the clouds.
830	Writing of the *Historia Brittonum*, attributed to Nennius. This early history includes the legend of King Vortigern and the Red and White Dragons of Dinas Emrys.

843	The Picts and Scots are united under Kenneth Macalpine.
c.935	Northern Britain finally becomes Scotland.
1069	The Saxon Princess Margaret marries King Malcolm Canmore. They rule Scotland from Dunfermline.
1073	Treaty of Abernethy between King Malcolm Canmore of Scotland and William the Conqueror of England.
1093	King Malcolm Canmore and Queen Margaret die.
1095	The First Crusade begins.
1099	The Crusaders, led by Godfrey of Bouillon, capture Jerusalem.
1104	Crusaders capture Acre.
1113	When monks from Laon in northern France travel through Cornwall, they discover that the Cornish still believe that Arthur, King of the Britons, will return.
1115	St Bernard founds the Abbey of Clairvaux in France.
1118	Nine knights join together under Hugh De Payens to found the Knights Templar.
1120-40	The Modena Archivolt, on the north portal of Modena Cathedral, is carved with Arthurian figures.

1128 St Bernard draws up the rule of the Knights Templar.

1128 Hugh de Payens visits Scotland on a recruiting and fundraising drive for the fledgling Templar order.

1130 Geoffrey of Monmouth composes the Prophesies of Merlin while working on the *History of the Kings of Britain*.

1131 Cistercian house of Rievaulx is founded in Yorkshire. It is the daughter house of Clairvaux.

1135 Geoffrey of Monmouth completes the *History of the Kings of Britain*.

1136 Cistercian house of Melrose is founded in southern Scotland. Melrose is the daughter house of Rievaulx. King David I of Scotland supports the Cistercian order.

1137 Stephen's Queen Maud gives the first gift of English land to the Knights Templar.

1141 King David I and Robert, Earl of Gloucester, support the cause of Matilda.

1141-2 Cistercian house of Newbattle founded in Midlothian, Scotland. In Newbattle's foundation documents, Edinburgh is referred to as the 'Castle of Maidens': an Arthurian name.

1141-2 Ailred, master of novices at Rievaulx, relates that the novices are moved to tears not by Scripture but by Arthurian tales.

1146   The Abbey Kirk is completed at Melrose.

1147-67 Jocelyn of Furness composes the *Vita Kentigerni*, the Life of Kentigern, for Jocelyn, Bishop of Glasgow. The Life includes the figure of Lailoken, Merlin the Wild, the prophet who lived and died in southern Scotland.

1147   Second Crusade launched following an appeal by Bernard of Clairvaux.

1149   Second Crusade ends.

1149   The Scottish King David I knights future Henry II of England at Carlisle on Whit Sunday.

1150   Geoffrey of Monmouth composes the *Vita Merlini*, the Life of Merlin.

1153   King David I dies. The Cistercian Ailred of Rievaulx writes his funeral oration.

1155   Wace completes his *Roman de Brut* based on Geoffrey's work, and introduces the Round Table to the Arthurian Matter of Britain.

1163-1235 Building of Notre Dame Cathedral in Paris, France.

1160-70 Chrétien de Troyes writes his five Arthurian poems: Erec and Enide, Cligés, Lancelot (the Knight of the Cart), Yvain, and Percival: the story of the Grail. The Grail appears for the first time in literature.

1187	Saladin takes Jerusalem. He has all of Jerusalem's holy places cleansed with rose water and allows the Christians within the Holy City to live.
1189-92	Third Crusade begins. It is led by Richard I, 'the Lionheart', of England, King Philip of France, and Frederick Barbarossa the Holy Roman Emperor.
1190	The monks of Glastonbury Abbey claim to discover the grave of Arthur and Guinevere. A lead cross is dug up baring the inscription: *'Hic iacet sepultus inclitus rex arturius in insula avalonia'* – 'Here lies buried the renowned King Arthur in the Isle of Avalon.'
1194-1260	Building of Chartres Cathedral in France.
1195-1200	Robert de Boron composes his three Arthurian romances. He introduces the notion of the Holy Grail as the vessel used by Christ at the Last Supper. Also introduces the Sword in the Stone.
1202-04	The Fourth Crusade. Crusaders are unable to pay the Venetians for transport so they agree to attack Constantinople. The city is taken and sacked.
1205	Wolfram von Eschenbach writes *Parzival*. He depicts the Grail as a magical stone.
1208-13	The Albigensian Crusade against heresy in France.
1212	The Children's Crusade. About 30,000 children set out from Europe for Palestine.
1215-35	The Vulgate Cycle of Arthurian legends is compiled.

1250   *The Black Book of Carmarthen*, the oldest surviving manuscript containing the Welsh tales of Arthur, is compiled.

1265   The *Book of Aneirin*, containing the surviving copy of the Gododdin, is compiled.

1280   Sir William de Sancto Claro becomes first Sinclair of Rosslyn. On 14 September the lands and barony of Roslin are granted to Sir William by King Alexander III.

1285   Sir William de Sancto Claro accompanies King Alexander's queen, Yolanda de Dreux, to Scotland.

1286   Thomas Rhymour prophesies the death of King Alexander III. King Alexander III falls to his death. Scotland is a land without a king.

1290   Margaret, the Maid of Norway, is drowned off coast of Orkney on her way to Scotland.

1291   William of Beaujeu, the Templar Grand Master, is slain at Acre and the Christians are expelled from Palestine.

1292   Sir William de Sancto Claro of Rosslyn and his son Henry swear fealty to King Edward I of England.

1296   Sir William de Sancto Claro and his son Henry are among the Scots nobles captured at Dunbar by the English army. They are imprisoned in Gloucester and St Briavels Castles.

1296	King Edward I has a large stone taken away from Scone, thinking it is the Stone of Destiny. It becomes the Coronation Stone.
1297	The Battle of Stirling Bridge. William Wallace leads the Scots to victory.
1297	Jacques de Molay is elected Grand Master of Knights Templar.
1298	The Battle of Falkirk. Wallace is defeated but escapes capture. Brian le Jay, Master of the Templars, is slain at the Battle of Falkirk. He had led Edward I north and fought with the English against Wallace and the Scots. Le Jay is killed by the Scots. He dies face down in a bog.
1299	Henry St Clair is exchanged for Sir William Fitz-Warin and returns to Scotland.
1301	King Edward I uses Arthurian sources to back his claim to the throne of Scotland in Rome.
1303	The Battle of Roslin. Three English forces, a total of 30,000 men, are defeated by a single Scottish force of 8,000.
c.1305	Work begins to build a new castle at Rosslyn.
1305	Wallace betrayed to the English. After a show trial in London he is hung, drawn and quartered.
1307	The Knights Templar are arrested across France.
1309	The trial of Knights Templar in Scotland takes

place at Holyrood in Edinburgh. Both Sir Henry St Clair of Rosslyn and Sir William St Clair testify against the Templars.

1314   The Battle of Bannockburn. The Scots, under King Robert the Bruce, defeat the English army. Sir Henry St Clair is among the victorious Scots.

1314   Templar Grand Master Jacques de Molay and the Templar Preceptor of Normandy Geoffrey of Charney are burned at the stake on the small island, the Ile-des-Javiaux, in Paris, France.

1314   Dante's *Alighieri's Inferno*, the first part of the *Divine Comedy*, is published.

1317   The Battle of Donibristle. William 'the fighting Bishop' of Dunkeld, brother of Sir Henry St Clair, leads the Scots to repel an invading English force which lands in Fife.

1320   Sir Henry St Clair of Rosslyn is among the Barons of Scotland who sign a letter to the Pope that is now known as the Declaration of Arbroath.

1322   The Cistercian Abbey at Melrose is pillaged and destroyed by troops under the English King Edward II.

c.1325   The *White Book of Rhydderch* compiled. Includes the tale of Lludd and Llefelys, and the red and white dragons.

1329   Robert the Bruce, King of Scots, dies at Cardross. His heart is removed, embalmed and placed in a silver casket. Sir William St Clair and Sir James Douglas are among the Scots knights who begin a journey to take Bruce's heart to Jerusalem.

1330   Sir William St Clair and his brother John are slain in battle by the Moors of Granada at Tebas de Ardales. Their bodies are taken from the battlefield, the flesh is boiled from their bones, and their bones and hearts are returned to Scotland.

1335   Sir Henry St Clair of Rosslyn dies.

1337   The start of the Hundred Years War between the English and French. The Scots fight alongside the French.

c.1350   Sir William St Clair marries Isabella de Strathearn, second daughter and main heiress of Malise, Earl of Caithness and Orkney.

1379   The St Clairs of Rosslyn acquire the ancient Norwegian earldom of Orkney. William and Isabella's son Henry has his claim to the earldom, lands and rights of Orkney accepted by the Norwegian King Hakon VI Magnusson. Henry becomes the first St Clair Earl of Orkney and is also titled 'lord of Rosslyn'.

c.1372   Geoffrey Chaucer begins to write the *Canterbury Tales*.

c.1400   The alliterative poem *Sir Gawain and the Green Knight* is written.

1400   Sir Henry St Clair, first Earl of Orkney and lord of Rosslyn, dies in Orkney: 'for the defence of the country he was slain there cruelly by his enemies'. He is succeeded by Henry St Clair, second Earl of Orkney and lord of Rosslyn.

c.1400   *The Red Book of Hergest* is compiled. Includes the tale of Lludd and Llefelys, and the red and white dragons.

1402   Henry St Clair, second Earl of Orkney, taken captive at the battle of Homildon Hill.

1405   Henry St Clair, second Earl of Orkney, leads the Scottish forces at the siege of Berwick. He becomes Guardian to Prince James, the future King James I of Scotland.

1406   Earl Henry attempts to take Prince James to France but their ship is captured by the English and they are both imprisoned in the Tower of London.

1407   Earl Henry either escapes with the aid of one of his servants or is released on payment of a ransom from the Tower, and returns to Scotland.

1411   The University of St Andrews is founded.

1415   Battle of Agincourt. Henry V, King of England, defeats the French.

1415   Sir William St Clair, the founder of Rosslyn Chapel, is born.

1418   Earl Henry is among the Scots notables who died

of 'le quhew', an epidemic recorded by Bower in 1420.

1424   The Battle of Vernuill in Normandy, France. Elizabeth Douglas loses her husband, her father, and one of her brothers.

1429   The Order of the Golden Fleece is founded.

1429   Joan of Arc leads the French against the English. Many Scots fight alongside the Maid. Sir Gilbert Hay is chamberlain to the Dauphin of France.

1432   Joan is put on trial and burned at the stake at Rouen.

1432   Sir William St Clair of Rosslyn marries Elizabeth Douglas. A papal dispensation was granted in 1432 for them to remain in matrimony.

1434   William St Clair is formally invested as Earl of Orkney by King Erik of Norway. William becomes the third and final St Clair Earl of Orkney.

1436   Earl William, as pantler and admiral of the fleet, escorts the Scots king's daughter Princess Margaret to France for her wedding to the Dauphin.

1445   Sir Gilbert Hay returns to Scotland from the French court. He lives in Rosslyn Castle and begins to translate manuscripts into Scots.

1446   Rosslyn Chapel, Collegiate Church of St Matthew the Evangelist, is founded by Sir William St Clair, third Earl of Orkney and lord of Rosslyn.

1447	Walter Bower records that Sir William is erecting an elegant structure at Rosslyn.
1447	A great fire consumes Rosslyn Castle.
1451	The end of the Hundred Years War.
1451	The University of Glasgow is founded.
1452	Birth of Leonardo da Vinci. His parents were Ser Piero, a notary, and Caterina, a peasant girl. They never married.
1452	William's first wife, Elizabeth Douglas, dies. They had four daughters and one son, William, who was known as 'the Waster'.
1454	Earl William marries Marjory Sutherland. They will have fourteen children including Sir Oliver, William, Alexander and Arthur.
1455	Earl William acquires the ancient earldom of Caithness.
1455-85	The War of the Roses, between the English houses of York and Lancaster.
1456	Roslin is erected into a burgh of barony with a weekly market on Saturday, a Mercat cross (Market cross) and 'a yearly fair on the feast of St Simon and St Jude'.
1460	Scottish King James II dies, blown up as a cannon explodes at Roxburgh. Earl William is one of the seven Regents for the minority of James III.

1470   Sir William St Clair resigns Earldom of Orkney. Orkney is transferred to the Scottish crown. William receives the castle of Ravenscraig and lands in Fife and an annual pension of four hundred marks in compensation.

1470   Sir Thomas Malory completes *Le Morte d'Arthur*.

1476   William St Clair gives his main estates to William and Oliver, the eldest sons of his second marriage, effectively disinheriting William 'the Waster', his son by his first marriage. He tries to pass Roslin and Ravenscraig to Oliver and the Earldom of Caithness to William.

1482   Infighting between William's children is resolved. Sir Oliver relinquishes the lands of Cowsland, the barony of Dysart, the castle of Ravenscraig, the lands of Dubbo, Carberry and Wilston to William 'the Waster'. In exchange, William renounces his claim to the barony of Rosslyn. It should be noted that 'a Waster' was the name of a wooden sword that squires fought with as they trained to become knights.

c.1484   Sir William St Clair, founder of Rosslyn Chapel, dies. He had lived to over 70 years old.

1492   Christopher Columbus sails to the New World.

1513   The Battle of Flodden. William St Clair, the second Earl of Caithness, slain.

1523   Sir William St Clair, lord of Rosslyn, grants land for dwelling houses and gardens to the Collegiate Church's provost, prebendaries and choristers.

1533   Elizabeth, the future Queen of England, is born.

1536   The English King Henry the VIII has his wife Anne Boleyn, Elizabeth's mother, executed. She is beheaded at the Tower of London.

1542   The Battle of Solway Moss. Ten thousand Scots under the command of Sir Oliver Sinclair of Rosslyn are defeated by King Henry VIII's English army.

1542   King James V dies at Falkland Palace as he hears that Marie of Guise has borne him a daughter. The child is Mary, future Queen of Scots.

1544   Rosslyn Castle is attacked by Henry VIII's troops during the 'Rough Wooing', when the English king tries to force the marriage of his young son Edward and the infant Mary, Queen of Scots. An English fleet lands at Edinburgh and the troops set fire to Holyrood Palace and burn the city when they fail to take Edinburgh Castle.

1546   Marie of Guise's letter mentions 'a secret' within Rosslyn.

1554   In the Acts of the Lords of Council in Public Affairs (1501-54) the lords ordain that William St Clair of Rosslyn should produce within three days all the jewels, vestments and ornaments of the Abbey and Palace of Holyroodhouse.

1558   Elizabeth I becomes Queen of England.

1558   John Knox sermonises against the iniquity of women.

1560   Scotland becomes Protestant. The Scots Parliament formally abolishes the authority of the Pope in Scotland and the celebration of the Catholic Mass is forbidden.

1565   John St Clair, the Bishop of Brechin and fourth son of Oliver St Clair, performs the marriage ceremony of Mary Queen of Scots and Lord Darnley at Holyrood.

1567   Lord Darnley is murdered: blown up with gunpowder at Kirk o' Field, Edinburgh. Mary is imprisoned and forced to abdicate in favour of her son, the infant James VI.

1571   The Catholic provost and prebendaries of the Collegiate College of St Matthew resign when their endowments are taken 'by force and violence'.

1587   Mary Queen of Scots is executed. She is beheaded in the red dress of a Catholic martyr.

1589   William Knox, brother of John Knox and minister of Cockpen, is censured for baptising the child of 'the Laird of Rosling'. The baptism is performed in Rosslyn Chapel, which is described in the Dalkeith Presbytery records as a 'monument of idolatrie'.

1590   Presbytery forbid Mr George Ramsay, minister of Lasswade, to bury the wife of Oliver St Clair in the chapel.

1592   Oliver St Clair is threatened with excommunication if he fails to have the altars within Rosslyn Chapel destroyed. By the end of August it is recorded that the altars have been demolished. Rosslyn Chapel finally ceases to be a place of worship and begins to fall into ruin.

1601   The first St Clair charter is written.

1603   Queen Elizabeth dies childless. James becomes King of England, as King James the VI of Scots and I of England, uniting the crowns.

1605   The gunpowder plot. Guy Fawkes and other conspirators are arrested and executed the following year.

1611   The King James Bible published.

1623   Rosslyn gypsies are persecuted. William St Clair had rescued a gypsy from hanging. Thereafter the gypsies gathered at Rosslyn each year to perform May plays.

1628   The second St Clair charter.

1642   English civil war begins.

1648   The Scots invade England in support of King Charles I. They are defeated at Preston by Cromwell's men.

1649   King Charles I executed and the monarchy abolished.

1650   Charles II lands in Scotland and is proclaimed king.

1650   Sir William Sinclair of Rosslyn dies at the Battle of

Dunbar. He becomes the last St Clair knight to be buried in full armour beneath Rosslyn Chapel.

1650   Cromwell's General Monk attacks Rosslyn Castle with cannon and an early form of grenade. His troops stable their horses within Rosslyn Chapel.

1658   Cromwell dies.

1660   King Charles II restored to the throne.

1677   Thomas Kirk from Yorkshire writes about the apprentice legend in his journal after visiting the ruined chapel.

1688   A Protestant mob attacks and damages Rosslyn Chapel.

1693   John Slezer records in his *Theatrum Scotia* the legend that the chapel appears 'all in fire' when a St Clair dies. He also mentions 'the Prince's pillar so much talk'd of'.

1700   Father Richard Augustine Hay, Canon of St Genevieve in Paris and Prior of St Piermont, completes his study of the history of Rosslyn and the St Clairs. Parts of it are published 135 years later as *A Genealogie of the Saintclaires of Rosslyn*. Hay's account is often unreliable. He was marrying into the family and was keen to win approval. As noted by the Rev. Professor H.J. Lawlor, 'it is probably universally admitted that Father Hay is not a writer whose unsupported testimony can be implicitly accepted'.

1707	The Act of Union between Scotland and England. The Scottish Parliament is suspended.
1715	Jacobite rising in support of the Old Pretender.
1736	Sir James St Clair has the windows of Rosslyn Chapel glazed, the stone floor relaid and the roof repaired.
1736	Scottish Masonic Grand Lodge formed. William St Clair elected first Grand Master.
1739	Repair work carried out under direction of Sir John Clerk of Penicuik. A sloping wooden roof is added to halt Rosslyn Chapel's further deterioration.
1746	The Battle of Culloden. 'Bonnie' Prince Charles Edward Stuart defeated. Sir James Sinclair of Rosslyn commanded the Royal Scots on the Hanoverian side.
1774	The first Rosslyn Chapel Guide-book is sold at the chapel. Written by Bishop Robert Forbes, it was first published as an article in the *Edinburgh Magazine*, January 1761, vol V.
1778	'The Last Rosslyn', Sir William St Clair, dies.
1806	George Meikle Kemp, the designer of the Scott Monument in Edinburgh, visits Rosslyn Chapel at the age of 10. The chapel creates so great an impression that the seeds of Kemp's future career are planted.
1807	William and his sister Dorothy Wordsworth visit Rosslyn Chapel. Dorothy notes that the chapel 'is

kept locked up, and so preserved from the injuries it might otherwise receive from idle boys, but as nothing is done to keep it together, it must, in the end, fall. The architecture within is exquisitely beautiful.'

1837   The black slabs in the north aisle of Rosslyn Chapel are removed. Two coffins are discovered lying across the inner opening, preventing access to the vault. The slabs are replaced.

1840-4   The Scott Monument is built in Edinburgh to commemorate the life and work of Sir Walter Scott. George Meikle Kemp's design was influenced by the gothic architecture of Melrose Abbey and Rosslyn Chapel.

1861   Controversial restoration work at Rosslyn Chapel under direction of architect and freemason David Bryce. 'Masonic' angels are added to the Lady Choir, stones are relaid in the sacristy and an altar is established.

1862   Rosslyn Chapel is rededicated by the Bishop of Edinburgh and the Bishop of Brechin. After two hundred years, Rosslyn is restored as a place of Christian worship.

1871   Francis Robert, the fourth Earl of Rosslyn, is elected the 69th Grand Master Mason of Scotland.

1880-1   The apse, which acts as a baptistry with an organ loft above, is added to Rosslyn Chapel. The work is led by Andrew Kerr. Kerr tells the Earl that a group of visitors remarked that 'it was wonderful that such young men should be entrusted to execute such carving' to which the estate factor 'very coolly replied, that it was not wonderful here, as the finest pillar in the chapel was the work of an apprentice boy!'

1915 Sir Robert Lorimer reports that 'the Chapel is in fairly good order . . . a few of the stones are crumbling but not to the extent to cause any alarm. The condition of the roof is not satisfactory.' Following Sir Robert's recommendation, the exterior of the roof is asphalted.

1942 During World War II, the congregation at Rosslyn Chapel's Sunday Services falls. It is suggested that it should be closed on account of the fuel the chapel uses. Gwilym Lloyd George MP, the Minister of Fuel, writes to the Secretary of State for Scotland, saying, 'from the fuel point of view, I doubt whether I would be justified in securing a small economy of fuel in this world at the possible cost of a disproportionate expenditure of it on myself in the next'.

1954 The interior masonry of Rosslyn Chapel is cleaned and scrubbed with stiff brushes then a coating of silica fluoride of magnesium is applied. The intention was to protect the stonework but in effect it trapped the dampness within the stone.

1989 *The Temple and the Lodge* is published. The authors Michael Baigent and Richard Leigh note parallels between the legend of the Murdered Apprentice and the Freemasonic legend of Hiram Abif. From then on, a series of 'alternative history' books with increasingly fantastical theories are produced by pseudo-history writers.

1997	In an attempt to allow the stonework to dry out, a free-standing steel roof is built over the chapel. A walkway allows visitors to climb to the level of the upper windows and gain a unique gargoyle's-eye view of the exterior details of the chapel. An ambitious repair, renovation and preservation strategy is undertaken.

1997   The Roslin Institute annouces the birth of Dolly the sheep, the first mammal cloned from a single adult cell.

2000   Phase two of the repair and preservation work at Rosslyn Chapel begins.

2002   An exhibition, Rosslyn – Country of Painter and Poet, is held by the National Gallery of Scotland.

2003   Dan Brown's novel *The Da Vinci Code* is published. It is phenomenally successful, selling tens of millions of copies.

2005   A Knights Templar seal is found less than a mile from Rosslyn Chapel.

2005   The Rosslyn Chapel Trust announces plans to create a medieval garden at Rosslyn.

APPENDIX TWO
The Story Of The Scottish Templars

THE FOLLOWING IS A chapter from Albert Gallatin Mackey's *The History of Freemasonry*, 1898. Mackey was a 33 degree Freemason from South Carolina. He was a member of St Andrew's Lodge No.10, he served as Grand Secretary of the Grand Lodge of South Carolina and became a Knight Templar in South Carolina Encampment No. 1 in 1842 and Commander in 1844. He was later made the honorary Past Grand Master of the Grand Encampment of Knights Templar of the United States.

Mackey's work cuts through Masonic legend in an attempt to separate the facts from the fiction.

The Story Of The Scottish Templars, Part One, Chapter XXIX

> The story, which connects the Knights Templars with Freemasonry in Scotland, after their return from the Crusades and after the suppression of their Order, forms one of the most interesting and romantic legends

connected with the history of Freemasonry. In its incidents, the elements of history and tradition are so mingled that it is with difficulty that they can be satisfactorily separated. While there are some writers of reputation who accept everything that has been said concerning the connection in the 14th century of the Freemasons of Scotland with the Templars who were then in that kingdom, or who escaped to it as an asylum from the persecutions of the French monarch, as an authentic narrative of events which had actually occurred, there are others who reject the whole as a myth or fable, which has no support in history.

Here, as in most other cases, the middle course appears to be the safest. While there are some portions of the story which are corroborated by historical records, there are others which certainly are without the benefit of such evidence.

In the present chapter I shall endeavor, by a careful and impartial analysis, to separate the conflicting elements and to dissever the historical from the legendary or purely traditional portions of the relation. But it will be necessary, in clearing the way for any faithful investigation of the subject, to glance briefly at the history of those events which were connected with the suppression of the ancient Order of Knights Templars in France in the beginning of the 14th century.

The Templars, on leaving the Holy Land, upon the disastrous termination of the last Crusade and the fall of Acre, had taken temporary refuge in the island of Cyprus. After some vain attempts to regain a footing in Palestine and to renew their contests with the infidels, who were now in complete possession of that country, the Knights had retired from Cyprus and repaired to their different Commanderies in Europe, among which those in France were the most wealthy and the most numerous.

At this period Philip IV, known in history by the sobriquet of Philip the Fair, reigned on the French throne, and Clement V was the Pontiff of the Roman Church. Never before had the crown or the tiara been worn by a more avaricious King or a more treacherous Pope. Clement, when Bishop of Bordeaux, had secured the influence of the French monarch toward his election to the papacy by engaging himself by an oath on the sacrament to perform six conditions imposed upon him by the king, the last of which was reserved as a secret until after his coronation.

This last condition bound him to the extermination of the Templars, an order of whose power Philip was envious and for whose wealth he was avaricious. Pope Clement, who had removed his residence from Rome to Poitiers, summoned the heads of the military orders to appear before him for the purpose, as he deceitfully pretended, of concerting measures for the inauguration of a new Crusade. James de Molay, the Grand Master of the Templars, accordingly repaired to the papal court. While there the King of France preferred a series of charges against the Order, upon which he demanded its suppression and the punishment of its leaders.

The events that subsequently occurred have been well called a black page in the history of the Order.

On the 13th of October, 1307, the Grand Master and one hundred and thirty-nine Knights were arrested in the palace of the Temple, at Paris, and similar arrests were on the same day made in various parts of France. The arrested Templars were thrown into prison and loaded with chains. They were not provided with a sufficiency of food and were refused the consolations of religion. Twenty-six princes and nobles of the court of France appeared as their accusers; and before the judgment of their guilt had been determined by the tribunals, the infamous Pope Clement launched a bull of excommunication against all persons who should give the Templars aid or comfort.

The trials, which ensued, were worse than a farce, only because of their tragic termination. The rack and the torture were unsparingly applied. Those who continued firm in a denial of guilt were condemned either to perpetual imprisonment or to the stake. Addison says that one hundred and thirteen were burnt in Paris and others in Lorraine, in Normandy, at Carcassonne, and at Senlis.

The last scene of the tragedy was enacted on the 11th of March, 1314. James de Molay, the Grand Master of the order, after a close and painful imprisonment of six years and a half, was publicly burnt in front of the Cathedral of Notre Dame, in Paris.

The Order was thus totally suppressed in France and its possessions confiscated. The other monarchs of Europe followed the example of the King of France in abolishing the Order in their dominions; but, in a more merciful spirit, they refrained from inflicting capital punishment upon the Knights.

Outside of France, in all the other kingdoms of Europe, not a Templar was condemned to death. The Order was, however, everywhere suppressed, and a spoil made of its vast possessions, notwithstanding that in every country beyond the influence of the Pope and the King of France its general innocence was sustained. In Portugal, it changed its name to that of the Knights of Christ – everywhere else the Order ceased to exist.

But there are writers who, like Burnes,[1] maintain that the persecution of the Templars in the 14th century did not close the history of the order, but that there has been a succession of Knights Templars from the 12th century down to these days.

Dr. Burnes alluded to the Order of the Temple and the pretended transmission of the powers of de Molay to Larmenius.

With this question and with the authenticity of the so-called 'Charter of Transmission', the topic which we are now about to discuss has no connection, and I shall therefore make no further allusion to it.

It is evident from the influence of natural causes, without the necessity of any historical proof, that after the death of the Grand Master and the sanguinary persecution and suppression of the Order in France, many of the Knights must have sought safety by flight to other countries. It is to their acts in Scotland that we are now to direct our attention.

There are two Legends in existence, which relate to the connection of Templarism with the Freemasonry of Scotland, each of which will require our separate attention.

The first may be called the Legend of Bruce, and the other the Legend of D'Aumont.

In Scotland the possessions of the Order were very extensive. Their Preceptories were scattered in various parts of the country. A papal inquisition was held at Holyrood in 1309 to try and, of course, to condemn the Templars. At this inquisition only two knights, Walter de Clifton, Grand Preceptor of Scotland, and William de Middleton appeared. The others absconded, and as Robert Bruce was then marching to meet and repel the invasion of King Edward of England, the Templars are said to have joined the army of the Scottish monarch.

Thus far the various versions of the Bruce Legend agree, but in the subsequent details there are irreconcilable differences.

According to one version, the Templars distinguished themselves at the Battle of Bannockburn, which was fought on St John the Baptist's Day, 1314, and after the battle a new order was formed called the Royal Order of Scotland, into which the Templars were admitted. But Oliver thinks very justly that the two Orders were unconnected with each other.

Thory says that Robert Bruce, King of Scotland under the title of Robert I, created on the 24th of June, 1314, after the Battle of Bannockburn, the Order of St Andrew of the Thistle, to which was afterward added that of Heredom, for the sake of the Scottish Masons, who had made a part of the thirty thousand men who had fought with a hundred thousand English soldiers. He reserved for himself and his successors the title of Grand Master and founded at Kilwinning the Grand Lodge of the Royal Order of Heredom.[2] The Manual of the Order of the Temple says that the Templars, at the instigation of Robert Bruce, ranged themselves under the banners of this new Order, whose initiations were based on those of the Templars. For this apostasy they were excommunicated by John Mark Larmenius, who is claimed to have been the legitimate successor of de Molay.[3]

None of these statements is susceptible of historical proof.

The Order of Knights of St Andrew or of the Thistle was not created by Bruce in 1314, but by James II in 1440.

There is no evidence that the Templars ever made a part of the Royal Order of Heredom. At this day the two are entirely distinct. Nor is it now considered as a fact that the Royal Order was established by Bruce after the Battle of Bannockburn, although such is the esoteric legend. On the contrary, it is supposed to have been the fabrication of Michael Ramsay in the 18th century. On this subject the remarks of Bro. Lyon, who has made the Masonry of Scotland his especial study, are well worth citation.

'The ritual of the Royal Order of Scotland embraces,' he says, 'what may be termed a spiritualization of the supposed symbols and ceremonies of the Christian architects and builders of primitive times, and so closely associates the sword with the trowel as to lead to the second degree being denominated an order of Masonic knighthood, which its recipients are asked to believe was first conferred on the field of Bannockburn, as a reward for the valor that had been displayed by a body of Templars who aided Bruce in that memorable victory; and that afterward a Grand Lodge of the Order was established by the King at Kilwinning, with the reservation of the office of Grand Master to him and his successors on the Scottish throne. It is further asserted that the Royal Order and the Masonic Fraternity of Kilwinning were governed by the same head. As regards the claims to antiquity, and a royal origin that are advanced in favour of this rite, it is proper to say that modern inquiries have shown these to be purely fabulous. The credence that is given to that part of the legend which associates the Order with the ancient Lodge of Kilwinning is based on the assumed certainty that that Lodge possessed in former times a knowledge of other degrees of Masonry than those of St John. But such is not the case. The fraternity of Kilwinning never at any period practiced or acknowledged other than the Craft degrees; neither does there exist any tradition worthy of the name, local or national, nor has any authentic document yet been discovered that can in the remotest degree be held to identify Robert Bruce with the holding of Masonic Courts, or the institution of a secret society at Kilwinning.' [4]

After such a statement made by a writer who from

his position and opportunities as a Scottish Mason was better enabled to discover proofs, if there were any to be discovered, we may safely conclude that the Bruce and Bannockburn Legend of Scottish Templarism is to be deemed a pure myth, without the slightest historical clement to sustain it.

There is another Legend connecting the Templars in Scotland with Freemasonry, which demands our attention.

It is said in this Legend that in order to escape from the persecution that followed the suppression of the order by the King of France, a certain Templar, named D'Aumont, accompanied by seven others, disguised as mechanics or Operative Masons, fled into Scotland and there secretly founded another order; and to preserve as much as possible the ancient name of Templars as well as to retain the remembrance of and to do honor to the Masons in whose clothing they had disguised themselves when they fled, they adopted the name of Masons in connection with the word Franc, and called themselves Franc Masons. This they did because the old Templars were for the most part Frenchmen, and as the word Franc means both French and Free, when they established themselves in England they called themselves Freemasons. As the ancient order had been originally established for the purpose of rebuilding the Temple of Jerusalem, the new order maintained their bond of union and preserved the memory and the design of their predecessors by building symbolically spiritual Temples consecrated to Virtue, Truth, and Light, and to the honor of the Grand Architect of the Universe.

Such is the Legend as given by a writer in the *Dutch Freemasons' Almanac*, from which it is cited in the London *Freemasons' Quarterly Review*.

Clavel, in his *Picturesque History of Freemasonry*,

gives it more in detail, almost in the words of Von Hund.
See *Freemasons' Quarterly Review*, London, 1843, p. 501,
where the Legend is given in full, as above.

After the execution of de Molay, Peter d'Aumont,
the Provincial Grand Master of Auvergne, with two
Commanders and five Knights, fled for safety and
directed their course towards Scotland, concealing
themselves during their journey under the disguise
of Operative Masons. Having landed on the Scottish
Island of Mull they there met the Grand Commander
George Harris and several other brethren, with whom
they resolved to continue the order. D'Aumont was
elected Grand Master in a Chapter held on St. John's
Day, 1313. To protect themselves from all chance of
discovery and persecution they adopted symbols taken
from architecture and assumed the title of Freemasons.
In 1361 the Grand Master of the Temple transferred the
seat of the order to the old city of Aberdeen, and from
that time it spread, under the guise of Freemasonry,
through Italy, Germany, France, Portugal, Spain, and
other places. It was on this Legend that the Baron Von
Hund founded his Rite of Strict Observance, and with
spurious documents in his possession, he attempted, but
without success, to obtain the sanction of the Congress
of Wilhelmsbad to his dogma that every Freemason was
a Templar.

This doctrine, though making but slow progress in
Germany, was more readily accepted in France, where
already it had been promulgated by the Chapter of
Clermont, into whose Templar system Von Hund had
been initiated.

The Chevalier Ramsay was the real author of the
doctrine of the Templar origin of Freemasonry, and to
him we are really indebted (if the debt have any value)
for the D'Aumont legend. The source whence it sprang is

tolerably satisfactory evidence of its fictitious character. The inventive genius of Ramsay, as exhibited in the fabrications of high degrees and Masonic legends, is well known. Nor, unfortunately for his reputation, can it be doubted that in the composition of his legends he cared but little for the support of history. If his genius, his learning, and his zeal had been consecrated, not to the formation of new Masonic systems, but to a profound investigation of the true origin of the Institution, viewed only from an authentic historical point, it is impossible to say what incalculable benefit would have been delved from his researches. The unproductive desert, which for three-fourths of a century spread over the continent, bearing no fruit except fanciful theories, absurd systems, and unnecessary degrees, would have been occupied in all probability by a race of Masonic scholars whose researches would have been directed to the creation of a genuine history, and much of the labors of our modern iconoclasts would have been spared.

The Masonic scholars of that long period, which began with Ramsay and has hardly yet wholly terminated, assumed for the most part rather the role of poets than of historians. They did not remember the wise saying of Cervantes that the poet may say or sing, not as things have been, but as they ought to have been, while the historian must write of them as they really were, and not as he thinks they ought to have been. And hence we have a mass of traditional rubbish, in which there is a great deal of falsehood with very little truth.

Of this rubbish is the Legend of Peter d'Aumont and his resuscitation of the Order of Knights Templars in Scotland. Without a particle of historical evidence for its support, it has nevertheless exerted a powerful influence on the Masonic organization of even the present day. We find its effects looming out in the most important rites and giving a Templar form to many of the high degrees. And it cannot be doubted that the incorporation of Templarism into the modern Masonic system is mainly to be attributed to ideas suggested by this D'Aumont Legend.

As there appears to be some difficulty in reconciling the supposed heretical opinions of the Templars with the strictly Christian faith of the Scottish Masons, to meet this objection a third legend was invented, in which it was stated that after the abolition of the Templars, the clerical part of the order – that is, the chaplains and priests – united in Scotland to revive it and to transplant it into Freemasonry. But as this legend has not met with many supporters and was never strongly urged, it is scarcely necessary to do more than thus briefly to allude to it.

Much as the Legend of D'Aumont has exerted an influence in mingling together the elements of Templarism and Freemasonry, as we see at the present day in Britain and in America, and in the high degrees formed on the continent of Europe, the dogma of Ramsay, that every Freemason is a Templar, has been utterly repudiated, and the authenticity of the Legend has been rejected by nearly all of the best Masonic scholars.

Dr Burnes, who was a believer in the legitimacy of the French Order of the Temple, as being directly derived from De Molay through Larmenius, and who, therefore, subscribed unhesitatingly to the authenticity of the 'Charter of Transmission', does not hesitate to call Von Hund 'an adventurer' and his Legend of D'Aumont 'a plausible tale.'

Of that part of the Legend which relates to the transfer of the chief seat of the Templars to Aberdeen in Scotland, he says that 'the imposture was soon detected, and it was even discovered that he had himself enticed and initiated the ill-fated Pretender into his fabulous order of chivalry. The delusions on this subject had taken such a hold in Germany, that they were not altogether dispelled until a deputation had actually visited Aberdeen and found amongst the worthy and astonished brethren there no trace either of very ancient Templars or of Freemasonry.' [5]

In this last assertion, however, Burnes is in error, for it is alleged that the Lodge of Aberdeen was instituted in 1541, though, as its more ancient minutes have been, as it is said, destroyed by fire, its present records go no further back than 1670. Bro. Lyon concurs with Burnes in the statement that the Aberdeenians were much surprised when first told that their Lodge was an ancient center of the High Degrees.[6]

William Frederick Wilke, a German writer of great ability, has attacked the credibility of this Scottish Legend with a closeness of reasoning and a vigor of arguments that leave but little room for reply.[7] As he gives the Legend in a slightly different form, it may be interesting to quote it, as well as his course of argument.

'The Legend relates,' he says, 'that after the suppression of the order the head of the Templar clergy, Peter of Boulogne, fled from prison and took refuge with the Commander Hugh, Wildgrave of Salm, and thence escaped to Scotland with Sylvester von Grumbach. Thither the Grand Commander Harris and Marshal D'Aumont had likewise betaken themselves, and these three preserved the secrets of the Order of Templars and transferred them to the Fraternity of Freemasons.' In commenting on this statement Wilke says it is true that Peter of Boulogne fled from prison, but whither he went never has been known. The Wildgrave of Salm never was in prison. But the legendist has entangled himself in saying that Peter left the Wildgrave Hugh and went to Scotland with Sylvester von Grumbach, for Hugh and Sylvester are one and the same person. His title was Count Sylvester Wildgrave, and Grumbach was the designation of his Templar Commandery. Hugh of Salm, also Wildgrave and Commander of Grumbach, never took refuge in Scotland, and after the abolition of the order was made Prebendary of the Cathedral of Mayence.

Wilke thinks that the continuation of the Templar order was attributed to Scotland because the higher degrees of Freemasonry, having reference in a political sense to the Pretender, Edward Stuart, were called Scotch. Scotland is, therefore, the cradle of the higher degrees of Masonry. But here I am inclined to differ from him and am disposed rather to refer the explanation to the circumstance that Ramsay, who was the inventor of the legend and the first fabricator of the high degrees, was a native of Scotland and was born in the neighborhood of Kilwinning. To these degrees he gave the name of Scottish Masonry, in a spirit of nationality, and hence Scotland was supposed to be their birthplace. This is not, however, material to the present argument. Wilke says that Harris and D'Aumont are not mentioned in the real history of the Templars and therefore, if they were Knights, they could not have had any prominence in the order, and neither would have been likely to have been chosen by the fugitive Knights as their Grand Master.

He concludes by saying that of course some of the fugitive Templars found their way to Scotland, and it may be believed that some of the brethren were admitted into the building fraternities, but that is no reason why either the Lodges of builders or the Knights of St John should be considered as a continuation of the Templar order, because they both received Templar fugitives, and the less so as the building guilds were not, like the Templars, composed of chivalrous and free thinking worldlings, but of pious workmen who cherished the pure doctrines of religion.

The anxiety of certain theorists to connect Templarism with Freemasonry has led to the invention of other fables, in which the Hiramic Legend of the Master's degree is replaced by others referring to events said to have occurred in the history of the knightly order. The most ingenious of these is the following:

Some time before the destruction of the Order of Templars, a certain sub-prior of Montfaucon, named Carolus de Monte Carmel, was murdered by three traitors. From the events that accompanied and followed this murder, it is said that an important part of the ritual of Freemasonry has been derived. The assassins of the sub-prior of Montfaucon concealed his body in a grave, and in order to designate the spot, planted a young thorn-tree upon it. The Templars, in searching for the body, had their attention drawn to the spot by the tree, and in that way they discovered his remains. The legend goes on to recite the disinterring of the body and its removal to another grave, in striking similarity to the same events narrated in the Legend of Hiram.

Another theory connects the martyrdom of James de Molay, the last Grand Master of the Templars, with the legend of the third degree, and supposes that in that legend, as now preserved in the Masonic ritual, Hiram has been made to replace De Molay, that the fact of the Templar fusion into Masonry might be concealed. Thus the events, which in the genuine Masonic Legend are referred to Hiram Abif are, in the Templar Legend, made applicable to De Molay; the three assassins are said to be

Pope Clement V, Philip the Fair, King of France, and a Templar named Naffodei, who betrayed the order. They have even attempted to explain the mystical search for the body by the invention of a fable that on the night after De Molay had been burnt at the stake, certain knights diligently sought for his remains amongst the ashes, but could find only some bones to which the flesh, though scorched, still adhered, but which it left immediately upon their being handled; and in this way they explain the origin of the substitute word, according to the mistranslation too generally accepted.

Nothing could more clearly show the absurdity of the legend than this adoption of a popular interpretation of the meaning of this word, made by someone utterly ignorant of the Hebrew language. The word, as is now well known to all scholars, has a totally different signification.

But it is scarcely necessary to look to so unessential a part of the narrative for proof that the whole legend of the connection of Templarism with Freemasonry is irreconcilable with the facts of history.

The Legend of Bruce and Bannockburn has already been disposed of. The story has no historical foundation.

The other Legend, that makes D'Aumont and his companions founders of the Masonic Order in Scotland by amalgamating the knights with the fraternity of builders, is equally devoid of an historical basis. But, besides, there is a feature of improbability if not of impossibility about it. The Knights Templars were an aristocratic order composed of highborn gentlemen who had embraced the soldier's life as their vocation, and who were governed by the customs of chivalry. In those days there was a much wider line of demarcation drawn between the various casts of society than exists at the present day. The 'belted knight' was at the top of the social scale, the mechanic at the bottom.

It is therefore almost impossible to believe that because their order had been suppressed, these proud soldiers of the Cross, whose military life had unfitted them for any other pursuit except that of arms, would have thrown aside their swords and their spurs and assumed the trowel; with the use of this implement and all the mysteries of the builder's craft they were wholly unacquainted. To have become Operative Masons, they must have at once abandoned all the prejudices of social life in which they had been educated.

That a Knight Templar would have gone into some religious house as a retreat from the world whose usage of his Order had disgusted him, or taken refuge in some other chivalric order, might reasonably happen, as was actually the case. But that these knights would have willingly transformed themselves into stonemasons and daily workmen is a supposition too absurd to extort belief even from the most credulous.

We may then say that those legendists who have sought by their own invented traditions to trace the origin of Freemasonry to Templarism, or to establish any close connection between the two institutions, have failed in their object. They have attempted to write a history, but they have scarcely succeeded in composing a plausible romance.

Notes:

1 *Sketch of the History of the Knights Templars* by James Burnes, LL.D., F.R.S., etc., London, 1840, p. 39.

2 *Acta Latomorum*, tome i, p. 6.

3 *Manuel des Chevaliers de l'Ordre du Temple*, p. 8.

4 *History of the Lodge of Edinburgh* by David Murray Lyon, ch. xxxii, p. 307.

5 *Sketch of the History of the Knights Templars*, p. 71.

6 *History of the Lodge of Edinburgh*, p. 420.

7 In his *Geschichte des Tempelherren's Orders*. I have not been able to obtain the work, but I have availed myself of an excellent analysis of it in *Findel's History of Freemasonry*, Lyon's Translation.

APPENDIX THREE
The Templar Trial In Scotland

IT HAS BEEN SUGGESTED that Scotland offered a safe haven to Templar knights who escaped persecution in France – and that they were never brought to trial in Scotland. Pseudo-histories claim that the St Clairs of Rosslyn protected Templar knights and that Sir William St Clair was in fact a Grand Master of the Knights Templar.

In reality, the Templars in Scotland were put on trial at the Abbey of Holyrood in Edinburgh in 1309. William, the Bishop of St Andrews, and a Master John of Solerius, clerk to Pope Clement V, presided over the trial.

The following Latin extracts from the original trial documents and complete English translation of the Holyrood trial show that the Templar Order was brought to trial in Scotland, and that the St Clairs of Rosslyn testified against the Templars. To our knowledge an English translation of the trial of the Knights Templar in Scotland has never been published before.

PROCESSUS FACTUS CONTRA TEMPLARIOS IN SCOTIA 1309

Hæc inquisitio facta per reverendum in Christo Patrem Dominum Willielmum, Dei gratia, Sancti Andreæ Episcopum, et Magistrum Johannem de Solerio, Domini Papæ clericum, contra ordinem Templariorum, et duos fraters ipsius ordinis inderius nominatos, solos in regno Scotiæ in suo habitu existents, de mandato Domini nostril Sanctissimi Domini Clementis, divina providential Papæ Quinti, in Abbatia Sanctæ Crucis de Edeneburgh, regni et episcopatus prædicti, 15 cal. mensis Decembris, Anno Gratiæ M.CCC.IX.

VICESIMUS SEXTUS AD 34 TESTES – Item domini Henricus de Leth, rector ecclesiæ de Restalrik, Walterus, rector ecclesiæ de Malavilla, Alanus, rector ecclesiæ de Stryvelyn, Nicolaus, vicarious de Laswald, Willielmus, capellanus de Stenton, Johannes, capellanus Hospitalis Sancti Leonardi prope Edeneburgh, Alanus de Theryngton, Johannes de Lyberton, Richardus de Anandia, Johannes de Clerkynton, et Walterus de Halbourn, capellani; vicini, et servitors Templariorum Scotiæ, et domus suæ de Blancrodoks, jurati. etc. dixerunt idem, quod Abbas de Dunfermelyn prædictus.

TRICESIMUS QUINTUS AD 40 TESTES – Item Willielmus de Preston, et Johannes de Wyggemer, senior, Willielmus de Sancto Claro, Adam Halybourtoun, Michæl Clenk, et Matthæus Constabularius, domicelli, jurati, et diligenter examinati super præmissis . . .

The Case Against The Templars In Scotland

This inquiry was set up by William, Reverend Father and Lord in Christ, by the grace of God, Bishop of Saint Andrews; and

Master John of Solerius, clerk to the Lord Pope; against the order of the Templars, and particularly against two brothers of that order, named below: the only two in their order that exist in the kingdom of Scotland. It is set up on the instructions of Lord Clement 5th, our most holy Master, by Divine Providence the Pope; and took place in the Abbey of Holy Rood in Edinburgh in the aforesaid Kingdom and Diocese, on 15 December AD 1309.

First Witness

First Brother Walter of Clifton was sworn in after placing his hand on the Holy Gospels. He was asked what nation he came from and he replied from England. Then he was asked what Order he belonged to and he replied to the Knights Templar. He was asked how many years he had been a member of the said Order and he replied for ten years last All Saints Day. Then he was asked where he had received the habit of the same Order and he replied that it was at Temple Bruer in Lincolnshire in England. He was asked who received him into the said Order and gave him his habit and he said it was Father William of More from Yorkshire, then and now Master of the said Order in England and Scotland. He was asked from which Master the brothers in the kingdom of Scotland received the observances of their Order and he replied that it was from the Master in England. When asked from whom the Master in England received the observances of his Order, he replied that it was from the senior Master of the Order of the Temple, established in Jerusalem, namely from the Master of Cyprus, and according to the statutes and observances of his General Chapter. He was asked whether the said Grand Master was in the habit of visiting the Order, or seeing to it that the Order of the Knights Templar in the kingdom of England and the members of that Order were visited by someone, and he said yes. He was asked what method was observed in his reception into the habit of the aforesaid Order and he replied that when the said Grand Master of the Order held his Chapter at Bruer in Lincolnshire the said brother Walter requested admission to the habit of that Order. The brothers who were already in existence there, namely Thomas of Toulouse, William of Ford, John of Faversham, Radulph, Prior of the London Temple, Henry of Wole, John of Hartil and John of Hufflet, from the Kingdom of England, and many other brothers of that Order, who have now left this world, these men said to him: 'This is a great thing that you seek, seeking entry into our religion, and giving up your own will, and binding yourself to obedience to the superiors of this Order. Who has ever sought the habit and membership of this Order more earnestly?' Then he was led into the Master's room, where the same men held their Chapter and again he knelt down and put his hands together and asked for the habit and membership of the Order. Then the said Master and the aforesaid brothers asked him to reply to some questions they would ask: whether he was bound by any other reason or obligation, or promised to any woman in marriage, or prevented from keeping his vows by any secret physical weakness or any other impediment, and he said no. And then the said Master asked the brothers standing round, 'Do you give your consent to the reception of Brother Walter?' and they replied unanimously, 'Yes.' Then the said Master and the aforesaid brothers standing round received the said Brother Walter in this way: namely: the said Brother Walter knelt down and put his hands together and promised that he would be the servant of the Master and the brothers of the Order for ever, for the defence of the lands in the East. Then the said Master stood up and took from a [capillanus? unshaven?] brother of the Order the book of the Gospels on which a cross was drawn. Walter put his hands on the book and the cross and promised with an oath to God and the Blessed Virgin Mary to be for ever chaste, obedient and to live without property. Then the Master gave him his mantle and put a hat upon his head and permitted him a kiss on the mouth. Then he made him sit upon the ground, enjoining him from then on to sleep in his shirt, trousers and linen boots, girded with one cord over the shirt and never to seek hospitality in a house where a woman lay in childbirth, nor to be present at a wedding, nor at the purification of a woman. And he instructed and informed him on a number of matters. When asked if any secular clerk or any brothers of another order were present at his reception, he said no, and that it was not the custom for them to be present at the reception of other brothers of the Order of the Templars. He knew this or had heard it said.

Then he was asked whether the observances of the Order, the reception of a brother and the profession of vows was the same throughout the world, and he said yes, as he believed and had heard tell from other brothers of the Order. However, he was certain only of what he saw in England in his own reception and in the reception of the brothers of his Order at which he had been present, but he could not remember their names. He was asked whether since he had been in the Order he had seen any visitor of his Order in France come and visit in England, and he said yes, namely Hugo Perraut, but he had not seen him hold a Chapter, but he believed and had been told that he had held a Chapter there, and had also visited. He was asked where he had spent his time since he had been in the Order and he replied that he was at Balintrodo in Scotland for three years, and at Temple Newsom in England for three years, and in London for one year, and at Temple Rockley and at Aslakeby for three years.

Then he was asked whether, because of the scandal that had arisen against the Order of the Temple, some brothers had given up their habit and left the Order because of this fear, and he said yes, Brother Thomas Toccus and Brother John of Huseflete, who had been Preceptor at Balintrodo in Scotland for two years. They were the two brothers mentioned who were from England. Then he was questioned thoroughly, in detail and word for word about each and every article included in the Papal Bull. He replied to all the articles with a simple no, but with one exception: he said that the Grand Master of the Order and the other Masters, Preceptors and Visitors, inferior brothers both ordained and lay could give absolution to the brothers who were subject to them from all sins except murder and laying violent hands on a priest. He said that the said Grand Master had this power from the grace of the Lord Pope and had received it long ago. He also said that he himself had seen at two Chapters celebrated in Dinesley in England that the aforesaid Master gave a general absolution to all the brothers in his area with the authority which he had, signing them with the sign of the Cross with his hand. He also said that there was considerable suspicion, and had been for a long time, because of the secret profession of vows and reception of brothers of the Order. He also said that in his aforesaid reception they had made him swear that he would never leave the Order, and he thought that all the others did the same. He also said that they didn't have a novitiate year in his Order, but that when someone was received he was considered to have taken life vows immediately. When he was asked who was the most senior Preceptor in his Order in the kingdom of Scotland, he said that he was, and that he was in charge of the whole of his Order there, and there were only two brothers there, himself and his associate mentioned below.

Second Witness

Next William Middleton, wearing the habit of the order of the Knights Templar, born near Newcastle in England, as he asserted. He was sworn in with his hand on the Holy Gospels and asked where he had been received into the said Order. He replied at Newsom near York on St Susanna the Virgin's day seven years ago last Autumn. Then he was asked who received him into the said Order and he said Brother Brian le Jay, then Master of his Order in England, in the presence of Brother Thomas of Toulouse, now still alive and wearing the habit, Brother John of Husflete, Brother Thomas Toccus and Brother John of Caraton. These men have now left the Order and fled at once overseas as he had heard said. Many others were there, who have now left this world. Then he was asked in which houses of his Order he had spent his life since the time of his aforesaid reception. He replied that it was in England in different places for five years, then in Scotland at Maryculter, and at Balintrodo for two years, and in Northumbria alternately in different places. Then he was asked whether he had seen anyone received into the habit of the Order in the kingdom of Scotland and he said no. Then he was asked about the rules and observances of his Order in Scotland, and he said that they received the same from the Master of England and the Master of England received them from the Master of France and the Master of France from the Master of Cyprus, as he had heard said. For this reason he thought that the manner of receiving and professing the brothers of his Order was the same all over the world. Then he was asked whether the Grand Master of the whole of his Order was in the habit of visiting or sending a visitor to his Order and the persons in it. He said yes, because he had seen Brother Hugo Perraut, who had come from France to visit England twice during his time, and on the one occasion this man had been with him in England and the other time he had not seen him because he himself had been then in Scotland, but he had heard it said that he had visited the Order in England. Then he said that the senior Master in England was in the habit of going to the Chapter in France every five years, as, so he said, he had always heard from the brothers; and when the same Brother Hugo Perraut visited England for the aforesaid second time Brother William of More, then the senior Master of England, had gone to the Grand Master over the seas, as to the Superior of his whole Order; then in his absence the said Brother Hugo removed some English preceptors and appointed others in their place. Then he was questioned thoroughly and examined in detail about all the questions previously put to the aforesaid Walter, his associate, and about each article contained in the Papal Bulls repeated to him word for word. He replied the same to everything as Brother Walter, with this addition: that he had been forbidden during his reception by the said Master who received him into the Order from accepting any service from women, not even water for washing his hands. And he said that he had seen and heard the Grand Master of his Order in England who was not a priest absolving brothers of his Order with these words: 'By the authority of God, and the blessed Peter and of the Lord Pope, committed to us, we absolve you of such and such a sin.' In addition he committed his authority to [ordain?] a brother priest of the same Order. However he said he thought that the [*casus*? cases, misfortunes?] of the Lord Pope were understood to be excepted.

Witnesses Summoned And Examined On This Matter Follow

First Witness
Lord Hugo, Abbot of Dunfermline, was sworn in as a witness and asked about the status and behaviour of the aforesaid brothers already examined and of other brothers of their Order, and all about the articles contained in the Papal Bull. He said that he had never known for certain, but had heard it said that they had done certain improper things. Nevertheless he had an unfavourable suspicion about them and always had had, because of the secret manner of the reception and profession of their brothers and because the celebration of their Chapter happened at night. Then he said that he thought that the observances and rules were the same everywhere in the whole Order. He thought this was so because the Visitor from France used to visit their Order in England and the English Visitor their Order in Scotland. Everywhere the brothers of the Order used to meet in their General Chapter and accordingly it seemed that the secrets of the Order were communicated. He also said that he had never heard tell of any brother of the said Order being received in Scotland, and so for this reason their secrets could not be known there.

Second Witness And Other Witnesses
Lord Elias, Abbot of Holy Rood in Edinburgh, Lord Gervasius of Newbattle, Master Robert of Kydlaw, and Brother Patrick, Prior of the Preaching Brothers of Edinburgh, were sworn in

and examined and in almost everything they agreed with Hugo, Abbot of Dunfermline.

Sixth Witness
Father Andrew of Douraid, [Guardian] of the lesser brothers of Haddington, was sworn in and questioned about the above, and he said the same as the aforesaid Lord Abbot of Dunfermline, with this addition: that he said he did not know that the brothers of the said Order of the Knights Templar made confessions to lesser brothers or preachers or other secular presbyters.

Seventh Witness
Brother Adam of Kenton, etc. agreed in everything with Andrew of Douraid.

Eighth Witness
Brother Adam of Wedale, a member of Newbattle Abbey, was sworn in and questioned about the above, and he said the same as the aforesaid Lord Abbot of Dunfermline, with this addition: that the Templars were criticised time and again for their unjust [seizures?] for they want to take for themselves indiscriminately the property and goods of their neighbours, by fair means or foul, and also because they do not offer hospitality except to the rich and powerful, [through fear that they might do acts of charity?].

Ninth And Three Other Witnesses
Then Brothers John of Bures, monk of the same Abbey, John of Munphut, Canon of Holy Rood in Edinburgh, Gilbert of Haddington, Canon of Holy Rood and Adam of Win, monk of Dunfermline, were sworn in etc. and they said the same as the aforesaid Adam of Wedale.

Thirteenth Witness
Then Master John of Lyndsey, Rector of the Church of Rachon

was sworn in etc. and he said the same as the aforesaid Abbot of Dunfermline.

Fourteenth Witness

Also Lord Robert, chaplain of Lyston, a neighbour of the Templars of Scotland, was sworn in on the subject of the above, and he said the same as the aforesaid Abbot of Dunfermline; with this addition; that it was common knowledge that the Templars in Scotland, and others of the same Order, are not completely exempt from offences confessed to their superiors in the assembly; and that this was because of the identity of their statutes and observances and of the mutual visitation. He also said he had never heard for certain or seen where any brother of the Temple was buried, or that any died a natural death. He also said that they were always against the Church, as far as they could, and that the general voice and reputation supported this.

Fifteenth Witness To Twenty-fifth

Also Lord Henry of Leith, Rector of the Church of Restalrig, Walter, Rector of the Church at Malavilla, Alan, Rector of the Church at Strivelin, Nicolas, Vicar of Lasswade, William, Chaplain of Stenton, John, Chaplain of the Hospital of St Leonard, near Edinburgh, Alan of Thrington, John of Liberton, Richard of Anandia, John of Clerkinton, and Walter of Halbourn, Chaplains. All of these were neighbours and servants of the Templars of Scotland, and of their house at Blancrodoks. They were sworn in, etc. They said the same as the aforesaid Abbot of Dunfermline.

Twenty-sixth Witness To Thirty-fourth

Also Lord Henry of St Clare, Fergus Marescal, William of Ramsay, Hugo of Rydale, William Bisset, Alan of Waldingford, Roger of Sutton, William of Disseford, and William [the president?] were sworn in and examined; and they agreed with the others above.

Thirty-fifth To Fortieth Witnesses

Also William of Preston, and John of Wyggemer, senior, William of St Clare, Adam Haliburton. Michael Clenk, and Matthew Constabularius, squires, were sworn in and carefully examined about the above. They said that they could say nothing about the characters of the said lord brothers, nor about the reception of the brothers of the said Order or about their profession of vows, because they had never seen anyone received into the brotherhood, either in Scotland or elsewhere, because they always did that secretly. For that reason both they themselves and their fathers had a bad opinion of the aforesaid Order and the brothers of it. This was particularly so when they saw certain other Religious beings publicly received and professed, and inviting friends, parents and neighbours and having great ceremonies and celebrations. They also said, as they firmly believed to be the case, that the reception and profession of the brothers was the same throughout the whole world and so were the statutes and observances; that everywhere in the world there were visitations of their superiors; and that brothers were sent to their chapters from everywhere. For this reason they believed that they all shared their secrets. Consequently it seemed that they were all entangled in the same accusations. They also said that they were not willing to offer hospitality to the poor, but through fear they welcomed only the rich and powerful. They were very anxious to acquire the property of others for their Order, by fair means or foul. They also said what their fathers had asserted, that if the Templars had been faithful Christians they would in no way have lost the Holy Land.

Forty-first Witness

John Thyng, who was a servant of the Templars for seventeen years in Scotland, was sworn in etc. and he said the same as the squires examined immediately before; with this addition that he said he had seen many lay brothers of the Templars indiscriminately absolving all who had been excommunicated, saying that they had authority in this from the highest Lord Pontiff. He also said that whether by day or by night they held their chapters so secretly that access to them was allowed to no one. His neighbours agreed with this witness in everything; and also those who cultivated the lands of the Templars, whose names are subscribed below: namely Adam Faber, Alan Pay, Michael Fyder, Thomas Stagger, Thomas Tenant, John Sergeant, Adam Lay, and John Gruub. This inquiry could not be more official because of enemy attack and the constant expectation of war.

And as testimony to the evidence of the above, Lord William, reverend Father in Christ, by divine providence Bishop of St Andrews, and the aforesaid Master John of Solerius set their seals to this inquiry, and with the same seals they close this same inquiry under my signature. As surer testimony of them, I, William Spottiswood, who was present at the aforesaid inquiry with the authority of the imperial notary, on the day, year and in the place aforesaid and with the aforesaid witnesses being present, have set my accustomed sign to the same as required, and have written it with my own hand as asked.

APPENDIX FOUR
Scottish Legends And Border Ballads

IT IS CLEAR THAT the legends of Rosslyn Chapel and Castle owe much to the work of Sir Walter Scott. Scott included local tales of Rosslyn in his poems and stories. It appears that he also contributed to local legends and proved an inspiration to the poets, writers and storytellers that followed him.

Characters from Borders legends and folk tales became particularly connected with the legends of Rosslyn's White Lady. The evil sorcerer Lord Soulis of Hermitage Castle was said to have enchanted the young maiden. Thomas the Rhymer, the Border prophet, used the magical spell book of Michael Scott the wizard to destroy Lord Soulis.

The following extracts illustrate the legends of Thomas, Lord Soulis, Michael Scott and Merlin the Wyld.

Extract from Letter IV, Letters on Demonology and Witchcraft, Sir Walter Scott

. . . the popular system of the Celts easily received the northern admixture of Drows and Duergar, which gave the belief, perhaps, a darker colouring than originally belonged to the British fairyland. It was from the same source also, in all probability, that additional legends were obtained of a gigantic and malignant female, the Hecate of this mythology, who rode on the storm and marshalled the rambling host of wanderers under her grim banner. This hag (in all respects the reverse of the Mab or Titania of the Celtic creed) was called Nicneven in that later system which blended the faith of the Celts and of the Goths on this subject. The great Scottish poet Dunbar has made a spirited description of this Hecate riding at the head of witches and good neighbours (fairies, namely), sorceresses and elves, indifferently, upon the ghostly eve of All-Hallow Mass. In Italy we hear of the hags arraying themselves under the orders of Diana (in her triple character of Hecate, doubtless) and Herodias, who were the joint leaders of their choir. But we return to the more simple fairy belief, as entertained by the Celts before they were conquered by the Saxons.

Of these early times we can know little; but it is singular to remark what light the traditions of Scotland throw upon the poetry of the Britons of Cumberland, then called Reged. Merlin Wyllt, or the wild, is mentioned by both; and that renowned wizard, the son of an elf or fairy, with King Arthur, the dubious champion of Britain at that early period, were both said by tradition to have been abstracted by the fairies, and to have vanished without having suffered death, just at the time when it was supposed that the magic of the wizard and the celebrated sword of the monarch, which had done so much to preserve British independence, could no longer avert the impending ruin. It may be conjectured that there was a desire on the part of Arthur or his surviving champions to conceal his having received a mortal wound in the fatal battle of Camlan; and to that we owe the wild and beautiful incident so finely versified by Bishop Percy, in which, in token of his renouncing in future the use of arms, the monarch sends his attendant, sole survivor of the field, to throw his sword Excalibar into the lake hard by. Twice eluding the request, the esquire at last complied, and threw the far-famed weapon into the lonely mere. A hand and arm arose from the water and caught Excalibar by the hilt, flourished it thrice, and then sank into the lake. The astonished messenger returned to his master to tell him the marvels he had seen, but he only saw a boat at a distance push from the land, and heard shrieks of females in agony:

And whether the king was there or not
He never knew, he never colde
For never since that doleful day
Was British Arthur seen on molde.

The circumstances attending the disappearance of Merlin would probably be found as imaginative as those of Arthur's removal, but they cannot be recovered; and what is singular enough, circumstances which originally belonged to the history of this famous bard, said to be the son of the Demon himself, have been transferred to a later poet, and surely one of scarce inferior name, Thomas of Erceldoune. The legend was supposed to be only preserved among the inhabitants of his native valleys, but a copy as old as the reign of Henry VII has been recovered. The story is interesting and beautifully told, and, as one of the oldest fairy legends, may well be quoted in this place.

Thomas of Erceldoune, in Lauderdale, called the Rhymer, on account of his producing a poetical romance on the subject of Tristrem and Yseult, which is curious as the earliest specimen of English verse known to exist, flourished in the reign of Alexander III of Scotland. Like other men of talent of the period, Thomas was suspected of magic. He was said also to have the gift of prophecy, which was accounted for in the following peculiar manner, referring entirely to the elfin superstition: As True Thomas (we give him the epithet by anticipation) lay on Huntly Bank, a place on the descent of the Eildon Hills, which raise their triple crest above the celebrated Monastery of Melrose, he saw a lady so extremely beautiful that he imagined it must be the Virgin Mary herself. Her appointments, however, were rather those of an Amazon or goddess of the woods. Her steed was of the highest beauty and spirit, and at his mane hung thirty silver bells and nine, which made music to the wind as she paced along. Her saddle was of royal bone (ivory), laid over with orfeverie, i.e., goldsmith's work. Her stirrups, her dress, all corresponded with her extreme beauty and the magnificence of her array. The fair huntress had her bow in her hand, and her arrows at her belt. She led three greyhounds in a leash, and three raches, or hounds of scent, followed her closely. She rejected and disclaimed the homage which Thomas desired to pay to her; so that, passing from one extremity to the other, Thomas became as bold as he had at first been humble. The lady warns him that he must become her slave if he should prosecute his suit towards her in the manner he proposes. Before their interview terminates, the

appearance of the beautiful lady is changed into that of
the most hideous hag in existence. One side is blighted
and wasted, as if by palsy; one eye drops from her
head; her colour, as clear as the virgin silver, is now of
a dun leaden hue. A witch from the spital or almshouse
would have been a goddess in comparison to the
late beautiful huntress. Hideous as she was, Thomas's
irregular desires had placed him under the control of
this hag, and when she bade him take leave of sun, and
of the leaf that grew on tree, he felt himself under the
necessity of obeying her. A cavern received them, in
which, following his frightful guide, he for three days
travelled in darkness, sometimes hearing the booming
of a distant ocean, sometimes walking through rivers of
blood, which crossed their subterranean path. At length
they emerged into daylight, in a most beautiful orchard.
Thomas, almost fainting for want of food, stretches out
his hand towards the goodly fruit which hangs around
him, but is forbidden by his conductress, who informs
him these are the fatal apples which were the cause of
the fall of man. He perceives also that his guide had no
sooner entered this mysterious ground, and breathed
its magic air, than she was revived in beauty, equipage,
and splendour, as fair, or fairer, than he had first seen
her on the mountain. She then commands him to lay
his head upon her knee, and proceeds to explain to him
the character of the country. 'Yonder right-hand path,'
she says, 'conveys the spirits of the blessed to Paradise;
yon downward and well-worn way leads sinful souls to
the place of everlasting punishment; the third road, by
yonder dark brake, conducts to the milder place of pain
from which prayer and mass may release offenders. But
see you yet a fourth road, sweeping along the plain to
yonder splendid castle? Yonder is the road to Elfland,
to which we are now bound. The lord of the castle is

king of the country, and I am his queen. But, Thomas, I would rather be drawn with wild horses, than he should know what hath passed between you and me. Therefore, when we enter yonder castle, observe strict silence, and answer no question that is asked at you, and I will account for your silence by saying I took your speech when I brought you from middle earth.'

Having thus instructed her lover, they journeyed on to the castle, and entering by the kitchen, found themselves in the midst of such a festive scene as might become the mansion of a great feudal lord or prince. Thirty carcases of deer were lying on the massive kitchen board, under the hands of numerous cooks, who toiled to cut them up and dress them, while the gigantic greyhounds which had taken the spoil lay lapping the blood, and enjoying the sight of the slain game. They came next to the royal hall, where the king received his loving consort without censure or suspicion. Knights and ladies, dancing by threes (reels perhaps), occupied the floor of the hall, and Thomas, the fatigues of his journey from the Eildon hills forgotten, went forward and joined in the revelry. After a period, however, which seemed to him a very short one, the queen spoke with him apart, and bade him prepare to return to his own country. 'Now,' said the queen, 'how long think you that you have been here?'

'Certes, fair lady,' answered Thomas, 'not above these seven days.'

'You are deceived,' answered the queen, 'you have been seven years in this castle, and it is full time you were gone. Know, Thomas, that the fiend of hell will come to this castle tomorrow to demand his tribute, and so handsome a man as you will attract his eye. For all the world would I not suffer you to be betrayed to such a fate; therefore up, and let us be going.' This terrible news reconciled Thomas to his departure from Elfin land, and the queen was not long in placing him upon Huntly bank, where the birds were singing. She took a tender leave of him, and to ensure his reputation, bestowed on him the tongue which could not lie. Thomas in vain objected to this inconvenient and involuntary adhesion to veracity, which would make him, as he thought, unfit for church or for market, for kings court or for lady's bower. But all his remonstrances were disregarded by the lady, and Thomas the Rhymer, whenever the discourse turned on the future, gained the credit of a prophet whether he would or not, for he could say nothing but what was sure to come to pass. It is plain that had Thomas been a legislator instead or a poet, we have here the story of Numa and Egeria. Thomas remained several years in his own tower near Erceldoune, and enjoyed the fame of his predictions, several of which are current among the country people to this day. At length, as the prophet was entertaining the Earl of March in his dwelling, a cry of astonishment arose in the village, on the appearance of a hart and hind, which left the forest and, contrary to their shy nature, came quietly onward, traversing the village towards the dwelling of Thomas. The prophet instantly rose from the board; and, acknowledging the prodigy as the summons of his fate, he accompanied the hart and hind into the forest, and though occasionally seen by individuals to whom he has chosen to show himself, has never again mixed familiarly with mankind.

Thomas of Erceldoune, during his retirement, has been supposed, from time to time, to be levying forces to take the field in some crisis of his country's fate. The story has often been told of a daring horse-jockey having sold a black horse to a man of venerable and antique appearance, who appointed the remarkable hillock upon Eildon hills, called the Lucken-hare, as the place where, at twelve o'clock at night, he should receive the price. He came, his money was paid in ancient coin, and he was invited by his customer to view his residence. The trader in horses followed his guide in the deepest astonishment through several long ranges of stalls, in each of which a horse stood motionless, while an armed warrior lay equally still at the charger's feet. 'All these men,' said the wizard in a whisper, 'will awaken at the battle of Sheriffmoor.' At the extremity of this extraordinary depôt hung a sword and a horn, which the prophet pointed out to the horse-dealer as containing the means of dissolving the spell. The man in confusion took the horn, and attempted to wind it. The horses instantly started in their stalls, stamped, and shook their bridles, the men arose and clashed their armour, and the mortal, terrified at the tumult he had excited, dropped the horn from his hand. A voice like that of a giant, louder even than the tumult around, pronounced these words:

Woe to the coward that ever he was born,
That did not draw the sword before he blew
the horn !

A whirlwind expelled the horse-dealer from the cavern, the entrance to which he could never again find. A moral might be perhaps extracted from the legend – namely, that it is best to be armed against danger before bidding it defiance. But it is a circumstance worth notice, that although this edition of the tale is limited to the year 1715, by the very mention of the Sheriffmoor, yet a similar story appears to have been current during the reign of Queen Elizabeth, which is given by Reginald Scot. The narrative is edifying as peculiarly illustrative of the mode of marring a curious tale in telling it, which was one of the virtues professed by Caius when he hired himself to King Lear. Reginald Scot, incredulous on the subject of witchcraft, seems to have given some weight to the belief of those who thought that the spirits of famous men do, after death, take up some particular habitations near cities, towns, and countries, and act as tutelary and guardian spirits to the places which they loved while in the flesh.

'But more particularly to illustrate this conjecture,' says he, 'I could name a person who hath lately appeared thrice since his decease, at least some ghostly being or other that calls itself by the name of such a person who was dead above a hundred years ago, and was in his lifetime accounted as a prophet or predicter by the assistance of sublunary spirits; and now, at his appearance, did also give strange predictions respecting famine and plenty, war and bloodshed, and the end of the world. By the information of the person that had communication with him, the last of his appearances was in the following manner: 'I had been,' said he, 'to sell a horse at the next market town, but not attaining my price, as I returned home I met this man, who began to be familiar with me, asking what news, and how affairs moved through the country. I answered as I thought fit; withal, I told him of my horse, whom he began to cheapen, and proceeded with me so far that the price was agreed upon. So he turned back with me, and told me that if I would go along with him I should receive my money. On our way we went, I upon my horse, and he on another milk-white beast. After much travel I asked him where he dwelt and what his name was. He told me that his dwelling was a mile off, at a place called Farran, of which place I had never heard, though I knew all the country round about. He also told me that he himself was that person of the family of Learmonths so much spoken of as a prophet. At which I began to be somewhat fearful, perceiving we were on a road which I never had been on before, which increased my fear and amazement more. Well, on we went till he brought me under ground, I knew not how, into the presence of a beautiful woman, who paid the money without a word speaking. He conducted me out again through a large and long entry, where I saw above six hundred men in armour laid prostrate on the ground as if asleep. At last I found myself in the open field by the help of the moonlight, in the very place where I first met him, and made a shift to get home by three in the morning. But the money I had received was just double of what I esteemed it when the woman paid me, of which at this instant I have several pieces to show, consisting of nine pennies, thirteen pence-halfpennies,' &c. It is a great pity that this horse-dealer, having specimens of the fairy coin, of a quality more permanent than usual, had not favoured us with an account of an impress valuable to medallists. It is not the less edifying, as we are deprived of the more picturesque parts of the story, to learn that Thomas's payment was as faithful as his prophecies. The beautiful lady who bore the purse must have been undoubtedly the Fairy Queen, whose affection, though, like that of his own heroine Yseult, we cannot term it altogether laudable, seems yet to have borne a faithful and firm character.

I have dwelt at some length on the story of Thomas the Rhymer, as the oldest tradition of the kind which has reached us in detail, and as pretending to show the fate of the first Scottish poet, whose existence, and its date, are established both by history and records; and who, if we consider him as writing in the Anglo-Norman language, was certainly one among the earliest of its versifiers. But the legend is still more curious, from

its being the first and most distinguished instance of a
man alleged to have obtained supernatural knowledge
by means of the fairies.

Sir Walter Scott, The Lay of the Last Minstrel, Canto II

Sir Walter Scott recounts the Borders legend that Michael Scott
was buried with his book of magic near a high altar at Melrose
Abbey. His grave slab, inscribed with a cross, can still be found
within the Abbey ruins:

> I buried him on St Michael's night,
> When the bell toll'd one, and the moon was bright,
> And I dug his chamber among the dead,
> When the floor of the chancel was stained red,
> That his patron's cross may over him wave,
> And scare the fiends from the Wizard's grave.
>
> In these far climes it was my lot
> To meet the wondrous Michael Scott,
> A wizard, of such dreaded fame,
> Than when, in Salmanca's cave,
> Him listed his magic wand to wave,
> The bells would ring in Notre Dame!
> Some of his skill he taught to me;
> And Warrior, I could say to thee
> The words that cleft Eildon hills in three,
> And bridled the Tweed with a curb of stone:
> But to speak them were a deadly sin;
> And for having but thought them my heart within,
> A treble penance must be done.
>
> When Michael lay on his dying bed,
> His conscience was awakened:
> He bethought him of his sinful deed,

And he gave me a sign to come with speed;
I was in Spain when the morning rose,
But I stood by his bed ere evening close.
The words may not again be said,
That he spoke to me, on death-bed laid;
They would rend they Abbay's massy nave,
And pile it in heaps above his grave.

I swore to bury his Mighty Book,
That never mortal might therein look;
And never to tell where it was hid,
Save at his Chief of Branksome's need:
And when that need was past and o'er,
Again the volume to restore.
I buried him on St Michael's night,
When the bell toll'd one, and the moon was bright,
And I dug his chamber among the dead,
When the floor of the chancel was stained red,
That his patron's cross might over him wave,
And scare the fiends from the Wizard's grave.

It was a night of woe and dread,
When Michael in the tomb I laid!
Strange sounds along the chancel pass'd,
The banners waved without a blast;
— Still spoke the Monk, when the bell toll'd one! —
'I tell you, that a braver man
Than William of Deloraine, good at need,
Against a foe ne'er spurr'd a steed;
Yet somewhat was he chill'd with dread,
And his hair did bristle upon his head.

Lo, Warrior! Now, the Cross of Red
Points to the grave of the mighty dead;
Within it burns a wondrous light,

To chase the spirits that love the night:
That lamp shall burn unquenchably,
Until the eternal doom shall be.' –
Slowly moved the Monk to the broad flagstone,
Which the bloody Cross was traced upon:
He pointed to a secret nook;
An iron bar the Warrior took;
And the Monk made a sign with his wither'd hand,
The grave's huge portal to expand.

The following extract relates the tale of Thomas the Rhymer and Canobie Dick.

Sir Walter Scott, Waverley, or 'Tis Sixty Years Hence, Appendix I

Fragment of a Romance which was to have been entitled Thomas the Rhymer.

No more of the proposed tale was ever written; but the Author's purpose was that it should turn upon a fine legend of superstition which is current in the part of the Borders where he had his residence, where, in the reign of Alexander III of Scotland, that renowned person, Thomas of Hersildoune, called the Rhymer, actually flourished. This personage, the Merlin of Scotland, and to whom some of the adventures which the British bards assigned to Merlin Caledonius, or the Wild, have been transferred by tradition, was, as is well known, a magician, as well as a poet and prophet. He is alleged still to live in the land of Faery, and is expected to return at some great convulsion of society, in which he is to act a distinguished part – a tradition common to all nations, as the belief of the Mahomedans respecting their twelfth Imaum demonstrates.

Now, it chanced many years since that there lived

on the Borders a jolly, rattling horse-cowper, who was remarkable for a reckless and fearless temper, which made him much admired, and a little dreaded, amongst his neighbours. One moonlight night, as he rode over Bowden Moor, on the west side of the Eildon Hills, the scene of Thomas the Rhymer's prophecies, and often mentioned in his story, having a brace of horses along with him which he bad not been able to dispose of, he met a man of venerable appearance and singularly antique dress, who, to his great surprise, asked the price of his horses, and began to chaffer with him on the subject. To Canobie Dick (for so shall we call our Border dealer) – a chap was a chap, and he would have sold a liaise to the devil himself, without minding his cloven hoof, and would have probably cheated Old Nick into the bargain. The stranger paid the price they agreed on; and all that puzzled Dick in the transaction was that the gild which he received was in unicorns, bonnet-pieces, and other ancient coins, which would have been invaluable to collectors, but were rather troublesome, in modern currency.

It was gold, however, and therefore Dick contrived to get better value for the coin than he perhaps gave to his customer. By the command of so good a merchant, he brought horses to the same slot more than once; the purchaser only stipulating that he should always come by night, and alone. I do not know whether it was from mere curiosity, or whether some hope of gain mixed with it, but after Dick had sold several horses in this way, he began to complain that dry-bargains were unlucky, and to hint that since his chap must live in the neighbourhood, he ought, in the courtesy of dealing, to treat him to half a mutchkin.

'You may see my dwelling if you will,' said the stranger; 'but if you lose courage at what you see there, you will rue it all your life.'

Dicken, however, laughed the warning to scorn, and having alighted to secure his horse, he followed the stranger up a narrow foot-path, which led them up the hills to the singular eminence stuck betwixt the most southern and the centre peaks, and called, from its resemblance to such an animal in its form, the Lucken Hare. At the foot of this eminence, which is almost as famous for witch meetings as the neighbouring wind-mill of Kippilaw, Dick was somewhat startled to observe that his conductor entered the hill-side by a passage or cavern, of which he himself, though well acquainted with the spot, had never seen or heard.

'You may still return,' said his guide, looking ominously back upon him; but Dick scorned to show the white feather, and on they went. They entered a very long range of stables; in every stall stood a coal-black horse; by every horse lay a knight in coal-black armour, with a drawn sword in his hand; but all were as silent, hoof and limb, as if they had been cut out of marble. A great number of torches lent a gloomy lustre to the hall, which, like those of the Caliph Vathek, was of large dimensions. At the upper end, however, they at length arrived, where a sword and horn lay on an antique table.

'He that shall sound that horn and draw that sword,' said the stranger, who now intimated that he was the famous Thomas of Hersildoune, 'shall, if his heart fail him not, be king over all broad Britain. So speaks the tongue that cannot lie. But all depends on courage, and much on your taking the sword or the horn first.' Dick was much disposed to take the sword; but his bold spirit was quailed by the supernatural terrors of the hall, and he thought to unsheathe the sword first might be construed into defiance, and give offence to the powers of the Mountain. He took the bugle with a trembling hand, and a feeble note, but loud enough to produce a terrible answer. Thunder rolled in stunning peals through the immense hall; horses and men started to life; the steeds snorted, stamped, grinned their bits, and tossed on high their heads; the warriors sprung to their feet, clashed their armour, and brandished their swords. Dick's terror was extreme at seeing the whole army, which had been so lately silent as the grave, in uproar, and about to rush on him. He dropped the horn, and made a feeble attempt to seize the enchanted sword; but at the same moment a voice pronounced aloud the mysterious words:

Woe to the coward, that ever he was born,
Who did not draw the sword before he blew
the horn!

At the same time a whirlwind of irresistible fury howled through the long hall, bore the unfortunate horse-jockey clear out of the mouth of the cavern, and precipitated him over a steep bank of loose stones, where the shepherds found him the next morning with just breath sufficient to tell his fearful tale, after concluding which he expired.

This legend, with several variations, is found in many parts of Scotland and England. The scene is sometimes laid in some favourite glen of the Highlands, sometimes in the deep coal-mines of Northumberland and Cumberland, which rim so far beneath the ocean. It is also to be found in Reginald Scott's book on Witchcraft, which was written in the sixteenth century. It would be in vain to ask what was the original of the tradition. The choice between the horn and sword may, perhaps, include as a moral that it is foolhardy to awaken danger before we have arms in our hands to resist it.

William Thomas Stead, Real Ghost Stories, 1891

William Thomas Stead spent a rather strange afternoon at Hermitage Castle in the Borders of Scotland. He wrote about his odd experience and recounted the legend of Lord Soulis in his book *Real Ghost Stories*. Twelve years later he was nominated for the Nobel Peace Prize, and was expected to receive it in 1912. However, when William Thomas Stead travelled to America to a speaking engagement at Carnegie Hall, he unfortunately chose to sail on the *Titanic*.

Real Ghost Stories

There is a certain uncanny fascination about haunted houses, but it is one of which it may emphatically be said that distance lends enchantment to the view. There is something much more thrilling in looking at a haunted house from the outside and reading of it at a distance of many miles, than spending a sleepless night within its walls. It has never been my good fortune to sleep in a haunted house, but on one occasion I went to sleep in the ruins of a haunted castle, and was awakened with a shuddering horror that I shall never forget as long as I live.

It was in Hermitage Castle, Hermitage, that grim old Border stronghold which stood in Liddes-dale, not many miles from Riccarton, that most desolate of railway junctions. I visited it when I was just out of my teens, with a mind saturated with legendary lore of the Scotch border. I made a pilgrimage to Brankesome Hall, taking Hermitage on my way. I write this, not to maintain the objectivity of any ghostly haunting of Hermitage

Castle, but to show that although it may all have been the merest delusion of a subjective character, I have at least gone through an experience which enables me to understand what it feels like to be in a haunted house.

Hermitage Castle, one of the most famous of the Border keeps in the days of its splendour, retains to this day a pre-eminence among the castles of the Scotch border:

Haunted Hermitage,
Where long by spells mysterious bound,
They pace their round with lifeless smile.
And shake with restless foot the guilty pile,
Till sink the mouldering towers beneath the
    burdened ground.

Lord Soulis, the evil hero of Hermitage, made a compact with the devil, who appeared to him, so runs the legend, in the shape of a spirit wearing a red cap, which gained its hue from the blood of human victims in which it was steeped. Lord Soulis sold himself to the demon, and in return he could summon his familiar whenever he chose to rap thrice on an iron chest, on condition that he never looked in the direction of the spirit. Once, however, he forgot or ignored this condition, and his doom was sealed. But even then the foul fiend kept the letter of his compact. Lord Soulis was protected by an unholy charm against any injury from rope or steel: hence cords could not bind him and steel would not slay him. When, at last, he was delivered over to his enemies, it was found necessary to adopt the ingenious and effective expedient of rolling him up in a sheet of lead and boiling him to death.

On a circle of stones they placed the pot,
On a circle of stones but barely nine;
They heated it red and fiery hot,
And the burnished brass did glimmer and shine.
They rolled him up in a sheet of lead—
A sheet of lead for a funeral pall;
They plunged him into the cauldron red,
And melted him body, lead, bones, and all.

That was the end of Lord Soulis's body, but his spirit still lingers superfluous on the scene. Once every seven years he keeps tryst with Red Cap on the scene of his former devilries:

And still when seven years are o'er,
Is heard the jarring sound,
When hollow opes the charmed door
Of chamber underground.

When I visited Hermitage Castle, I was all alone, with my memory teeming with associations of the past. I unlocked the door with the key, which I brought with me from the keeper's cottage, at a little distance down the valley. As it creaked on its hinges and I felt the chill air of the ruin, I was almost afraid to enter. Mustering my courage, however, I went in and explored the castle, then lying down on the mossy bank I gave myself up to the glamour of the past. I must have been there an hour or more when suddenly, while the blood seemed to freeze down my back, I was startled by a loud prolonged screech, over my head, followed by a noise which I could only compare to the trampling of a multitude of iron-shod feet through the stone-paved doorway. This was alarming enough, but it was nothing to the horror which filled me when I heard the heavy gate swing on its hinges with a clang which for the moment seemed like the closing of a vault in which I was entombed alive. I could almost hear the beating of my heart. The rusty hinges, the creaking of the door, the melancholy and unearthly nature of the noise, and the clanging of the gate, made me shudder and shiver as I lay motionless, not daring to move, and so utterly crushed by the terror that had fallen upon me that I felt as if I were on the very verge of death. If the evil one had appeared at that moment and carried me off I should have but regarded it as the natural corollary to what I had already heard. Fortunately no sulphureous visitant darkened the blue sky that stretched overhead with his unwelcome presence, and after a few minutes, when I had recovered from my fright, I ventured into the echoing doorway to see whether or not I was really a prisoner. The door was shut, and I can remember to this day the tremour which I experienced when I laid my hand upon the door and tried whether or not it was locked. It yielded to my hand, and I have seldom felt a sensation of more profound relief than when I stepped across the threshold and felt that I was free once more. For a moment it was as if I had been delivered from the grave itself which had already closed over my head. Of course, looking back upon this after a number of years, it is easy to say that the whole thing was purely subjective. An overwrought fancy, a gust of wind whistling through the crannies and banging the door close were quite sufficient to account for my fright, especially as it is not at all improbable that I had gone to sleep in the midst of the haunted ruins.

So I reasoned at the moment, and came back and stayed another hour in the castle, if only to convince myself that I was not afraid. But neither before nor after that alarm did any gust of wind howl round the battlements with anything approaching to the clamour which gave me such a fright. One thing amuses me in looking back at a letter which I wrote at the time, describing my alarm. I say, 'Superstition, sneer you? It may be. I rejoiced that I was capable of superstition; I thought it was dried out of me by high pressure civilisation.' I am afraid that some of my critics will be inclined to remark that my capacities in that direction stand in need of a great deal of drying up.

Geoffrey of Monmouth: Merlin's Prophecies

Geoffrey of Monmouth, *The History of the Kings of Britain*, Book VII, Chapter III & IV.

The following extracts are taken from the 1718 Latin to English translation of *Geoffrey's History of the Kings of Britain*, by Aaron Thompson. The extracts are from Geoffrey's account of the prophecies of the boy Merlin made to King Vortigern at Dinas Emrys in Wales. Dinas Emrys is a real hill in North Wales. Strangely, the hill is built of red and white stone:

> . . . the two dragons, one of which was white, the other red, came forth, and approaching one another, began a terrible fight, and cast forth fire with their breath. But the white dragon had the advantage, and made the other fly to the end of the lake. And he, for grief at his flight, renewed the assault upon his pursuer, and forced him to retire. After this battle of the dragons,

the king commanded Ambrose Merlin to tell him what it portended. Upon which he, bursting into tears, delivered what his prophetical spirit suggested to him, as follows:

'Woe to the red dragon, for his banishment hasteneth on. His lurking holes shall be seized by the white dragon, which signifies the Saxons whom you invited over; but the red denotes the British nation, which shall be oppressed by the white. Therefore shall its mountains be levelled as the valleys, and the rivers of the valleys shall run with blood. The exercise of religion shall be destroyed, and churches be laid open to ruin. At last the oppressed shall prevail, and oppose the cruelty of foreigners. For a boar of Cornwall shall give his assistance, and trample their necks under his feet. The islands of the ocean shall be subject to his power, and he shall possess the forests of Gaul. The house of Romulus shall dread his courage, and his end shall be doubtful. He shall be celebrated in the mouths of the people and his exploits shall be food to those that relate them . . .

'. . . It shall rain a shower of blood, and a raging famine shall afflict mankind. When these things happen, the red one shall be grieved; but when his fatigue is over, shall grow strong. Then shall misfortunes hasten upon the white one, and the buildings of his gardens shall be pulled down . . .

'. . . After this shall the red dragon return to his proper manners, and turn his rage upon himself. Therefore shall the revenge of the Thunderer show itself, for every field shall disappoint the husbandmen. Mortality shall snatch away the people, and make a desolation over all countries. The remainder shall quit their native soil, and make foreign plantations. A blessed king shall prepare a fleet, and shall be reckoned the twelfth in the court among the saints. There shall be a miserable desolation of the kingdom, and the floors of the harvests shall return to the fruitful forests. The white dragon shall rise again, and invite over a daughter of Germany. Our gardens shall be again replenished with foreign seed, and the red one shall pine away at the end of the pond . . .

'. . . There shall be gilding in the temples, nor shall the edge of the sword cease. The German dragon shall hardly get to his holes, because the revenge of his treason shall overtake him. At last he shall flourish for a little time, but the decimation of Neustria shall hurt him. For a people in wood and in iron coats shall come, and revenge upon him his wickedness. They shall restore the ancient inhabitants to their dwellings and there shall be an open destruction of foreigners. The seed of the white dragon shall be swept out of our gardens, and the remainder of his generation shall be decimated. They shall bear the yoke of slavery, and wound their mother with spades and ploughs. After this shall succeed two dragons, whereof one shall be killed with the sting of envy, but the other shall return under the shadow of a name . . .

'. . . The camp of Venus shall be restored; nor shall the arrows of Cupid cease to wound. The fountain of a river shall be turned into blood; and two kings shall fight a duel at Stafford for a lioness . . .

'. . . After this shall be produced a tree upon the Tower of London, which having no more than three branches, shall overshadow the surface of the whole island with the breadth of its leaves. Its adversary, the North wind, shall come upon it, and with its noxious blast shall snatch away the third branch; but the two remaining ones shall possess its place, till they shall destroy one another by the multitude of their leaves: and then shall it obtain the place of those two, and shall give sustenance to birds of foreign nations. It shall be esteemed hurtful to native fowls; for they shall not be able to fly freely for fear of its shadow. There shall succeed the ass of wickedness, swift against the goldsmiths, but slow against the ravenousness of wolves. In those days the oaks of the forests shall burn . . .

'. . . Fishes shall die with the heat thereof; and of them shall be engendered serpents. The baths of Badon shall grow cold and their salubrious waters engender death. London shall mourn for the death of twenty thousand; and the river Thames shall be turned into blood. The monks in their cowls shall be forced to marry, and their cry shall be heard upon the mountains of the Alps . . . '

Book VII. Chapter III.

'. . . For earth shall be turned into stones; stones into water; wood into ashes; ashes into water, if cast over it. Also a damsel shall be sent from the city of the forest of Canute to administer a cure, who, after she shall have practised all her arts, shall dry up the noxious fountains only with her breath. Afterwards, as soon as she shall have refreshed herself with the wholesome liquor, she shall bear in her right hand the wood of Caledon, and in her left the forts of the walls of London. Wherever she shall go, she shall make sulphureous steps, which will smoke with a double flame. That smoke shall rouse up the city of Ruteni, and shall make food for the inhabitants of the deep. She shall overflow with rueful tears, and shall fill the island with her dreadful cry. She shall be killed by a hart with ten branches, four of which shall bear golden diadems but the other six shall be turned into buffalo's horns, whose hideous sound shall astonish the three islands of Britain . . .

'. . . there shall come a worm with a fiery breath, and with the vapour it sends forth shall burn up the trees. Out of it shall proceed seven lions deformed with the heads of goats. With the stench of their nostrils they shall corrupt women, and make wives turn common prostitutes. The father shall not know his own son, because they shall grow wanton like brute beasts. Then shall come the giant of wickedness, and terrify all with the sharpness of his eyes . . .

'. . . Men shall be drunk with wine, and, regardless of heaven, shall be intent upon the earth. From them shall the stars turn away their faces, and confound their usual course. Corn will wither at their malign aspects; and there shall fall no dew from heaven. The roots and branches will change their places, and the novelty of the thing shall pass for a miracle. The brightness of the sun shall fade at the amber of Mercury, and horror shall seize the beholders. Stilbon of Arcadia shall change his shield; the helmet of Mars shall call Venus. The helmet of Mars shall make a shadow; and the rage of Mercury pass his bounds. Iron Orion shall unsheath his sword: the marine Phoebus shall torment the clouds; Jupiter shall go out of his lawful paths; and Venus forsake her stated lines. The malignity of the star Saturn shall fall down in rain, and slay mankind with a crooked sickle. The twelve houses of the stars shall lament the irregular excursions of their guests; and Gemini omit their usual embraces, and call the urn to the fountains. The scales of Libra shall hang obliquely, till Aries put his crooked horns under them. The tail of Scorpio shall produce lightning, and Cancer quarrel with the Sun. Virgo shall mount upon the back of Sagittarius, and darken her virgin flowers. The chariot of the Moon shall disorder the zodiac, and the Pleiades break forth into weeping. No offices of Janus shall hereafter return, but his gate being shut shall lie hid in the chinks of Ariadne. The seas shall rise up in the twinkling of an eye, and the dust of the ancients shall be restored. The winds shall fight together with a dreadful blast, and their sound shall reach the stars.'

Book VII. Chapter IV

APPENDIX SIX
The White Lady Of Blenkinsopp

THE LEGEND OF THE White Lady of Blenkinsopp in Northumbria, England, appeared in the *Monthly Chronicle of North-Country Lore and Legend*, March 1888. It is a fine example of a local legend of a White Lady who haunts a castle and guards a buried treasure.

> Like almost all the old Northumbrian castles and peels, Blenkinsopp has the reputation of being haunted. A gloomy vault under the castle is said to have buried in it a large chest of gold, hidden in the troubled times: some say by a lady whose spirit cannot rest so long as it is there, and who used formerly to appear – though not, that we have heard, for the last four or five decades – clothed in white from head to foot, and so was known as 'The White Lady'.
>
> About the beginning of this century several of the least ruinous apartments in the castle were still occupied

by a hind [an agricultural labourer] on the estate and some cottars. Indeed, two or three of them continued to be so down to the year 1820 or thereabouts. The visits of the White Lady seem to have been infrequent latterly, and for some considerable time they had ceased. One night, however, shortly after retiring to rest, the hind and his wife (so the story goes) were alarmed on hearing loud and reiterated screams coming from an adjoining room, in which one of the children, a boy of about eight years of age, had been laid to sleep. On hastily rushing in to see what was the matter, they found the boy sitting trembling on his pillow, terror-struck and bathed in perspiration. 'The White Lady! The White Lady!' he screamed, as soon as he saw them.

'What Lady?' cried the astonished parents, looking round the room. 'There is no lady here.'

'She is gone,' replied the boy, 'and she looked so angry at me because I would not go with her. She was a fine lady, and she sat down on my bedside and wrung her hands and cried sore. Then she kissed me and asked me to go with her, and she would make me a rich man, as she had buried a large box of gold many hundred years since, down in the vault; and she would give it to me, as she could not rest so long as it was there. When I told her I durst not go, she said she would carry me, and she was lifting me up when I cried out and I frightened her away.'

The hind and his wife, both very sensible people, concluded that the child had been dreaming and at length succeeded in quieting him and getting him to sleep. But for three successive nights they were disturbed in the same manner, the boy repeating the same story with little variation, so that they were forced to let him sleep in the same apartment with themselves, when the apparition no longer visited him. The effect upon the boy's mind, however, was such that nothing ever afterwards would induce him to enter into any part of the old castle alone even in daylight.

The legend of the White Lady is not one of those that unsophisticated country people willingly let die; and the belief that treasure lies hidden under the grim old ruin, waiting to be disinterred, is probably still entertained by not a few. Indeed, there is hardly a place of the kind, either in this country or any other, regarding which some such impression does not exist.

About fifty years since, we are told, a strange lady arrived at the village of Greenhead, and took up her quarters at the inn there. She told the landlady, in confidence, that she had had a wonderful dream, to the effect that a large chest of gold lay buried in the vault of Blenkinsopp Castle, and that she was to be the person to find it. She stayed several weeks, awaiting the return of the owner of the property to ask leave to search; but she either got tired of waiting, or could not obtain permission, and so she went away without accomplishing her purpose, and the hidden treasure, if there be such a thing there, remains for some more fortunate person to bring to the light of day.

Tradition accounts for the alleged hiding of the gold in the following way: one of the castellans in the middle ages, named Bryan de Blenkinsopp, familiarly Bryan Blenship, was as avaricious as he was bold, daring, and lawless. He was once heard to say, when taunted with being a fusty old bachelor, that he would never marry until he met with a lady possessed of a chest of gold heavier than ten of his strongest men could carry into his castle; and fate, it seems, had ordained that he would keep his word. For, going to the wars abroad, whether to the Holy Land to fight against the Saracens, or to Hungary to oppose the Turks, we cannot tell, and staying away several years, he met with a lady in some far country who came up to his expectations, courted her, married her, and brought her home, together with a chest of gold which it took twelve strong men to lift. Bryan Blenkinsopp was now the richest man in the North of England; but it soon transpired that his riches had not brought him happiness, but the reverse. He and his lady quarrelled continually, a fact which could not long be concealed and one day, when the unhappy couple had had a more serious difference than usual, Sir Bryan was heard to utter threats, in reply to his wife's bitter reproaches, which seemed to indicate that he meant to get rid of her as soon as he could without any more formality or fuss than if they had merely been 'handfasted', that is, pledged to each other for a year and a day. The lady muttered something in return, which could not be distinctly heard by the servants, and so the affair, for the nonce, seemed to end. But a very short time afterwards – possibly the next night – the indignant, ill-used lady got the foreign men-servants who had accompanied her to the castle to take up the precious chest and bury it deep in some secret place out of her miserly husband's reach, where it lies to this day. Accounts differ as to what followed. Some say Sir Bryan disappeared shortly after he discovered his loss; others say the lady disappeared first; but it is affirmed that they both disappeared in a mysterious manner, and that neither of them was ever afterwards seen. It was, moreover, sagely hinted that the lady was 'something uncanny' – in plain terms, an imp of darkness, sent with her wealth to ensnare Sir Bryan's greedy soul. At any rate folks were sure that she was an infidel, for she never went to church, and used on Sundays to sing . . . in an unknown tongue in her own room.

BIBLIOGRAPHY

Rosslyn Chapel and Castle

Brydon, R., F.S.A. Scot., *History of the Guilds, the Masons and the Rosy Cross*, Edinburgh, 1994

Carlo, F.G., (ed.) Stevenson, W. and Meikle V., *The Battle of Rosslyn 1303: A Short History to Commemorate the 700th Anniversary*, Roslin Heritage Society, 2003.

Dickson, J., *Roslin Castle and the St Clairs: Their History*, Edinburgh, 1897.

Forbes, Dr R., Bishop of Caithness, *An Account of the Chapel of Rosslyn 1778*, Pub. 1774, reprinted 1778.

Grant, W., *Rosslyn: The Chapel, Castle and Scenic Lore*, Dysart & Rosslyn Estates, 1954.

Hay, R.A., Father, *The Genealogie of the Sainteclaires of Rosslyn*, Edinburgh, 1835.

Jackson, J., *Tales of Roslin Castle*, Edinburgh, 1836.

Kerr, A., Esq., F.S.A. Scot., *The Collegiate Church or Chapel of*

Rosslyn, Its Builders, Architect, and Construction, Proceedings of Society of Antiquaries of Scotland, 1877.

Kerr, A., Esq., F.S.A. Scot., *Rosslyn Castle, Its Buildings Past and Present*, Proceedings of Society of Antiquaries of Scotland, 1877.

Kerr, A., Esq., F.S.A. Scot., *Glencorse and Its Old Buildings*, Proceedings of Society of Antiquaries of Scotland, 1879.

Kirk, T. and Thoresby, R. (ed.), Hume Brown, *Tours of Scotland 1677 and 1681*, Edinburgh, 1892.

Lawlor, Rev. Professor H.J. D.D., F.S.A. Scot., *Notes on the Library of the Sinclairs of Rosslyn*, Proceedings of Society of Antiquaries of Scotland, 1898.

Ralls-MacLeod, K. and Robertson, I., *The Quest for the Celtic Key*, Luath Press, 2002.

Rosslyn, H. and Maggi, A., *Rosslyn: Country of Painter and Poet*, National Gallery of Scotland, 2002.

Rosslyn, P. St Clair-Erskine, Earl of, *Rosslyn Chapel*, Rosslyn Chapel Trust, 1997.

St Clair, R.W., *The St Clairs of the Isles*, Auckland, 1898.

Stringer, K.J., (ed.), *Essays on the Nobility of Medieval Scotland*, Edinburgh, 1985. (Crawford, B.E., *William Sinclair, Earl of Orkney, and His Family: A Study in the Politics of Survival*)

Scottish, British and Medieval History

Ashmore, P. J., *Neolithic and Bronze Age Scotland*, B.T. Batsford Ltd. with Historic Scotland, 1996.

Barber, R., *The Knight and Chivalry*, Sphere Books, 1974.

Camille, M., *Gothic Art: Visions and Revelations of the Medieval World*, Everyman Art Library, 1996.

Carver, M., *Surviving in Symbols: A Visit to the Pictish Nation*, Canongate with Historic Scotland, 1999.

Clerk, Sir J., *Memoirs of Sir John Clerk of Penecuik*, Edinburgh, 1893.

Cowan, E.J., 'For Freedom Alone': The Declaration of Arbroath 1320, Tuckwell Press, 2003.

Foster, S.M., Picts, Gaels and Scots, B.T. Batsford Ltd. with Historic Scotland, 1996.

Fraser, A., Mary Queen of Scots, Weidenfeld and Nicolson, 1969.

Frayling, C., Strange Landscape: A Journey Through the Middle Ages, BCA, 1999.

Hay, Sir G., The Buke of the Order of Knyghthood, Abbotsford Club, 1847.

Hay, Sir G., (ed.) Cartwright, J., The Buik of King Alexander the Conquerour, Scottish Text Society, 1986.

Hay, Sir G., (ed.) Cartwright, J., The Buik of King Alexander the Conquerour Vol. 3, Scottish Text Society, 1990.

Hay, Sir G., (ed.) Stevenson, J.H., Gilbert of the Haye's Prose Manuscript, Scottish Text Society, 1901.

Hay, Sir G., (ed.) Glenn J. A., The Prose Works of Sir Gilbert Hay. Vol. 3, The Buke of the Ordre of Knychthede and The Buke of the Gouernaunce of Princis, Scottish Text Society, 1993.

Hutton, R., The Stations of the Sun, Oxford University Press, 1996.

Hutton, R., The Pagan Religions of the Ancient British Isles, Blackwell, 1991.

Kelvingrove Museum and Art Gallery, Scotland's Ancient Treasures from the National Museum of Antiquities, Scotland, 1951.

Legg, R., Romans in Britain, BCA, 1983.

MacKenzie, A.M. (ed.), Scottish Pageant 55 BC to AD 1513, Oliver and Boyd for the Saltire Society, 1946.

Mackenzie, D.A., Scotland: The Ancient Kingdom, Blackie & Son, 1933.

Macquarrie, A., Scotland and the Crusades, John Donald, 1997.

McHardy, S., The Quest for Arthur, Luath Press, 2001.

McHardy, S., The Quest for the Nine Maidens, Luath Press, 2003.

McHardy, S., Tales from the Picts, Luath Press, 2005.

McNamee, C., The Wars of the Bruces, Tuckwell Press, 1997.

Morris, W.J., A Walk through Glasgow Cathedral, Society

of Friends of Glasgow Cathedral, St Mungo Museum and Cathedral Centre, 1986.

Piggot, S., *Scotland Before History*, Nelson, 1958.

Powell, T.G.E., *The Celts*, Thames and Hudson, 1991.

Proctor, C., *Ceannas nan Gaildheal — The Headship of the Gael*, Clan Donald Lands Trust, 1985.

Ross, A., *Pagan Celtic Britain: Studies in Iconography and Tradition*, Routledge and Kegan Paul, 1967.

Simpson, W.D., *The Celtic Church in Scotland*, Aberdeen University Press, 1935.

Smyth, A.P., *Warlords and Holy Men: Scotland AD 80–1000*, Edward Arnold, 1984.

Taylor, R., *How to Read a Church*, Rider, 2003.

Tranter, N., *The Story of Scotland*, Neil Wilson, 2003.

Watt, F., *Edinburgh and the Lothians*, London, 1912.

Whidden Green, C., *Saint Kentigern, Apostle to Strathclyde: A Critical Analysis of a Northern Saint*, master's thesis, University of Houston, 1998.

Wood, M., Richardson, J.S., Tabraham, C.J., *Melrose Abbey*, HMSO, 1981.

Templar History

Lord, E., *The Knights Templar in Britain*, Longman, 2002.

Nicolson, H. J., *Love, War and the Grail: Templars, Hospitallers, and Teutonic Knights in Medieval Epic and Romance 1150–1500*, Brill Academic Publishers, 2004.

Nicolson, H.J., *The Knights Templar: a new history*, Sutton, 2001.

Ralls-MacLeod, K., *The Templars and the Grail*, Quest Books, 2003.

Read P.P., *The Templars*, Phoenix, 2003.

Slezer, J., *The Spottiswoode Miscellany.* 2 vols., Spottiswoode Society, 1844–5.

King Arthur

Aneirin, trans. Jackson, K., *The Gododdin*, Edinburgh University Press, 1969.

Barber, R., *The Holy Grail: Imagination and Belief*, Allen Lane, 2004.

Barber, R., *King Arthur: Hero and Legend*, Boydell Press, 1986.

Barber, R., *King Arthur in Legend and History*, Boydell Press, 1973.

Chrétien de Troyes, trans. and intro. Owen, D.D.R., *Arthurian Romances*, Everyman, 1993.

Geoffrey of Monmouth, trans. and intro. Clarke, B., *Vita Merlini: The Life of Merlin*, University of Wales Press, 1973.

Geoffrey of Monmouth, trans. and intro. Thorpe, L., *The History of the Kings of Britain*, Penguin Books, 1966.

Gerald of Wales, trans. O'Meara, J.F., *The History and Topography of Ireland*, Penguin Books, 1982.

Gerritsen, W.P. and van Melle, A.G. trans. Guest, T., *A Dictionary of Medieval Heroes*, Boydell Press, 1998.

Trans. Gantz, J., *The Mabinogion*, Penguin Books, 1976.

Gildas, ed. and trans. Winterbottom M., *De Excidio Britanniae: The Ruin of Britain and Other Works*, Phillimore, 1978.

Graeme Ritchie, R.L., *Chrétien de Troyes and Scotland*, Oxford at the Clarendon Press, 1952.

Guillaume Le Clerc, trans. and intro. Owen, D.D.R., *Fergus of Galloway, Knight of the King Arthur*, Everyman, 1991.

Jenkins, E., *The Mystery of King Arthur*, Dorset Press, 1990.

Lacy, N.J., assoc. ed. Ashe, G., et al., *The Arthurian Encyclopedia*, Boydell Press, 1988.

Loomis, R.S., *The Grail, From Celtic Myth to Christian Symbol*, Constable, 1993.

Loomis, R.S., *Scotland and the Arthurian Legend*, Proceedings of Society of Antiquaries of Scotland, 1955–56.

Loomis, R.S., *Arthurian Tradition and Chrétien de Troyes*, New York, 1949.

MacQueen, W. and J., *Vita Merlini Silvestris*, Scottish Studies 29, 1989.

Malory, Sir Thomas, (ed.) Vinaver. E., *Sir Thomas Malory: Works*, Oxford, 1967.

Moffat, A., *Arthur and the Lost Kingdoms*, Weidenfeld and Nicolson, 1999.

Morris, J., *The Age of Arthur: A History of the British Isles from 350 to 650*, Charles Scribner's Sons, 1973.

Randall, J., *Arthur & Merlin: The Tweedale Connection*, John Randall, 1997.

Strachan, Rev. G., *Jesus the Master Builder*, Floris, 1998.

Stuart Glennie, J.S., *Arthurian Localities*, Edinburgh, 1869.

Tolstoy, N., *The Quest for Merlin*, Hodder and Stoughton, 1985.

Treharne, R.F., *The Glastonbury Legends*, Abacus, 1975.

Ziolkowski, J., *The Nature of Prophecy in Geoffrey of Monmouth's Vita Merlini*, Cornell University Press, 1990.

Myths, Legends and Folk Tales

Alexander, M., *British Folklore, Myths and Legends*, Weidenfeld and Nicolson, 1982.

Ashe, G., *Mythology of the British Isles*, Methuen, 1996.

Barber, R., *Myths and Legends of the British Isles*, Boydell Press, 1999.

Bord, J. and C., *Mysterious Britain*, Paladin, 1974.

Briggs, K.M., *The Vanishing People: A Study of Traditional Fairy Beliefs*, Batsford, 1978.

Briggs, K.M., *The Fairies in English tradition and Literature*, Bellew, 1989.

Briggs, K.M., *A Dictionary of Fairies: Hobgoblins, Brownies, Bogies and Other Supernatural Creatures*, Penguin Books, 1977.

Cooper, Q. and Sullivan, P., *Maypoles, Martyrs and Mayhem*, Bloomsbury, 1994.

Crossley-Holland, K., *The Norse Myths*, Penguin, 1982.

Dubois, P., *The Great Encyclopedia of Faeries*, Pavilion, 1999.

Edwards, G., *Hobgoblin and Sweet Puck: Fairy Names and Natures*, Geoffrey Bles, 1974.

Evans-Wentz, W.Y., *Fairy Faith in Celtic Countries*, Henry Frowde, 1911.

Henderson, L. and Cowan, E.J., *Scottish Fairy Belief: A History*, Tuckwell Press, 2001.

Hope, A.D., *A Midsummer Eve's Dream*, Viking Press, 1970.

Oxbrow, M.I., *Halloween: Pagan Festival to Trick or Treat*, Strega, 2001.

Stoneman, R., *Legends of Alexander the Great*, Everyman, 1994.

Westwood, J., *Albion: A Guide to Legendary Britain*, BCA, 1986.

Templar Myths

Baigent, M. and Leigh, R., *The Temple and the Lodge*, Jonathan Cape, 1989.

Baigent, M., Leigh, R. and Lincoln, H., *The Messianic Legacy*, Jonathan Cape, 1986.

Baigent, M., Leigh, R. and Lincoln, H., *The Holy Blood and the Holy Grail*, Jonathan Cape, 1982.

Coppens, P., *The Stone Puzzle of Rosslyn Chapel*, Frontier/ Adventures Unlimited Press, 2002.

Gardner, L., *Bloodline of the Holy Grail*, Element, 1996.

Knight, C. and Lomas, R., *The Hiram Key*, Century, 1996.

Laidler, K., *The Head of God*, Weidenfeld and Nicolson, 1998.

Lincoln, H., *Chronicle: The Lost Treasure of Jerusalem . . . ?* BBC, 1978.

Picknett, L. and Prince, C., *The Templar Revelation*, Bantam Press, 1997.

Sinclair, A., *The Sword and the Grail*, Birlinn, 2002.

Sinclair, A., *The Secret Scroll*, Sinclair-Stevenson, 2001.

Wallace-Murphy, T. and Hopkins, M., *Rosslyn: Guardian of the Secrets of the Holy Grail*, Element, 1999.

Wallace-Murphy, T., *The Templar Legacy & the Masonic Inheritance within Rosslyn Chapel*, Friends of Rosslyn, 1994.

Miscellaneous, Including Novels and Poetry

Brown, D., *The Da Vinci Code*, Bantam Press, 2003.

Cox, S., *Cracking the Da Vinci Code*, Michael O'Mara, 2004.

Eco, U., trans Weaver, W., *Foucault's Pendulum*, Secker & Warburg, 1989.

Scott, Sir W., *The Lay of the Last Minstrel*, David Bogue, 1839.

Scott, Sir W., *Waverley Novels*, Edinburgh 1829–33.

INDEX